Building of Faith

VENIT HORA UT CLARIFICETUR FILIUS HOMINIS

AMEN AMEN
DICO VOBIS
NISI GRA
NUM FRU
MENTI CAD
ENS IN TER-
RAM MORTU-
UM FUERIT
IPSUM SOLU
MANET SI
AUTEM
MORTU
FUERIT
MULTUM
FRUCTUM
AFFERT

QUI AMAT ANIMAM SUAM
PERDET EAM ET QUI ODIT
ANIMAM SUAM IN HOC
MUNDO IN VITAM AETER-
NAM CUSTODIT EAM

JESUS IS LAID IN THE TOM

Westminster Cathedral

Building of Faith

John Browne Timothy Dean

Booth-Clibborn Editions

Acknowledgements

Many people have helped us in a variety of ways to produce this book. Some have offered special insights, others have contributed something no-one else remembers. Our thanks are also due to all those who assisted us but whose names may not appear here. To all, we are grateful for valuable help, magnanimously given.

At Cathedral Clergy House: Monsignor George Stack, Adminstrator of Westminster Cathedral, Father Mark Langham, Rector and Sub-Adminstrator, The College of Cathedral Chaplains, in particular Father Thomas Allan, Father Daniel Cronin, Monsignor Walter Drumm, Monsignor David Norris VG, Father Kevin O'Callaghan SJ, Father Philip Whitmore. At Vaughan House: Monsignor Ralph Brown VG. Staff and Volunteers in the Cathedral precinct: Harry Bailey, Evaline Brown, Heather Craufurd, Father James Curry, Franciscan Sisters of Our Lady of Victories, Jean Esposito (Secretary to The Friends of Westminster Cathedral), Paul Gillham, James and Irene Hanratty, Ivan Kightley, Margaret LeFoe for her floral arrangements, John MacGregor, Margaret McKerrow, John Moss, Aidan Oliver, Patrick O'Rourke, Barry Palmer, Michael Parkinson, Denis Reynolds, Sisters of Mercy, Gerard Skinner, Frank Warrender, Gordon Wilkinson.

Igor and Anabel Anrep, Phil Baines, Anthony Bartlett, Aelred Bartlett, Lady Freda Berkeley for permission to photograph Boris Anrep's model proposing a scheme for the sanctuary mosaics, Delian Bower, Roger Brightmore for his photograph of The Holy Face by William Christian Symons, Fiona Cowan, Father Ian Dickie (Archivist, Diocese of Westminster), Father Michael Donaghy, Michael Dover, Franciscan Missionary Sisters of Littlehampton, Miranda Goodby (Newcastle Museum, Staffordshire), HE Archbishop Bruno Heim, the late Louis Heren, Monsignor Anthony Howe, The National Portrait Gallery for permission to reproduce the painting of John Bentley by William Christian Symons, John Outram for his essay on the future completion of the interior, Jean-Claude Peissel, Graham Piggot, Lieutenant-Colonel N.W. Poulson for information on the Irish regiments commemorated in the Chapel of Saint Patrick, Gillian Roy, Camberwell School of Art, Peter Smith for his photographs of the Henry Clutton drawings for a projected cathedral, Lord Snowdon, Peter and Elizabeth Symons, Elizabeth Thomas (Victoria Art Gallery, Bath), Marianne Topham, Stephen and Elizabeth Usherwood, Right Reverend W Gordon Wheeler, Emeritus Bishop of Leeds. Father Patrick Daly, Administrator of St Chad's Cathedral, Birmingham, Dries Lecluyse, Leuven, and Marie Gascoigne, whose marriage to John Browne took place at Westminster Cathedral whilst Building of Faith was being written.

In our review of the Liturgical Treasury of Westminster Cathedral, a great deal of new and unexpected information came to light during the preparation of this book. For this we thank the specialists in a number of disciplines. They have all been generous with their time and expertise, enabling the authors to augment, complete and amend the received knowledge about many items in the collection. Staff at the British Library for manuscripts and early printed books: Janet Backhouse, Patricia Basing, Michelle Brown, John Goldfinch. Staff at the Victoria and Albert Museum, metalwork collection: Marian Campbell, Louise Hofman, textiles and dress collection: Jennifer Wearden, Linda Woolley, Paul Harrison, Linda Parry. Charles Truman of Aspreys Ltd, London.

We are sincerely grateful to our publisher Edward Booth-Clibborn for providing the remarkable standard of quality and design which are the hallmark of Booth-Clibborn Editions, for this portrait of Westminster Cathedral. To the people he assembled for the project we would like to express our admiration for their creativity, knowledge and skill: Silvia Gaspardo Moro and Angus Hyland, designers, Susanne Atkin and Vicky Hayward, editors. Finally, to the cool and gentlemanly Phil Sayer we wish to express our gratitude for his unique photographer's eye and the pains he took in creating a wide-ranging portfolio of evocative and memorable photographs.

Architectural and still-life photography
Phil Sayer

Design
Angus Hyland and Silvia Gaspardo Moro

Design Assistant
Deborah West

Endpapers
Phil Baines

Portrait of Cardinal George Basil Hume OSB
Snowdon

Published by
Booth-Clibborn Editions
12 Percy Street
London W1P 9FB
UK

Distributed in the UK and world-wide by
Internos Books
12 Percy Street
London W1P 9FB
UK

Distributed in France by
InterArt
1 Rue de l'Est
75020 Paris
France

ISBN 1-873968-45-0

AMDG

Lord Jesus, King and Redeemer, save us by your blood

Contents

**HE Cardinal George Basil Hume OSB with his
gentiluomo Mr Anthony Bartlett by Snowdon.**

The Church adapts continously to the circumstances
of a changing world. Equally it is proud of its
traditions and can be at ease with aspects of its
history and culture which are clearly from another
age. As a Benedictine, Cardinal Hume often wears
the simple black habit of a monk. As an archbishop
and cardinal he wears the robes proper to his office.
In former times each Cardinal had a suite comprising
master of ceremonies, chaplain, cross-bearer, train-
bearer and gentiluomo - a gentleman-in-waiting.
Anthony Bartlett succeeded his father as *gentiluomo*
to the Cardinal Archbishop of Westminster. This
office was dispensed with at the time of the Second
Vatican Council (1962-65) although due to the historic
visit to Westminster Cathedral of Michael Ramsay,
Archbishop of Canterbury, on 23 January 1968 the
role of *gentiluomo* was reinstated here for the lifetime
of the present office-holder. Mr Bartlett was awarded
the OBE in 1992 in recognition of his 60 years of
charitable work among the poor in Westminster with
the Society of Saint Vincent de Paul.

Pax Inter Spinas

In a great Cathedral like Westminster, it is right that we should use all that is fine and magnificent to give honour and glory to God.

We cannot look directly at the sun with a naked eye. Yet in searching for meaning and purpose in life, we are trying to catch glimpses of God's glory. From time to time the cloud of unknowing is pierced by a shaft of light - the kind of beam that can break through the windows of our Cathedral in the most unforgettable way on a fine day.

Our senses receive shafts of His glory in accordance with their different capacities: sight, taste, hearing are windows through which we receive shafts of the glory of God. Those experiences are ways of bringing that glory into our lives. It is much more so in the experience of loving, as in our appreciation of beauty and our response to it.

The eye perceives proportion, shape and colour. But the beauty which the eye beholds, or which pleases the ear, speaks of something other than itself - it speaks of God.

When we strive to acknowledge what we believe Him to be, we use those things which are noblest and best in God's creation and man's achievement. A thing of beauty speaks to us of the beauty of God. To praise His goodness and His majesty we communicate with Him in language which has dignity, with music that is noble and in buildings of distinction and merit.

But there is a beauty which is the most pleasing to Him, more than the greatest music, the finest architecture. We call it beauty of the heart, which is another way of speaking of the first of the eight Beatitudes: 'blessed are the poor in spirit for they shall see God'. The remarkable creation which is Westminster Cathedral exists to help us search for God and to offer Him worship. It is a home for all. It is here to serve the needs of all men and women, to help them on their journey through life. The Cathedral should be a chink in the cloud of unknowing, enabling parishioners and visitors to glimpse something of divine beauty. It is a place where they meet Christ, and, in and through Him, gain strength and courage to take another step along the road to God.

Basil Hume

Archbishop of Westminster

Coat of Arms
Azure a lion rampant between three mascles Argent on a chief three escallops counterchanged. On the dexter side Gules a Pall proper surmounted by a fleur-de-lys Argent.
Motto: Peace among thorns

Preface

Cathedrals are one of the glories of England and visiting them has always been an enriching experience. Most of these great churches are the better part of a thousand years old and although much is known of their history, the story of their creation can only be guessed at. The personalities, ecclesiastical figures, architects, artists, craftsmen and noble sponsors and the stories associated with their interaction are beyond the reach of historical research.

Not so with a cathedral conceived and built a mere century ago. A great deal is understood about the vision and motives of those who built Westminster Cathedral. Also known in ample detail is the social and cultural setting of late Victorian London. So a visit to Westminster Cathedral creates not so much a challenge to the visitor's imagination as a need for access to known facts. Why a particular chapel looks the way it does, how the architect got along with his client, even how the money was raised to complete a particular stage of the project.

Working at Westminster Cathedral gave us the opportunity to look at the sources of this kind of knowledge. Not only were the archives to hand, many of the people who know most about the place were also about. But the greatest source of information is the Cathedral itself which casts an exotic spell on all who give it their time and attention. Even those who admit a preference for Exeter, York or Canterbury can find themselves falling in love with the sincerity and quiet passion of John Bentley's *chef-d'oeuvre*. A profusion of decorative detail absorbs the eye and there is always some new vista, some play of light on marble or sooty brick to contemplate.

We were conscious that the Cathedral is a complex environment, capable of bewildering some of its visitors, particularly those with only a passing acquaintance with Christian symbols and iconography. So we have attempted to provide this background along the way, whether scriptural or moderately theological. In a church so richly endowed with craft and artistry the designers have often drawn attention to some nuance of shape or colour that caught the photographer's eye, well aware that the observant will light on a hundred other intriguing details.

Finally, it will be clear that Westminster is a working cathedral, demonstrably good at fulfilling its purpose as a house of prayer and worship. The people who use it day by day and fill it to capacity on the great occasions, attest to its success as as a building of faith.

John Browne and Timothy Dean

The Chief Pastors of the Catholic Church in England
showing their Communion with the Apostolic See of Rome

Pope	Date		Name	Date and place of receiving pallium
St Peter				
Silvester	314		Restitutus (Archbishop of Canterbury)	
Gregory I	500			
		507	St Augustine	601 England
Sabinian	604		St Laurence	
Boniface III	607			
St Boniface IV	608			
St Aedeodatus I	615			
Boniface V	619		St Mellitus	
		624	St Justus	624 England
Honorius I	625			
		627	St Honorius	634 England
Severinus	630			
John IV	640			
Theodore I	642			
St Martin I	649			
St Eugene I	655		Deusdedit	
St Vitalian	657			
		668	St Theodore	
Adeodatus II	672			
Donus	676			
St Agatho	678			
St Leo II	682			
St Benedict II	684			
John V	685			
Canon	686			
St Sergius I	687			
		693	St Berchtwald	
John VI	701			
John VII	705			
Sisinnius	708			
Constantine	708			
St Gregory II	715			
St Gregory III	731		St Tatwine	733 England
		735	Nothelm	736 England
			Cuthbert	741 England
St Zachary	741			
Stephen II	752			
St Stephen III	752			
St Paul I	757			
		759	Bregowine	
		766	Iaenberht	766 England
Stephen IV	768			
Hadrian I	772			
		793	Aethelheard	
St Leo III	795			
		805	Wulfred	
Stephen V	816			
St Paschal I	817			
Eugene II	824			
Valentine	827			
Gregory IV	827			
		832	Feologeld	
		833	Ceolnoth	833 England (died at Rome)
Sergius II	844			
St Leo IV	847			
Benedict III	855			
St Nicholas I	858			
Hadrian II	867			
		870	Aethelred	
John VIII	872			
Marinus I	882			
Hadrian III	884			
Stephen VI	885			
		890	Plegmund	(c. 891)
Formosus	891			
Stephen VII	896			
Romanus	897			
Theodore II	898			
John IX	898			
Benedict IV	900			
Leo V	903			
Sergius III	904			
Anastasius III	911			
Lando	913			
		914	Athelm	
John X	915			
		923	Wulfhelm	(went to Rome c. 925)
Leo VI	928			
Stephen VIII	929			
John XI	931			
Leo VII	936			
Stephen IX	939			
		942	St Odo	
Marinus II	943			
Agapitus II	946			
John XII	956			
		960	St Dunstan	960 Rome
Benedict V	964			
John XIII	965			
Benedict VI	972			
Benedict VII	975			
John XIV	984			
John XV	985			
		988	Aethelgar	
		990	Sigeric	990 Rome
		995	Aeleric	995 Rome
Gregory V	996			
Silvester II	999			
John XVII	1003			
John XVIII	1004			
		1005	Aelfheah (Alphege)	1007 Rome
Sergius IV	1009			
Benedict VIII	1012			
		1013	Lyfing	
		1020	Aethelnoth	1022 Rome
John XIX	1024			
Benedict IX	1032			
		1038	Eadsige	(went to Rome c. 1040)
Gregory VI	1045			
Clement II	1046			
Damasus II	1047			
St Leo IX	1048			
		1051	Robert	c. 1058 Rome
		1052	Stigand (deprived)	(from Anti-Pope Benedict X)
Victor II	1054			
Stephen X	1057			
Nicholas II	1058			
Alexander II	1061			
		1070	Lanfranc	1070 Rome
St Gregory VII	1073			
Victor III	1086			
Urban II	1088			
		1093	St Anselm	1095 Canterbury
Paschal II	1099			
		1114	Ralph d'Ecures	1115 Canterbury
Gelasius II	1118			
Callistus II		1119	(Legates of the See Apostolic)	
		1123	William de Corbeuil	1123 Rome
Honorius II	1124			
Innocent II	1130			
		1139	Theobald	1139 Rome
Celestine II	1143			
Lucius II	1144			
Eugene III	1145			
Anastasius IV	1153			
Hadrian IV	1154			
Alexander III	1159			
		1162	St Thomas M	1162 Canterbury
		1174	Richard	1174 Anagni
Lucius III	1181			
Urban III	1185		Baldwin	1185 Canterbury
Gregory VIII	1187			
Clement III	1187			
Celestine III	1191			
		1193	Hubert Walter	1193 Canterbury
Innocent III	1198			
		1207	Stephen Langton, Cardinal of Chrysogonus	1207 Viterbo
Honorius III	1216			
Gregory IX	1227			
		1229	Richard Le Grant	1229 England
		1234	St Edmund Rich	1234 Canterbury
Celestine IV	1241			
Innocent IV	1243			
		1245	Bl Boniface of Savoy	1244-5 England
Alexander IV	1254			

Urban IV	1261			
Clement IV	1265			
Bl Gregory X	1271			
		1273	Robert Kilwardby, Cardinal Bishop of Porto	1273 Teynham
Innocent V	1276			
Hadrian V	1276			
John XXI	1276			
Nicholas III	1277			
		1279	John Peckham	1279 Rome
Martin IV	1281			
Honorius IV	1285			
Nicholas IV	1288			
St Celestine V	1294		Robert Winchelsey	1294 Aquila
Boniface VIII	1294			
Bl Benedict XI	1303			
Clement V	1305			
		1313	Walter Reynolds	1314 Chatham
John XXII	1316			
		1328	Simon Mepeham	1328 Avignon
		1333	John Stratford	1334 Rue in Ponthieu
Benedict XII	1334			
Clement VI	1342			
		1349	Thomas Bradwardine	died before investiture
		1349	Simon Islip	1350 Esher
Innocent VI	1352			
Urban V	1362			
		1366	Simon Langham, Cardinal of St Sixtus and Cardinal Bishop of Palestrina	1366 St Stephen's, Westminster
		1368	William Whittlesey	1369 Lambeth
Gregory XI	1370			
		1375	Simon Sudbury	(1376 Enthroned)
Urban VI	1378			
		1381	William Courtenay	1382 Croydon
Boniface IX	1389			
		1397	Thomas Arundel	1397 Westminster
		1398	Roger Walden	1398 High Clere
		1399	Thomas Arundel	(restored)
Innocent VII	1404			
Gregory XII	1406			
Alexander V	1409			
		1414	Henry Chicheley	1414 King's Sutton
Martin V	1417			
Eugene IV	1431			
		1443	John Stafford	1443
Nicholas V	1447			
		1452	John Kemp, Cardinal of St Balbina Cardinal Bishop of St Rufina	1452 Fulham
		1454	Thomas Bouchier, Cardinal of St Cyriacus in Thermis	(1455 enthroned)
Callistus III	1455			
Pius II	1458			
Paul II	1464			
Sixtus IV	1471			
Innocent VIII	1484			
		1486	John Morton, Cardinal of St Anastasia	1487 England
Alexander VI	1492			
		1501	Henry Dean	1501 St Stephen's, Westminster
Pius III	1503			
Julius II	1503			
Leo X	1513			
Hadrian VI	1522			
Clement VII	1523			
		1533	Thomas Cranmer (deprived for heresy)	1533 England
Paul III	1534			
Julius	1550			
Marcellus II	1555			
Paul IV	1555			
		1556	Reginald Pole, Cardinal of St Maria in Cosmedin	1556 Bow Church, London
Pius IV	1559			

Catholic Church in England and Wales ruled by Archpriests and Vicars Apostolic under immediate jurisdiction of the Holy See

St Pius V	1556			
Gregory XIII	1572			
Sixtus V	1585			
Urban VII	1590			
Gregory XIV	1590			
Innocent IX	1591			
Clement VIII	1592		(Archpriests)	
		1599	George Blackwell Archpriest	
Leo XI	1605			
Paul V	1605			
		1608	George Birkhead Archpriest	
		1615	William Harrison Archpriest	
Gregory XV	1621		(Vicars Apostolic)	
Urban VIII	1623	1623	William Bishop VA	
		1625	Richard Smith VA	
Innocent X	1644			
Alexander VII	1655			
Clement IX	1667			
Clement X	1670			
Innocent XI	1676			
		1685	John Leyburn VA	
Alexander VIII	1689			
Innocent XII	1691			
Clement XI	1700			
		1703	Bonaventure Giffard VA	
Innocent XIII	1721			
Benedict XIII	1724			
Clement XII	1730			
		1734	Benjamin Petre VA	
Benedict XIV	1740			
Clement XIII	1758	1758	Richard Challoner VA	
Clement XIV	1769			
Pius VI	1775			
		1781	James Talbot VA	
		1790	John Douglass VA	
Pius VII	1800			
		1812	William Poynter VA	
Leo XII	1823			
		1827	James Yorke Bramston VA	
Pius VIII	1829			
Gregory XVI	1831			
		1836	Thomas Griffiths VA	
Pius IX	1846			
		1848	Thomas Walsh VA	
		1849	Nicholas Wiseman VA	
			(Archbishops of Westminster)	
		1850	Nicholas Wiseman, Cardinal of St Pudenziana	1850 Rome
		1865	Henry Edward Manning, Cardinal of SS Andrew and Gregory on the Coelian Hill	1865 Rome
Leo XIII	1878			
		1892	Herbert Vaughan, Cardinal of SS Andrew and Gregory on the Coelian Hill	1892 The Oratory, London
Pius X	1903	1903	Francis Bourne, Cardinal of St Pudenziana	1903 Rome
Benedict XV	1914			
Pius XI	1922			
		1935	Arthur Hinsley, Cardinal of St Susanna	1935 Rome
Pius XII	1939			
		1943	Bernard Griffin, Cardinal of SS Andrew and Gregory on the Coelian Hill	1946 Rome
		1956	William Godfrey, Cardinal of SS Nereus and Achilleus	1958 Rome
John XXIII	1958			
Paul VI	1963	1963	John Carmel Heenan, Cardinal of St Silvestro in Capite	1963 Rome
		1976	George Basil Hume, Cardinal of St Silvestro in Capite	1976 Rome
John Paul I	1978			
John Paul II	1978			

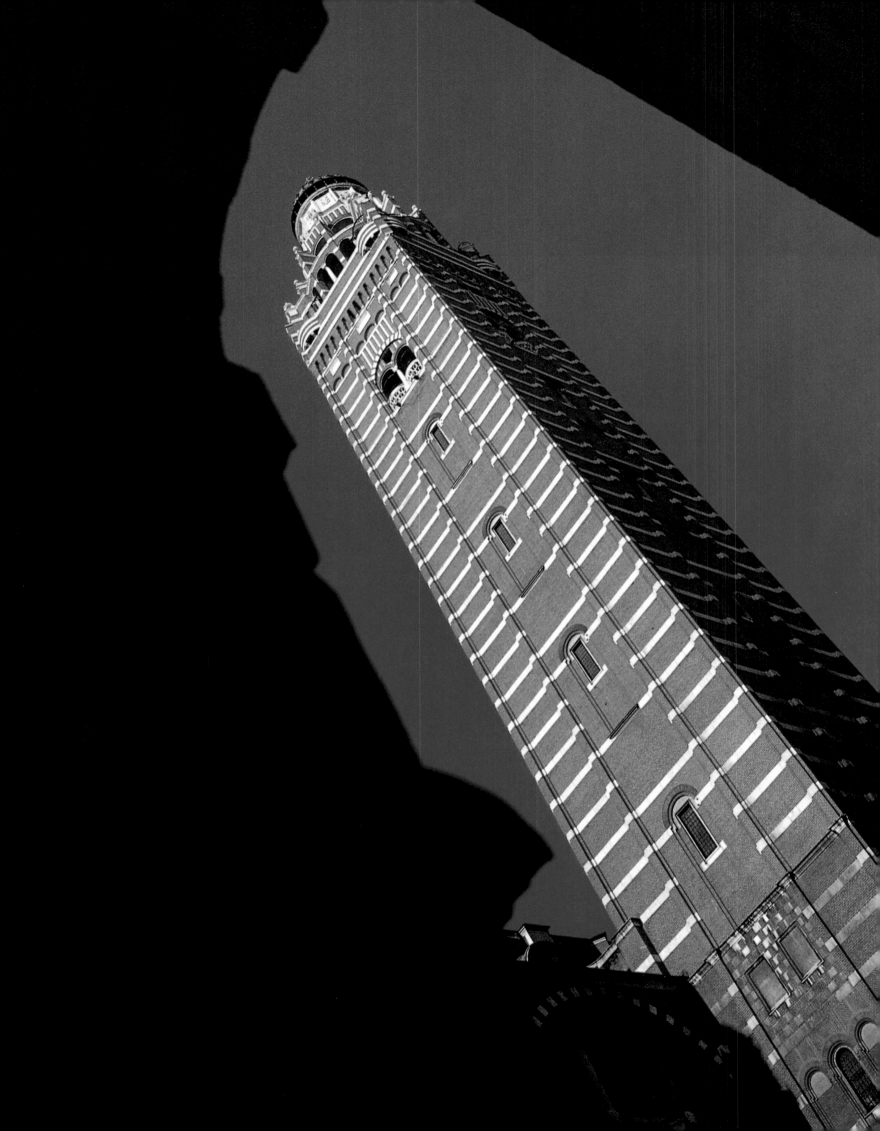

Faith finds its place in London

Archbishop's throne or cathedra

What makes a cathedral is not its grandeur or impressive size but the presence of a particular chair, the *cathedra* ($\chi\alpha\theta\epsilon\delta\rho\alpha$) or ceremonial throne of the bishop or archbishop. It represents his right and responsibility to teach the Christian faith in his diocese.

As shepherd he oversees the flock in his own area and the church that houses the *cathedra* is the cathedral of the diocese. In the case of Westminster, that diocese consists approximately of London north of the Thames together with the county of Hertfordshire. The bishop's authority extends no further, but this does not prevent people thinking of the Archbishop of Westminster as the senior Roman Catholic churchman in England and Wales. Certainly, all Archbishops of Westminster have been made Cardinals by the pope of the day, but that may be seen, in part, as a courtesy from the Holy See to the nation of which London is the capital.

With the restoration in the mid-nineteenth century of the hierarchy of Catholic bishops came the necessity to establish the characteristics of their dioceses. The natural focus for Westminster was the heart of London. However the absence here of a visible centre for Catholic worship, commensurate with the Church's newly public identity and emerging self-confidence, became more of an embarrassment with each passing decade. It had always been the desire of Cardinal Nicholas Wiseman, the first Archbishop of Westminster, that a cathedral might be built for his Metropolitan See and he is known to have expressed this earnest wish a few months before his death. With Wiseman's passing on 15 February 1865, the project was immediately taken up seriously by friends, in acknowledgement of his contribution to the life and development of the Catholic Church in England. The approval and blessing of Pope Pius IX were obtained. Then a fortnight before the consecration of Henry Edward Manning on 25 May 1865, the new Archbishop, later Cardinal, presiding at a public meeting of clergy and laity, undertook the task as a matter of duty. There was one condition. He insisted that before the foundations of the Cathedral were laid, the foundations of the *spiritual* Church in his diocese must be completed. This was to be done by providing for the religious education of thousands of poor Catholic children, especially those in non-Catholic workhouses, industrial schools and reformatories whose ecclesial birthright was considered to be at risk. (Catholics like Jews have generally considered faith in the context of family to be an inheritance in need of safeguards.) After this meeting a Cathedral Account was opened, efforts were begun to obtain an adequate site and strenuous fund-raising began with senior clergymen travelling to Austria, Germany, Italy, and Spain while Manning's nephew left with a companion to tour the United States in a bid to raise the necessary funds.

A Time to Seek

Back in London it was by no means clear that a site could be obtained within the City of Westminster. A week after returning from receiving the *pallium* at the hands of Pope Pius IX, the archbishop wrote to Monsignor Talbot on 8 November 1865 in Rome, 'I believe that I can now tell you of the site for the cathedral - namely, the Chelsea Cemetery ... London is travelling westward. From Belgrave Square to Kensington will be the best part of London. It is within ten minutes walk of Eaton Square and twenty of Westminster.' The negotiations came to nothing and the delays in obtaining a suitable site cost Manning the resignations of the Earl of Gainsborough and Sir Charles Clifford from their trusteeships of the Wiseman Memorial. Money already collected was handed over in trust to the Archbishop who, in September 1867, after two years of searching was able to purchase a first piece of land in Westminster. This freehold site, bought for £16,500 was a long narrow strip on the right-hand side of Carlisle Place (approaching from Victoria Street which had been opened in 1851) between the present convent of the Sisters of Charity and the large, purpose-built Guards' Institute on the corner.

Concept for a gothic cathedral at Westminster prepared by the draughtsman William Brewer and submitted to Cardinal Vaughan by Archibald Dunn in 1893

*Nicholas Wiseman 1802-65
by (?) Ferdinando Cavalleri 1828*

Despite the unpromising narrowness of the site, several designs for a cathedral were produced by Henry Clutton, a distinguished architect. Clutton was related to the Cardinal by marriage and there were rumblings in the Catholic press over his selection. The fact is that throughout his involvement he gave his work free of charge except for expenses, and bishops have to be practical! In August the following year another large parcel of freehold land was purchased for £20,000 on the opposite side of Carlisle Place. With it came the right to build on the intervening roadway increasing the area to about two and a third acres. New designs were drawn for a cathedral suited to the enlarged space. Four years later, in 1872, the Guards' Institute at the south corner of the cathedral site came on the market. This was purchased with money not contributed towards a cathedral but from private sources including, it seems, the Cardinal's personal funds. This spacious building which had not been paying its way as a club for the Brigade of Guards became 'Archbishop's House', where Cardinal Manning took up residence in March 1873, after the necessary internal alterations. (It still stands in the 1990s, but after a modern reconstruction inside is now a sophisticated office building.)

Further designs for a cathedral were drawn by Clutton - the final one, which the Cardinal accepted, was for a gothic building not unlike the cathedral at Cologne, Germany. It was to be 450 feet long and 250 feet wide across the transepts, much larger than the church that now exists (360 feet by 156 feet). The problem was that with its vast size and great cost the Clutton design might have taken a century to build, and the Cardinal could have done little more than lay the first stone. Every penny would have to be raised from scratch, even though - not surprisingly for the times - the Church relied heavily on aristocratic patronage and leading citizens. During the remainder of the decade fund-raising slowed down. Those responsible may well have grown anxious as they counted

the cost of building a magnificent gothic pile. It was the time in London *par excellence* for extravagant piles - Tower Bridge, the Albert Hall, the Albert Memorial, the Natural History Museum. Clearly, however, the Catholic community was not made of money; yet here was a proposed church that in some dimensions would be larger than any cathedral in England. Back in 1867 the Cardinal had laid the foundation stone for the Church of Our Lady of Victories - forerunner of the present building in Kensington - destined to serve for thirty-five years as 'pro-cathedral' for the diocese of Westminster. Now, in the 1870s, thousands of pounds were being spent on a seminary at Hammersmith for the training of much-needed priests to serve the diocese.

Towards the end of 1882, Cardinal Manning received an encouraging message from Sir Tatton Sykes, which led him to believe that his greatest financial challenge - that of paying for the construction of a cathedral - was about to be met. This prospect freed him to plan for a church of great beauty and richness of design, though smaller than the one last designed by Henry Clutton, being erected by private means without any need for public contributions. Convinced of this, in 1883 he paid off the debt that remained on his plot of land with the help of the Duke of Norfolk, Baron Petre, Baron Gerard, Baroness Weld, Countess Tasker, F.M. Spilsbury and a generous donor who chose to remain anonymous in perpetuity. With justification these notable Roman Catholics have been described as the Pioneers of Westminster Cathedral.

In the same year, to provide a more spacious and open site than the one in Carlisle Place, the Cardinal arranged with the Westminster Land Company, which had been formed for the purchase of the old Middlesex County Prison of Tothill Fields and the plot on which it stood, to buy the site on which the Cathedral with its adjacent buildings was destined to stand. It follows that Westminster

Cathedral is built largely on the foundations of a Penitentiary.

Winefride de l'Hôpital wrote: 'The land on which had stood for many years the Middlesex County Prison of Tothill Fields (in earlier days part of the Abbey lands of Westminster Abbey) came at this juncture into the property market. Cardinal Manning, realizing the advantage of such a position over that of the land bought in 1867 and 1868, decided on its acquisition if within the bounds of possibility. Thereupon in November 1882 he sent for his solicitor, the late Mr Alfred J Blount. The interview opened in the usual brief, laconic, and somewhat imperious fashion. Drawing Mr Blount to the window of his room from which the prison site could be seen, and waving his hand to indicate the ground, he said: "That land is for sale. I wish you to buy it for me!" The finding of ways and means was left to Mr Blount, who at once set to work to carry out the Cardinal's wishes.'

The price of the prison and its site was ascertained to be £115,000; the manner in which the large sum was raised may perhaps best be told in the words of the late Bishop Johnson, for over forty years diocesan secretary, and therefore more intimately acquainted than any other with the business of the archdiocese. His record has been slightly compressed.

'Mr Blount, after the interview [related above], put the matter before Mr Herman Lescher, chartered account, who drew up an admirable scheme for the formation of a limited company which became, as it were, the machinery that gave effect to the Cardinal's wishes. The Memorandum and Articles of Association of the Westminster Land Company ... were dated September 12th, 1883. The subscribers thereto were the late Earl of Denbigh, the Count de Torre Diaz, the late Sir Charles Clifford Bart, the late Hon H.W. Petre, Mr Alfred J. Blount, the late Mr Herman Lescher, and Mr (now the Rev) F.C. New.... On August 16th, 1883, a Conditional Agreement for the purchase had been entered into between

Sixteenth Century Burse with symbols of the passion (Catalogue number 115)

Fifteenth Century hood of an embroidered cope showing the Assumption of the Virgin surrounded by four angels (Catalogue number 117)

Sir Richard Nicholson, Clerk of the Peace for Middlesex, and the late Earl of Denbigh, the Count de Torre Diaz, the ninth Baron Beaumont, and the late Sir Charles Clifford, Bart. Beside those names who have already appeared in the Articles of Agreement, etc, the subscribers were Lord Arundel of Wardour, Lord Clifford of Chudleigh, the late Mr T. Weld-Blundell, Mr Robert Vigers, Mr W. Hussey Walsh, and Mr E.F.D. Walshe.

'The property was conveyed to the Westminster Land Company by Sir Richard Nicholson, as Clerk of the Peace for Middlesex, by two indentures of February 19th, 1884; and the part of the prison site which Cardinal Manning had selected as the new site for the Cathedral was conveyed to the Cardinal and others by the company for its cost price of £55,000 by a deed of the same date.'

The £55,000 price of this new site was met by conveying to the company the plot in Carlisle Place at its estimated value of £35,000, and by borrowing by means of a mortgage on the new site the additional £20,000 required. The whole outlay, up to the time of the sale of the Carlisle Place site, was £36,500 for the purchase of the two portions; £5,723 paid from 1867 to 1883 for interest on the unpaid balance of the purchase money and more than £2,000 for legal costs, architect's expenses and others, making a total of over £44,223. This was in addition to the money which Manning himself provided for the purchase of the first Archbishop's House, which had brought the diocesan administration from Wiseman's inconveniently located premises at 8 York Place, Baker Street.

'Tothill Fields were, within three centuries, part of a marshy tract of land lying between Mill Bank and Westminster Abbey, on which were a few scattered buildings, some of which were residences of noble personages' (Archer, *Vestiges of Old London*). This great salt-water lagoon formed by the Thames had centuries earlier been reclaimed in part by the monks, who were brought there and settled on Thorney (or Bramble) Island by King Edgar, acting under the influence of Saint Dunstan. The King erected monastic buildings, and restored the Church of Saint Peter, which had suffered seriously from the recent Danish raids. He further gave the new community by way of endowment all the land lying between the Fleet and the Tyburn east and west, and between the Thames and what is now Oxford Street, north and south. The Fleet and the Tyburn were of course both tributary streams of London's river. The actual site of the Cathedral was under water, and was known then as Bulinga Fen.

It was reclaimed by Benedictine monks, the builders and owners of Westminster Abbey, and used as a market and fairground. Tothill is a contraction of 'Toot Hill', a beacon or observation post. Appropriately, the top of the campanile of Westminster Cathedral provides one of the finest vantage points for observing the London panorama of today. Since the Middle Ages this easily-flooded land had a number of uses from bear gardens to duelling and often a rubbish tip. There were two fairs in Westminster, Saint Edward's and Saint Mary's. The latter, which took place on Tothill Fields annually on 22 July - the Feast of Saint Mary Magdalene - was founded by a charter of Edward III and continued until the end of the sixteenth century. After the Reformation and the eviction of the monks from their abbey and lands, the area served in turn for a maze, a pleasure garden and a ring for bull-baiting. In 1651, after the defeat of Charles II at Worcester, 4,000 Scottish prisoners were quartered here of whom 1,200 died - the marshy environment evidently giving rise to a virulent fever. Fifteen hundred survivors were sold to slave merchants and shipped off to Guinea and Barbados. During the plague in London in 1665 the fields provided burial pits as recorded by Samuel Pepys in his *Diary* entry for 18 July 1665: 'I was much troubled this day to hear at Westminster how the officers do bury the dead in the open Tuttle Fields, pretending want of room elsewhere.' A view of Tothill Fields in the time of Charles I was described as follows: 'They appear to be dead level, broken only by a clump of trees in the centre, forming a sort of maze. The foreground is broken by a row of slight terraces ...'. The fields retained their solitary and uncultivated character until 1810, with only a group of lonely cottages in their midst. But they ceased to be prone to flooding after embankments were constructed for the Thames in the latter part of the nineteenth century. Nowadays the only area of open ground which formed part of the old Tothill Fields is the centre of Vincent Square, the playing fields of Westminster School.

A 'house of correction' had existed in the neighbourhood since 1618. This had been enlarged in 1655 and in the reign of Queen Anne it began housing criminals. An 1826 Act of Parliament gave powers for a new, larger prison to be built and an eight-acre site was chosen costing £16,000. In the next sixty years the value of the site increased sevenfold. In 1884, Cardinal Manning would have to find £55,000 to pay for half of it.

Strong, deep foundations set for the prison were destined to save a great deal of labour and expense when it came to building the Cathedral in Herbert Vaughan's time as Archbishop. The prison was opened in 1834 at a cost of £186,000. Prisoners were received there until 1850 after which it received only women and males under 17. Once admired as 'a solid and handsome structure' and a 'fine specimen of good brickwork' it came to be regarded as a costly blunder. By 1883, the Middlesex authorities were glad to be rid of it. When Manning bought the site the building had been demolished and the ground lay idle.

When the purchase of the final configuration of land was completed in February 1884, Cardinal Manning hoped that construction would soon begin. But this expectation, based on an absolute

View of the foundations 10 October 1895

Herbert Cardinal Vaughan

certainty that the building would be erected by the generosity of one non-Catholic benefactor, was soon dashed. Sir Tatton Sykes had offered his support on the understanding that the architect should be Baron Heinrich von Ferstel. who had designed the Votivkirche in Vienna and was architect to the Emperor of Austria. When in the same year von Ferstel died, Manning's agreement with the eccentric Yorkshire baronet fell apart. It was a bitter blow for the Cardinal. With the many needs of the diocese to consider and the weight of increasing years, he was now stymied in doing more for the future Cathedral than pay the interest on the £20,000 mortgage for the new site. He died on 14 January 1892. He had written in his journals: 'My successor may begin to build a cathedral. I have often said that Wiseman's death bought the land; perhaps mine will begin the building.' He was correct. Having delivered by strenuous efforts an adequate site of about four acres in the heart of London, it was left to the zeal and stamina of his successor Cardinal Vaughan to erect the Cathedral that the first two Archbishops of Westminster had been under such pressure to provide.

There was never any doubt as to who would be chosen to succeed Cardinal Manning. At the age of 60 Herbert Vaughan, the energetic and accomplished Bishop of Salford, was appointed Archbishop of Westminster on 29 March 1892. Arriving at King's Cross from Manchester one afternoon in May, he gave a two-hour interview to a writer from The Tablet, the famously thoughtful Catholic journal Vaughan had himself purchased in 1868. Together they paced up and down the driveway in front of the Midland Station Hotel and as Vernon Blackburn told it: 'The whole time he talked eagerly and earnestly, pouring out his hopes, plans and fears. His scheme for a Central Seminary, his plans for bringing clergy and laity together, the Catholic Social Union, the Society of the Ladies of Charity and above all, Westminster Cathedral, were all put forward as so many things to be accomplished. When

he told me he meant to build a great cathedral I was dismayed. I thought the task of collecting the money completely beyond his strength. He admitted the difficulty of doing the thing, but preferred to dwell upon the importance of getting it done. He looked to a cathedral not only as necessary for the perfection of the liturgy and worship of the Church, but also as the centre of all Catholic life and activity. He had no money for building a cathedral but was confident that the Catholics of England would come to his help if only the right appeal were made to their hearts. I have often wondered since at the method and perseverance with which the words of that afternoon were redeemed in the years that followed' (Snead-Cox, Life of Cardinal Vaughan).

The background of this energetic priest shows that his later achievements at Westminster were thoroughly in character. He was born at Gloucester on 15 April 1832, the son of Colonel John Vaughan and Louise Elizabeth (née Rolls) who had become a Catholic shortly before her marriage in 1830. She was clearly a woman of prayer and must have encouraged the idea of the religious calling among her children. All five of her daughters entered convents and of her eight sons, six became priests, three of them bishops. Herbert, her eldest, went to school at Stonyhurst, Lancashire, from 1841 to 1847, moving to another Jesuit college in Belgium for three years. It seems his father hoped he would become a soldier, but after the Belgian sojourn he went for a year to Downside Abbey near Bath as an ecclesiastical student. In 1851 he arrived in Rome to study at the Collegio Romano but poor health made his seminary years a particularly trying time. Friends were concerned he might never be ordained. For this reason permission was sought for his ordination day to be brought forward. Herbert Vaughan was ordained priest in Lucca, Italy, on 28 October 1854 at the age of 22. He celebrated his first Mass the following day at the famous Servite church of the Annunziata in Florence.

(Opposite)
Cardinal Herbert Vaughan

Vaughan's considerable abilities were employed without delay. On return to England, Cardinal Wiseman appointed him Vice-President of Saint Edmund's College, Ware, Hertfordshire, the main seminary for southern England. It was a difficult time - he was probably too young for such responsibilities - and Vaughan suffered disappointing setbacks. He started to take on external tasks, including the founding of a mission at Enfield and building a church at Hertford, the county town.

Father Vaughan had always been drawn to the work of the Church's missionaries. As a boy he had wanted to be a missionary in Wales, no doubt conscious of his Welsh forbears. Later he was resolved to consecrate himself to the work of the foreign missions. His hero was Blessed Peter Claver and he saw himself setting off for Africa and Japan. He came to the conclusion that a great college was needed, able to train missionary priests and send them out to the world. He wanted to raise funds for the project internationally and obtained Cardinal Wiseman's permission to do so. Sailing for the Caribbean in December 1863 and starting work in Panama he found a situation in which priests were forbidden to celebrate Mass. The churches were all closed and people were dying of smallpox. Father Vaughan went into high gear. He celebrated the Eucharist, heard confessions and was keeping an appointment to say Mass at the house of a dying woman when he was arrested and finally expelled. He then headed for California, stayed five months and raised $25,000 for his college before setting out for South America - Panama again, Peru, Chile, then round the Horn on HMS *Charybdis* to Brazil. In June 1865, Manning as new Archbishop of Westminster summoned him home. Vaughan opened his college in a rented house the following year. Since he intended the money he had raised abroad to be used as a permanent endowment for students' maintenance, he was soon begging again. It is a tribute to his powers of persuasion that people

rallied round enthusiastically and in March 1871 a new college was opened with a community of thirty-four. This was the start of Saint Joseph's Missionary Society, Mill Hill, which exists to this day. Vaughan visited America again where he became fascinated by the power of the American press. Back in England, his purchase of *The Tablet* gave him the opportunity to work as an editor for a while.

Herbert Vaughan was made Bishop of Salford in 1872. He founded a pastoral seminary and Saint Bede's College, Manchester, working for the welfare of poor Catholic youngsters - an echo of Cardinal Manning's preoccupations in London. In Lancashire he established two homes, obtaining the approval of the local authority. His years in Salford were remembered for his ability to get things done. As Manning's successor at Westminster, Vaughan began fund-raising immediately - a task which he did not relish but at which he was now uniquely experienced. In the words of Edward Norman, 'his success as archbishop was precisely the achievement of the objectives he had laid down; essential work, quietly and effectively completed.' (Norman, *The English Catholic Church in the Nineteenth Century*).

The Cathedral, now more urgently needed than when the pledge for its building was first given to London's Catholics, would now be the monument to Vaughan's two great predecessors, Wiseman and Manning. The new Cardinal had a fine site on which to build - admittedly burdened with a £20,000 mortgage and shut away from the main street by tall houses on its western side, but his chief assets were faith in divine providence, boundless energy and the ability to enthuse others.

The site obtained by Manning had remained unoccupied for ten years, when Herbert Vaughan, after much reflection, resolved in 1894 to begin the construction of the Cathedral as soon as possible. Following a generous response from people to whom the project was presented privately, he declared his intentions in public and turned his attention to the choice of the right architect. Although confident in his ability to raise the necessary funds, he was less sure of his judgement regarding the style of architecture to be adopted and the best man for the job. Commendably Vaughan spent a full eighteen months after his return from Rome in the autumn of 1892, sounding out the opinions of those best qualified to guide him. Although the discussions were private, news of their substance leaked out and as many as a dozen architects approached the Cardinal with a view to presenting their ideas. John Francis Bentley, after thirty years' work on British church architecture, knew what was going on but made no attempt to promote his interests - beyond keeping himself abreast of developments. His lifelong practice had been to wait for work to come to him. Vaughan knew Bentley's work and was well-disposed towards him but was coming to the conclusion that an architectural competition - much in vogue at the time - was going to be necessary. This dismayed Bentley's supporters. One said: 'He hated competition and more than once told me he did not approve of the principle and moreover thought the results were always unsatisfactory.' The Finance Board wanted an architect appointed without a competition and Vaughan's own preference would have been for Bentley. But before making the decision it occurred to him to take soundings among the leading British architects of the day. When asked for one suggestion they were unanimous in proposing the name of John Bentley. The architect's offices were off the Strand at 13 John Street, Adelphi, and the Cardinal called personally to give him the news. Bentley relates that when thanked the Archbishop replied: 'You are not to thank *me*; it is your fellow architects you have to thank!'

John Bentley was born in Doncaster in 1839, the third surviving son among the seventeen children of Charles Bentley, a wine merchant, and his wife Ann (née

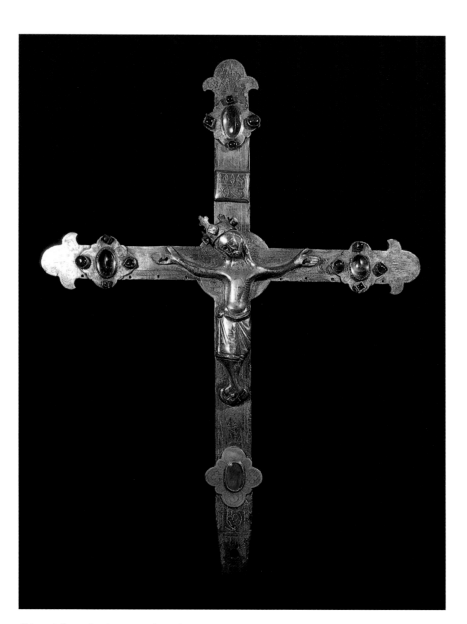

Thirteenth Century French processional cross, Limoges
(Catalogue number 86)

Bacchus). The family lived in an old house in French-gate, close to the parish church of Saint George which he loved and knew intimately from an early age. It was greatly renowned for the dignity and magnificence of its central tower giving it a cathedral-like quality. He attended a private school and was a voracious reader. He had a speech impediment but had virtually overcome it by the time he reached maturity. With his father, elder brothers and sisters he visited the Great Exhibition of 1851 which made a strong impression on him. Back home he loved to spend time in local masons' yards and joinery workshops where craftsmen were happy to share their knowledge with an intelligent youngster. Then on the night of 27 February 1853 the great church near his house caught fire and John, from the lane outside and wrapped in a blanket watched the hissing, crackling flames shoot into the night sky. In a short time the whole church was a glowing furnace and at 2 am, the roof fell in with a deafening crash. By 3.30 the church was a smouldering ruin. For John Bentley at 14, the loss of a building whose every inch he knew was a personal grief. He made a perfect scale model of the church from memory. The architect chosen to rebuild the Doncaster church was Sir Giles Gilbert Scott and work began immediately, with John Bentley haunting the site office of George Cleverley, a local mason appointed Clerk of Works. He was a willing assistant and so committed that his father agreed to let him leave school while still only fifteen. Soon he was a sort of Under Clerk of Works for repairs on Loversall Church, three miles from Doncaster. He was never satisfied with anything but the finest workmanship and once took over some carving from a slow craftsman and did it himself. Yet he was responsive to sincerity and had the ability to create enthusiasm in a diffident worker. In those early years, Bentley was developing a great interest in crafts and manual skills - knowledge that would serve him well when he came to design the details of Westminster Cathedral. After a brief stay at a Manchester engineering works it was clear that he

had no interest in the railways, so his father put him into the building trade. A friend introduced them to Richard Holland of Winslow & Holland in London, who could see from his superb drawing skills that the boy should be in an architect's office, but on the sceptical father's insistence, took him on as an apprentice in the building trade. Living on £60 a year, he would walk each day from lodgings with a clergyman at Camberwell Green to the firm's offices in Bloomsbury. Working in the drawing office he soon attracted the attention of the partners who generously proposed to release him from his indentures, should any ecclesiastical architect be keen to take him on. They already had in mind an architect who had been intrigued by some drawings he had seen from Winslow & Holland. The contractors told him they were the work of one of their apprentices and before long Bentley was working for Henry Clutton, the architect who would in due course provide Cardinal Manning with the first ideas for a cathedral at Westminster.

Bentley was never articled to Clutton, although he spent a number of years at his busy and well-connected practice and was offered a partnership in the firm at the age of 21. He chose instead to set up on his own, and experienced the chill winds of uncertainty that often accompany such a move. In 1862 he took a couple of rooms for his practice at 14 Southampton Street, overlooking Maiden Lane near the Strand. With the start of his independent career John Bentley's chambers became an informal meeting point for architects and other professional people, young and old. Many remembered him as a loyal friend and stimulating company but deeply serious about his work and aspirations.

Bentley was of medium height but broad-shouldered with a large head, wide brow and a mane of tousled hair. He had deep-set blue eyes with a 'faraway look' noticed by many and a humorous smile which clearly stayed with him into middle age. His daughter would later write: 'It lit up his whole countenance, beginning with an indescribable twinkle of merriment in the eyes, impossible to forget. His children would often repeat things that had amused him before, in the hope that he would again break into laughter.' All his life, however, he suffered from severe headaches which in the early years of striving sometimes gave way to depression. He was careless about exercise and diet, saying, 'If I were to eat in the middle of the day I should lose so much time ...' and his passion for work kept him at his desk until late at night. Friends passing his rooms very late often saw the lamp still burning. They would come in to remonstrate only to find he had not been out all day.

In parallel with his professional independence John Bentley had also reached a new point of departure in terms of religious faith. Having got to know a good number of Roman Catholics and members of the clergy in the course of his work, including the first Archbishop of Westminster, Nicholas Wiseman, Bentley moved steadily but unhurriedly from his nonconformist beginnings towards the Roman Catholic Church. On Wednesday of Holy Week 1862, Cardinal Wiseman received him into the Roman Catholic community at Saint Francis Church, Pottery Lane, Notting Hill, a building designed by Henry Clutton which Bentley had helped supervise. Bentley had also provided the design for a Byzantine monstrance for this church, his first work in that style. For his confirmation name he chose Francis.

By July 1868 Bentley had moved his work to new premises at 13 John Street, Adelphi. This enabled him to accommodate as his housekeeper Mrs Cleverley, the widow of the Clerk of Works whom John had worked alongside as a boy; she had come to London from Doncaster to look after 'Master Johnnie'. He occupied these premises for thirty-four years until his death in March 1902. John Bentley was 35 when he married.

Chalice and ciborium, gift of Cardinal Manning in commemoration of the First Vatican Council (Catalogue numbers 44 and 45)

His mother had recently died and the loss seemed to awaken in him a need for the partnership of a woman that his career had somehow displaced. Margaret Fleuss was fourteen years younger than Bentley, the daughter of a German anglophile who had settled in London. They met at the home of mutual friends in Hampstead. A fortnight on, during a walk on Hampstead Heath, he proposed marriage. Before the wedding she took instruction in the Catholic faith, staying for a while with Franciscan nuns in Bayswater. It was there that she was received into the Catholic Church and confirmed by Cardinal Manning on 8 September 1874. They were married in October. After a brief honeymoon on the Isle of Wight they settled down in furnished rooms in Belmont Road, Clapham, while looking for a permanent home in the area. Bentley eventually discovered to his great delight that one of three old terrace houses, the work of Sir Christopher Wren, would soon be available at 43 Old Town.

For the next twenty years the income derived from his profession was considerable - upwards of £1,700 per annum. In 1874 he was engaged on such lucrative and widely varied projects as decorative work for Lord Beaumont at Carlton Towers, the Roman Catholic seminary in Hammersmith, a distillery at Finsbury, together with stained glass, organ cases and a host of church furnishing designs. His social life in London had given way to an absorbing home life in Clapham and a busy work schedule, although he rarely mentioned his work at home. By 1894 he was able to purchase the freehold of a substantial new home, about eighty years old, one of three set back in a drive known as 'The Sweep'. Bentley set about remodelling the interior just as Cardinal Vaughan was about to appoint an architect at Westminster. Now, in July 1894, the decision of the Archbishop that John Francis Bentley would be the architect of Westminster Cathedral had brought him to the threshold of the greatest challenge of his professional life. As he was

congratulated warmly by his friends he put the work on his new home into other hands. One of his first colleagues wrote to him:

Dear Bentley,

Just a line of hearty congratulation on the glorious news in your letter this morning .... You have had many a disappointment, but at last, the reward has come .... The Cardinal's action will gratify all thinking men who appreciate intellect and true art ...

The Road to Byzantium

The first decision to be addressed by architect and client was the style of architecture to be chosen. Cardinal Vaughan had inherited the Clutton drawings from his predecessor but the projected cost of realising the plans had slowed the pace of fund-raising - so ambitious and costly were they perceived to be. Expertise was not a problem. Since the days of Pugin, the Victorians had become masters of neo-gothic splendour - Bentley was a practitioner himself. He had several fine neo-gothic Catholic churches to his credit, including Holy Rood, Watford and Corpus Christi, Brixton. But it was also in the nature of the style that structure and ornament were inseparable. They were completed together or not at all, so the whole cost would be payable at the same time. When the decision-makers finally settled on the Byzantine style they were doing so in part for economic reasons. The complete structure of a neo-Byzantine basilica could be erected rapidly, leaving ornamentation to be completed 'at leisure', if necessary by later generations. Vaughan had already expressed his preference for the form of a basilica to which Bentley eventually agreed, but he later said: 'Personally, I should have preferred a Gothic church, yet on consideration I am inclined to think the Cardinal was right.' The Cardinal's thinking was also bound up in the matter of the dedication or title to be chosen for the Cathedral as we shall see later. 'He wanted a large building, in the Roman

basilican tradition, on the model of Constantine's original Church of Saint Peter in Rome, itself used as the model for the first cathedral at Canterbury' (Norman, *The English Catholic Church in the Nineteenth Century*).

Bentley was unmoved by the idea of a specifically Italianate building and forwarded a proposal of his own. He was equally interested in a return to the tradition that flowed from the Romans with their mastery of brick and concrete construction. But he wanted to link hands with a more specific historical trend. In 324 AD, the Emperor Constantine had moved the capital of the Roman Empire from Rome to Byzantium, renamed Constantinople, a move which brought about a new synthesis of the architectural styles of east and west. This is generally described as Byzantine. The eastern contribution was the use of domes to cover polygonal and square plans. This Byzantine influence is found in Venice, especially with Saint Mark's Basilica, and other centres. Santa Sophia in Constantinople (532-537 AD) also shows the successful use of a central domed

space. While the building plan is square, semi-domes or apses are built against the arches which support the main dome so that flowing curvilinear shapes are the predominant impression given, especially inside the building. Byzantine theology also brought its own symbolism - the cruciform ground plan was a reminder of the sacrifice of Christ, while domes represented his burial and resurrection, as well as heaven itself.

A Time to Speak

John Bentley believed that the principal Catholic church in England should not be built in a style which was 'confined to Italy, England or any other nation', but rather that it should be absolutely primitive Christian (i.e. Byzantine), a style which by the ninth century had spread over many countries. Bentley's London was on the crest of a wave, basking in the successes of imperial expansion and no English professional would have been unaffected by such a strong national self-image. To Bentley it seemed inappropriate that a cathedral in the centre of what was then the world's

leading metropolis might be limited by some national or insular characteristic of style. Vaughan was won over, but the architectural world was still divided. Divided or not, the Cardinal wanted to bring this phase of the process to a rapid conclusion and press on with the work. So he gave three reasons in support of his decision to build a neo-Byzantine edifice. Firstly, that a church of this type, with a wide nave and a view of the sanctuary unimpeded by columns, screens or organs, was best-suited to the congregational needs of a metropolitan cathedral. All the great liturgies could take place in the sight, as well as the hearing of the people. The second reason was the financial one. As the Cardinal explained in the first edition of the *Westminster Cathedral Record* in 1896: 'Fortunately, the Christian-Byzantine style which has been adopted lends itself to an economical and most advantageous mode of procedure. We can cover the whole space, we can erect the whole building, apart from decoration and ornament, which in other styles would form a substantial and costly part of the structure. In this way the essentials of space and proportion are

obtainable at once for a moderate sum, while the decoration may be applied as time goes on, according to the devotion and generosity of succeeding generations.' The third reason proceeded from the second. Vaughan felt that it would be impossible to erect a new gothic cathedral that would be a worthy counterpart to the ancient Westminster Abbey nearby and it would be foolish to attempt it. Since gothic ornament is integral with structure the entire cost would have to be met as the building took shape - far beyond the means of one generation of Catholics.

In the event, the fabric of the building would be completed by 1903, just seven years after the laying of the foundation stone. The first major religious service would be the funeral of the Cardinal, who, like his architect, died just before the completion of the primary structure. A hundred years on, both men can be seen to have been far-sighted, practical and courageous.

While Vaughan turned to the job of raising funds for building, Bentley was left to his own devices to produce a design. Until that time, he had gained little experience of Byzantine architecture nor the opportunity to study original models. He had therefore decided to make an extensive tour of sites in Europe where such churches could be examined at first hand. With the choice of style now settled, he started making arrangements to visit Italy and Constantinople spending the summer of 1894 setting his professional house in order in readiness for a prolonged absence from London. It also occurred to him that some study of Italian would be useful: he had not a single word of the language and his Latin was unlikely to get him very far in the more rural areas he planned to visit.. On the evening of 22 November 1894 the architect left for Milan, armed with an open circular letter from the Cardinal designed to coax favours from the various clerical officials he was likely to along the way.

In the brick-built church of Sant'Ambrogio, Milan, founded in the fourth century and, as it now stands, a Roman basilica of the twelfth, Bentley contemplated a powerful tradition. The curious galleries over its facade, the baldachino, supported by four ancient porphyry columns (on which he would model the one at Westminster), the lofty brick campanile of the ninth century, all fascinated him. He proceeded to Pavia and described Certosa as 'the most sumptuous church I have yet beheld'. In the cathedral at Pisa he found Byzantine influences; a Latin cross in plan, with a single cupola at the intersection of the nave and transepts. This feature would also be incorporated at Westminster. Bentley's tour included Lucca with its Romanesque churches of San Michele and San Martino, then Pistoia with a cathedral of similar type, before proceeding to Florence. His opinion of the Duomo at Florence, taken from books and plans was confirmed on viewing the reality - 'architecturally the worst large building I have ever seen.' The Campanile and the Baptistry made up for it, however, as did a visit to the delightful Fiesole before heading for Rome. He wrote: 'The morning after my arrival I made straight for Saint Peter's - not looking into the many churches I passed on the road, that my first act might be one of veneration to him who is the centre and keystone of Christian unity. I venerate the place more than I can say and my only regret is that the human part of it is not more worthy of so august a purpose. I cannot conceive that any architect can sing its praises. Of course, the effect is fine, but produced at the sacrifice of scale.' So much for Saint Peter's Basilica!

He spent six weeks in Rome and was warmly received by friends and acquaintances. The Rector of the Scots College, Monsignor Campbell, went with him to the catacombs of Saint Callistus and Saint Lucina and Bentley appreciated his considerable knowledge of the subject. He received willing help from Monsignor Stonor, Archbishop of

Interior brick work completed. The dome of Saint Edward's Tower is ready to cap the Camponile

Monstrance, Toledo c.1620. Surmounted by Saint Dominic, thus probably from a Dominican House (Catalogue number 95)

Trebizond, Monsignor Stanley, later to be an assistant bishop at Westminster, and the Father General of the Redemptorists. With the help of these friends, he obtained a private audience with Pope Leo XIII, attended his early morning Mass and later talked with him in French. The pope held the architect's hands in his own, finally bestowing a special blessing on the great work of designing a new Cathedral in London. Later he was invited to attend the annual Requiem for Pope Pius IX in the Sistine Chapel, where a seat was assigned to him next to the assembled cardinals.

The month of January passed in a deep study of early Christian art, together with pagan Roman structures such as the Basilica of Maxentius and the Baths of Caracalla whose massive forms find an echo in the interior brickwork at Westminster. Next the architect spent a week in Naples, visiting the ruins of Pompeii and climbing Vesuvius. He was back in Rome in the first week of February, then visiting Assisi and moving on to Perugia in the Umbrian Hills. It turned out to be the coldest winter in living memory but the intrepid Londoner continued his studies. We can imagine John Bentley shivering in unheated churches while the snow piled up outside. He warmed to Perugia's fifteenth-century gothic Cathedral of San Lorenzo and the sixth-century circular church of Sant' Angelo with its sixteen antique columns inside. Then he pushed on to Ravenna and the ancient churches of the Adriatic seaboard which delighted him. The sixth-century church of San Vitale, completed by Justinian, showed him an octagonal plan with a small apsidal choir extended to the east. At Sant' Appollinare-in-Classe, outside Ravenna, of similar date and history with its nave and aisles carried out by Byzantine artists on Roman models, he pondered the challenge of adapting the Byzantine idea for modern congregational needs.

In Bologna, which he reached by 18 February, the brick church of S Stefano interested him greatly together with the unfinished sixteenth-century Municipal Palace. He arrived in Venice via Ferrara (where he wanted to see its twelfth-century cathedral) pretty well exhausted from cold and the strains of travel. His letters relate that he managed to avoid a serious chill by means of a hot bath and fourteen hours of uninterrupted sleep. After that, refreshed in mind and body, Bentley began a minute examination of Saint Mark's. His affection for this church never left him and the lion heads seen throught the buildings at Westminster are a subtle reference to its influence. Only a year before his death he obtained a copy of the monumental and detailed survey of Saint Mark's by Ongania, first published in Venice in 1881.

He had planned to continue his journey with a visit to Constantinople, but news of a cholera epidemic reached him and he had to cancel his plans. It is a surprise to find that he was not particularly put out by this turn of events. Instead, he continued to develop his knowledge and understanding of Saint Mark's. Regarding Santa Sophia in Constantinople, he had brought with him a newly-published book on Justinian's great church by Lethaby and Swainson, the leading Byzantine experts of the day. Although Bentley never saw it, Santa Sophia was to be a recognisable influence on the design of Westminster Cathedral. Yet later on he remarked: 'San Vitale at Ravenna and Lethaby's book really told me all I wanted.' In fact, Bentley abhorred the idea of slavish imitation.

He was not in the habit of making sketches or written notes on his travels. John Bentley's lifelong practice had been to cultivate interior vision and he was returning to London with a clear mental picture of the church he would create. 'Everything,' he would say, 'the reality as though before me solidly - light and shade, colour, all is there - and not until I see this in its entirety do I ever begin to draw.' Years after Bentley's death, William Lethaby, (1857-1931), whose book he had relied on, would be generous in his praise of the Cathedral after seeing over every part of it:

'Spectators have a way of thinking that "a
piece of architecture" is erected so that
they shall come and say whether they like
it or not. And they usually say that they
don't quite like it and something ought to
be different. A younger man may not
understand the burden of such a work -
the thousands of decisions, adjustments,
compromises, the power of getting things
done, the responsibility, the strain - all are
hidden. Mr Bentley's cathedral is a
building nobly planned, carefully balanced,
serious and serene. The great things are
the masterly structure and the sincerity of
the whole work. Throughout all the
preliminary talk about the choice of a
style, Bentley must have known what he
wanted to build' (de l'Hôpital,
Westminster Cathedral and its Architect).

John Bentley's Grand Tour was coming to
an end. From Venice he visited Torcello
Cathedral with its early Christian
foundations of a bishop's throne in the
apse, followed by the thirteenth-century
basilica of Saint Anthony at Padua, with
its seven cupolas. Starting for home on 7
March 1895, by way of Verona, Turin,
Dijon and Paris, Bentley was back in
London on 19 March. Immediately, plans
and sketches were prepared and
submitted to Cardinal Vaughan. These
were studied with alacrity and although
the first ground-plan was replaced by
another and then a third, their rapport
was good. As a first-class administrator,
Vaughan knew when decisions had to be
taken rapidly. He summed up his
approach: 'Having laid down certain
conditions as to size, space, chapels and
style, I left the rest to him. He offered me
the choice between a vaulted roof and
one of saucer-shaped domes: I chose the
latter. He wished to build two
campaniles; I said one would be enough
for me. For the rest he had a free hand.'
With equal despatch, arrangements went
ahead for the ceremony of laying the
foundation stone.

The date of the founding ceremony was
set for 29 June, the Feast of Saints Peter
and Paul. Although the day started
overcast, it soon turned warm and sunny.

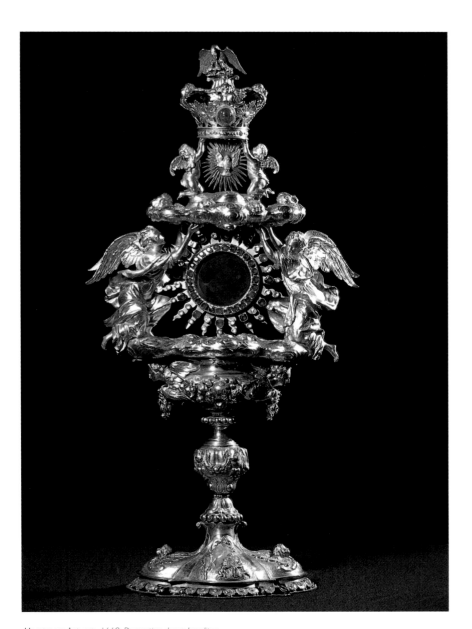

*Monstrance Antwerp, 1669. Decoration shows Israelites
gathering manna and the Last Supper
(Catalogue number 97)*

Flags and bunting decorated the tiered seats erected for the occasion with space for 2,500 dignitaries and invited guests, although 10,000 are estimated to have been present. An altar had been set up with a large plain red cross at the spot where the permanent altar would be placed. This large cross was the first reference to the dedication or title that was given to the new Cathedral that day. It is generally described as The Metropolitan Cathedral of the Precious Blood but the full dedication is as follows;

To the Most Precious Blood of Our Lord Jesus Christ
To his Blessed Mother,
His Foster Father Saint Joseph
and Saint Peter his Vicar.

Secondary Patrons

Saint Augustine and all British saints
Saint Patrick and all saints of Ireland

Every Christian church has such a dedication, chosen from a hierarchy of possible titles. The origins of the practice can be traced to the early days of the Church in Rome. Cardinal Vaughan must have pondered these things, seeking as he did to recall the earliest origins of the Christian Church, both in England and in Rome. Catholics had been inspired by John Henry Newman's memorable reference to a 'Second Spring' in a famous address in 1852 and had long been praying for a renaissance of Catholic life in England. In terms of commitment, dedication and hope, a rebirth did take place, but not quite on the lines envisaged at the time. Yet in this context and conscious of the long, linear history of the Christian centuries, Cardinal Vaughan chose the *Precious Blood of the Saviour* to be the dedication of Westminster Cathedral - an echo of Canterbury as the Cathedral Church of Christ and the original title of the foremost cathedral in Rome - the ancient church of the Lateran, as the Church of the Saviour. It is interesting to note that Augustine had followed the order of the great patriachal basilicas in Rome when

founding principal churches in England, with *Saint Peter* for York and *Saint Paul* for London. Indeed for many centuries Saint Paul's in Rome was placed under the protection of the English kings.

A feast-day honouring the Most Precious Blood of Christ had been instituted by Pope Pius IX as recently as 1849 and anyone entering Westminster Cathedral today can see immediately how this primary title has been visually expressed. Looking up the long nave towards the sanctuary where the foundation stone rests, the view is dominated by the great rood or crucifix suspended from the roof. In the narthex - close to the entrance - two central columns of deep red Norwegian granite frame the view; pillars that symbolise the redeeming blood of Christ poured out in powerful streams across the earth.

The foundation ceremony began as a long procession of clergy left Archbishop's House in Carlisle Place and made its way to the site, leading Cardinal Vaughan and Cardinal Michael Logue, Archbishop of Armagh, to their thrones. By a special accommodation of the Holy See, the Archbishop of Westminster completed his vesting by donning the *pallium* which he would normally wear only during Mass. The *pallium* has the most ancient history and is worn by a metropolitan archbishop. Derived from a priestly stole, it is woven from lambswool and held in place by jewelled pins - a symbol of his pastoral responsibility to care for Christ's sheep and lambs (John 21:15-17). Some of the earliest sculptures from the Roman catacombs show Christ as a young shepherd, clean-shaven and carrying a lamb slung across his shoulders (John 10:11). With these simple bands of white wool embroidered with crosses about his shoulders and clad in a magnificent cope of white and gold, Cardinal Vaughan, together with the Irish Cardinal, advanced towards the massive corner-stone of Cornish granite (a gift of the Freeman family firm from their Penryn quarries), suspended over its bed of concrete.

Pyx - travelling container for the Eucharist - from the reign of Charles I. Engraved with crucifix before the Holy City (Catalogue number 103)

A Time to Gather Stones

Quietly, the architect and attendant masons rose to assist them in locating the stone in its precise position. In a cavity beneath, a cylinder had been placed containing a record of the event and a copy of the dedication. The stone was laid *'In the name of the Father, and of the Son and of the Holy Ghost, that true faith may flourish here, and the fear of God and brotherly love, and that this place may be devoted to prayer'* and the choir sang psalm 127: 'NISI DOMINUS AEDIFICAVERIT DOMUM …' (Unless the Lord builds the house, those who build it labour in vain...). The Cardinal then set out to bless the marked-out boundaries of the foundations, beyond the sight of those in the stands but watched by great numbers who had crowded the roofs and windows of surrounding buildings. After a Mass sung by Cardinal Logue, both prelates gave a lunch for 1,100 in a marquee on the south side of the site. During his speech Vaughan described the role he foresaw for Westminster Cathedral: 'The Catholic body must have a Cathedral in which the sacred liturgy of the Church is carried out in all its fulness day by day, and many times a day, as it was of old in Westminster and in Canterbury.'

Meanwhile the crowds milling round the newly-laid foundation stone examined the chiselled inscription, and made what they could of the following:

DIE XXIXO IUNII AD MDCCCLXXXXV
ANNO XVIIIO PONT LEONIS PAPAE
XIII

REGNI VICTORIAE REGINAE LIXO
BIENNIO POST ANGLIAM BEATISSIMAE
VIRGINI ET S PETRO APOST PRINCIPI
CONSECRATAM

HIC LAPIS PRIMARIUS
ECCL CATHEDRALIS WESTMON
DOMINO NOSTRO IESU CHRISTO
QUI SUO NOS REDEMIT SANGUINE
BEATAE MARIAE MATRI EIUS
IMMACULATAE
S PETRO PRIMO EIUS VICARIO
S IOSEPH ECC CATH PATRONO

AC DEINDE S AUGUSTINO APOST
ANGLIAE S EDUARDO REG CONF
ET O O SS BRITANN S PATRITIO ET O
O SS HIBERNIAE DEDICANDAE
AB EMO ET RMO DOMINO HERBERTO
CARD VAUGHAN ARCHIEPO
WESTMON IIIO EMO ET RMO
DOMINO MICHAELE CARD LOGUE
ARCHIEPO
ARMACH TOTIUS HIBERNAE PRIMATE
ASSISTENTE
POSITUS EST

IESU REDEMPTOR MISERERE ANGLIAE
SANCTA MARIA CUIUS DOS EST
ANGLIA
S PETRE APOST S IOSEPH SPONSE
BVM ET O O SS BRIT ET HIB

ORATE PRO ANGLIA

On the 29 June 1895, in the eighteenth year of the pontificate of Pope Leo XIII in the 59th year of the reign of Queen Victoria, two years after England was consecrated to the Blessed Virgin and Saint Peter, Prince of Apostles this foundation stone of the Cathedral Church of Westminster dedicated to Our Lord Jesus Christ who redeemed us with his blood to Blessed Mary, his Immaculate Mother to Saint Peter, his first Vicar to Saint Joseph, Patron of the Cathedral Church and thereafter to Saint Augustine, Apostle of the English to Saint Edward, King and Confessor, and all the Saints of England to Saint Patrick and all the Saints of Ireland was laid by the Most Eminent and Reverend Lord, Herbert Cardinal Vaughan, Third Archbishop of Westminster, assisted by the Most Eminent and Reverend Lord, Michael Cardinal Logue, Archbishop of Armagh, Primate of All Ireland.

Jesus our Redeemer, have mercy on England. Holy Mary, whose dowry is England, Saint Peter the apostle, Saint Joseph, husband of the Blessed Virgin Mary, and All Saints of England and Ireland, pray for England.

No sooner had the foundation stone been laid than preparation of the site began for the laying of the foundations of Westminster Cathedral. It was found that under the old prison there had been a great platform of concrete nine foot thick, covering more than half the area within the new boundary lines. Although this needed supplementing, the existence of so much valuable concrete resulted in a considerable economy. Bentley's biographer, his daughter, Winefride de l'Hôpital, provides ample information regarding the construction of the Cathedral for anyone studying Victorian building methods of the period (de l'Hôpital, *Westminster Cathedral and its architect*). However, some of the details she provides are also of general interest.

14,500 tons of earth and old brickwork were removed from the excavations by means of cranes - one large Scotch crane able to lift 3 tons at the maximum reach of 50 feet and two steam travelling cranes (2 tons minimum) for which 800 feet of temporary railway was laid. Most of the earth was taken up river in barges and on to Dagenham, to fill a disused dock. 6,000 tons of concrete, combining

Thames ballast and Portland cement were required for the new foundations, its composition decided only after a series of careful tests by the contractors, Mowlem of Westminster. The second contract, for brickwork foundations, was taken over by Perry of Bow in January 1896 and completed by the following October. Over 2 million hand-made bricks were needed for the foundations alone. Progress was rapid, despite a strike by unskilled labourers in May 1895. The action was due to a recent rise in bricklayers' wages with the men holding out for a similar rate rise. Work came to a standstill, but by June a full complement of men was back at work. By October, Perry was ready to withdraw and hand over to the contractor responsible for the superstructure. Five firms had tendered; Shillitoe and Sons of Bury Saint Edmunds was awarded the contract, having recently worked on Truro Cathedral, additions to the National Gallery and the restoration of Westminster Hall. Their task was to erect the building up to the level of the domes, with the price of brickwork fixed at £20 per rod. Every two weeks Bentley's long-term surveyor, Mr Gate measured up the progress, whereby the contractor on presentation of the architect's certificate was paid immediately. The risk of debts piling up was avoided by the Cardinal's practice of raising the money and paying for the work continuously as it was carried on. The builders were contracted to employ at least 260 men full-time. When the Cardinal was in funds, they were at liberty to take on as many more hands as they could find work for.

A Time to Build

A battery of tests had been done by the architect on the wide choice of bricks available to him. Those selected for the piers and walls were put through rigorous weight-sustaining tests by Kirkaldy and Sons, his stress-testing engineers. Ordinary London brick offered only half the bearing strength of Fletton wire-cut bricks which resisted 185.6 tons per square foot, while Poole wire-cut bricks

could bear 398.6 tons. Blue Staffordshire
bricks, impervious to water and used for
outside facing of underground work and
damp-courses, showed satisfactory
resistance to pressure of up to 700 tons
per square foot. For the exterior, Bentley
chose Bracknell red facings, supplied by
Lawrence and Sons, an exceptionally fine,
thin brick giving five courses to the foot.
The building interior was lined with
Faversham stocks left rough and
unpointed to provide a satisfactory
surface for the adherence of marble and
mosaic when the time came. The beauty
and originality of the Cathedral brickwork
is self-evident. Each of the twelve and a
half million bricks was hand-made -
machine-made bricks being outlawed by
the architect. At first, the difficulty of
getting adequate supplies caused
troublesome delays, until the contractors
bought a brickfield at Fletton, near
Peterborough, able to deliver 60,000
bricks a week.

When English granite prices were high,
there was talk of importing the stone
from Baveno which had supplied the
eighty massive columns for the
reconstruction of Saint Paul's Basilica in
Rome. Fortunately, at the moment it was
needed for the plinth of the external
walls, the price of English granite fell and
the order was placed with Freeman and
Sons of Penryn. Many varieties of the best
hard freestones were considered for
masonry, both plain and decorated.
Eventually a strong Portland was chosen
for the external dressings, so important
for the distinctive white banding of the
exterior. All the masonry was worked on
site, although supplies were not always
readily available and delays were caused.
C.H. Mullis, the Clerk of Works, had
worked for Bentley before and was
chosen again for his capacity and integrity.
But soon it was necessary to provide him
with an assistant, Percy Lamb, and the
two men continued their joint supervision
until the campanile was finished in 1903.
Lamb stayed on in sole charge until 1905
when all structural work was completed.
In 1896 Cardinal Vaughan sent Canon
(later Bishop) Patrick Fenton to see Pope

*1845 reliquary of the true cross, School of Pugin
(Catalogue number 105)*

John Francis Bentley

Leo XIII, taking with him a set of plans for the new cathedral, complete with Italian measurements and intended for the Vatican Library.

In April 1897, Bentley wrote cheerfully that 'the red brick facing is making a great show'. Progress was so steady and encouraging that early in 1898 Cardinal Vaughan was pressing for an opening date of 1900 - fifty years on from the restoration of the Roman Catholic Hierarchy. At the outset he had actually reckoned on the building being completed in two years - a manifest impossibility when it is considered that the foundations alone took fifteen months. But his monthly disbursements were at their highest yet and March of the following year found him writing in the *Cathedral Record* appealing for more help. It was now well-known that Cardinal Vaughan would authorise nothing he could not pay for, and once again his building fund received the contributions that were urgently required. A new contract was drawn up with Shillitoe in May 1899 for the erection of the domes and vaulting. By June it was announced that the brick and stonework, excluding that of the campanile, were up to their full height and that it only remained to finish the various turrets. Brickwork pointing would be completed as the external scaffolding was removed. Inside, work began on the first part of the vaulting, that of the Blessed Sacrament Chapel. Then followed the ceiling over the choir and the sanctuary dome. From this time, the interior of the building 'looked like a great forest whose trees had been struck dead and stripped of bark and foliage. Vast avenues of timber, designed to carry the wooden centering of the domes, were constructed with such scientific skill and strength as had never before been required except possibly for the dome of Saint Paul's' (de l'Hôpital, vol. I, p. 87). The construction of the domes exercised Bentley greatly. Various methods were possible and had to be carefully assessed. From the beginning he was determined to avoid the use of iron, for wherever there is iron

there is some expansion under heat. He wanted domes wholly made of concrete combining Portland cement with broken brick. The domes were constructed during fourteen months of great concentration and anxiety for the architect and his clerk of works. The easternmost dome of the nave was positioned first, together with the vault and choir apse, completed in June 1899. Then came the sanctuary dome, the middle nave dome and finally, the westernmost. In 1896, funding had been invited for the twenty-one nave and transept pillars, the six in the sanctuary and fourteen others needed. By May 1899 only five of the twenty-one main monoliths had been subscribed for, although the whole number had been ordered. Some deliveries were delayed due to war conditions between Greece and Turkey in the summer of 1897. The Turks had seized the columns as spoils of war but later released them to arrive safely in London. By December 1900, all were paid for and in position. Two months later the galleries were complete. The tower, which measures 273 feet to the top of the cupola had reached a height of 182 feet. When the architect visited the building for the last time on 1 March 1902 it had risen another 40 feet.

For the last years of Bentley's life, the Cathedral at Westminster was the central and engrossing theme. There were other commissions, including a consultancy to the Bishop of Brooklyn for a gothic cathedral that took him to the United States, but by far the greatest share of his attention and energy was concentrated on completing his greatest work. The first warning sign that his health was not what it should be for a man of 59, was a slight, paralysing stroke in November 1898. He knew then that with so much yet to be accomplished, time was fast running out. Nothing would persuade him to take the absolute rest that was recommended. As soon as he could, he began laying down details of the work of completion that would need to follow the public opening of the shell of the building. It is clear that he was working under immense pressure.

Saint Dunstan's Studio
Seymour Place, Fulham Road
South Kensington, S.W.

From
Omar Ramsden & Alwyn C. E. Carr
to His Grace The Archbishop of Westminster.

Bifel that on a day from his high shrine
Saint Dunstan rose, ful gracious and benigne,
And when that he had blest his follwers tweye
And good dog Lippo, thus this Saint did saye:
'My Sons,' quod he, 'ye've wrought this long, long, yeare
A Monstrance fit for Holy Westminstere;
Gold-bete it is, with precious stonés rare,
That once did glitter on a ladye faire.
And since that it is done, 'tis mete and wel
Ye bid all friendés round about that dwell
To joy with you. Ther nis namo to tell.'

Lordinges and ladyes, therefore, one and all,
We bid you for to hold high festivall
Upon the Nineteenth day of leafy June
From Nine o' the clock til midnight comes too soon.
Most tender Musick shall your soules witch,
And songes swete - ther never nas noon swich
Since Chaunticleer gan tune his merrie throte
To maken melodye for Pertelote.

Come then, good Sir, faire Mistress! Pray attend
Saint Dunstan's shrine, would ye be clepéd friend;
Ne fail not, would ye not be clépéd foe,
To send us worde if that ye come or no.

Monstrance with stand. Omar Ramsden
and Alwyn Carr, 1906
(Catalogue number 99)

Fortunately he was fairly impervious to the soubriquets going around at the time - 'Cardinal Vaughan's Railway Station' and 'The Roman Candle' referring to the ever-rising height of the campanile. Nor would he live to hear the completed side-chapels compared to 'bathrooms designed by Harrods' or read Ian Nairn's muted praise in 1966:

'For me, this building shows the difference between actually being and trying very-hard-to-be, better than any in London. For very many thousands of others, the Cathedral is a holy place and a house of God. If I offend them, I am sorry. J. F. Bentley was a man who never found himself. Competent and full of feeling, he built in many styles yet was at home in none of them. This, a kind of free Byzantine, was just one more style. The marble, which is glorious, can mesmerize momentarily and so can the detail which, like the tower, seems to depend more on the Imperial Institute than on anything from across the Channel' (Nairn, *Nairn's London*).

By contrast, at the turn of the century, the scaffolding came down to reveal a building which the architectural establishment were happy to applaud without reservation. Representing the profession, Professor William Lethaby and Norman Shaw visited the Cathedral in December 1901. Shaw wrote: 'Beyond all doubt the finest church that has been built for centuries. The design is superb in scale and character. The architect has converted conditions which to many would have been serious obstacles into stepping stones to a great triumph.' Lethaby was also fulsome: 'The constructive ideas are finely conceived and realised with great daring, assurance and success. What appeals to me is the masterly simplicity by which a huge unit bay, 60 feet square, four times repeated, and a noble apse form the effective interior. The scale is very large - the span equal to the largest known - and the height ample. Subsidiary parts like the side chapels are themselves large, but the main church carries them proudly, as a

liner carries little boats on davits' (*Architectural Review,* January 1902).

In February 1902, The Royal Institute of British Architects nominated Bentley for the King's Gold Medal. He would have been nominated a year earlier, but for the death of Queen Victoria - no medal was awarded in 1901. He was delighted. 'I appreciate', he wrote, 'the Gold Medal, coming as it does from my confreres, to whose judgement I attach the utmost importance.' It was an honour he would never receive. Bentley died on 2 March, the day before the committee met and Edward VII decided that the medal should not be awarded posthumously. Nevertheless, in the entrance hall of the Institute in Portland Place, where the names of the Royal Gold Medalists of the RIBA from 1848 are incised in stone, the following inscription appears alone on an adjoining wall:

John Francis Bentley was nominated for the award of the gold medal in 1902 but died before the nomination could be confirmed.

By the early part of 1903 the whole exterior of Westminster Cathedral was finished, except for the mosaic in the entrance-arch of the west front. Bentley's friend Christian Symons produced a number of designs for this tympanum which still exist but eventually the project was completed in 1916 by Robert Anning Bell whose other work in the Cathedral is the altarpiece mosaic in the Lady Chapel. Here above the West Door this deeply recessed tympanum represents Christ seated and holding an open book displaying the words:

EGO SUM HOSTIUM; PER ME SI QUIS INTROIERIT SALVABITUR
(I am the gate: if anyone enters by me, he shall be saved. John 10:9).

On the left stands the Blessed Virgin and on the right, Saint Joseph. Kneeling on either side are Saint Peter and Saint Edward the Confessor, patrons of Westminster, the latter holding a cramp

ring. Cardinal Bourne was less than delighted with the result and others criticised the choice of a white background rather than the more traditional blue or gold. Above the mosaic the following words appear:

DOMINE JESU REX ET REDEMPTOR PER SANGUINEM TUUM SALVA NOS
(Lord Jesus, King and Redeemer, save us by your blood).

The doorway below is surmounted by a bas-relief of the sacred host and a chalice. On either side are sculpted medallions containing busts of twelve of the Archbishops of Canterbury. From left to right these are: Saint Augustine 597, Saint Laurentius 604, Saint Mellitus 619, Saint Justus 624, Saint Honorius 627, Saint Theodore 668, Saint Dunstan 960 - The West Door - Saint Elphege 1005, Saint Anselm 1093, Saint Thomas 1162, Saint Edmund 1234, Boniface 1254. On either side of the north-west porch in Ambrosden Avenue are medallions of four of the Doctors of the Church. From the left: Saint Augustine of Hippo 430, Saint Gregory the Great 604, Saint Francis de Sales 1622 and Saint Alphonsus Liguori 1787. Above the doorway on the left, Saint Peter is shown as key-bearer and on the right, Saint Edward the Confessor close to the base of the campanile which bears his name. In his hands he carries a model of Westminster Abbey which he founded.

The Campanile or Bell Tower is 30 foot square and 284 feet high to the top of the cross. This contains a fragment of the wooden cross reputedly found by the Empress Helena at Jerusalem in 326 AD. The mother of Constanstine, the first Christian Emperor, she had come to the Holy Land in her old age, to honour the sites associated withg the life and death of Jesus. The cross she uncovered near the site of the Holy Sepulchre became an object of veneration and a strong tradition remains that it was the instrument of Christ's crucifixion.

The Cathedral tower is faced with red brick and Portland stone and at a level of 218 feet there is an intricate detail comprising arched, coupled balconies on each side. Twelve small buttresses support a circular drum beneath the cupola, each one surmounted by a boldly carved stone eagle, symbol of John the Evangelist, patron saint of the architect.

The campanile, dedicated to Saint Edward the Confessor, patron of Westminster contains a single bell. It is inscribed in honour of the donor as follows:

Pray for Gwendolen, Duchess of Norfolk, who has given this bell to the glory of God and in honour of Saint Edward the Confessor in the year 1910. Whilst the sound of this bell travels through the clouds, may the bands of angels pray for those assembled in thy Church. Saint Edward, pray for England.

The tympanum above the north-west porch contains a mosaic crafted in 1981 by Trevor John Caley to a design by Nicolete Gray with the inscription:

PORTA SIS OSTIUM PACIFICUM QUI SE OSTIUM APPELLAVIT JESUM CHRISTUM
(May this door be the gate of peace through Jesus Christ who called himself the gate).

The phrase 'Porta sis ostium pacificum' is superimposed on the large letters of 'Jesum Christum' to reflect the theology of Jesus Christ represented as The Door (John 10:2-4).
Cardinal Vaughan had always intended the Cathedral to be a living church in which there should be daily Mass and both the singing and recital of the *Divine Office* - the official daily prayer of the Catholic Church consisting mainly of psalms and other readings from Scripture. On Ascension Day in 1902 he formed a body of Cathedral Chaplains under a formal Constitution, and provided for a well-trained choir under Richard Terry, a former Choirmaster at Downside Abbey, as the first Master of

Cruet set made for Roman Catholic Chapel at Westminster by John Angell, 1822
(Catalogue number 91)

Music. From Ascension Day 1902 until December 1903, since the Cathedral had yet to be made available, the adjoining Chapter Hall (now known as the Cathedral Hall) was used for the daily liturgical services. Vaughan was delighted and said jauntily: 'The Hall has been arranged like the Sistine Chapel and looks beautiful.' On Lady Day, 1 May 1903, the future Lady Chapel was screened off to be used as a temporary parish church. The following month the stark shell of the Cathedral became an auditorium when Sir Edward Elgar conducted the first performance in England of his choral masterpiece, *The Dream of Gerontius,* but the Cardinal was not present. He had been far from well for a number of years and on the morning of 25 March had left Archbishop's House for the last time. He wanted to end his life at Saint Joseph's, the missionary college he had founded at Mill Hill. He continued to receive visitors although many could barely recognise him, he had become so frail. The Cardinal talked of work he was

leaving undone, especially the Cathedral. He spoke of the provision he had made for its future and his hope that the sale of surplus land would provide an ample endowment. With surprising frankness, a friend asked him whether it would be a great disappointment not to see the public opening. 'The slow look of wonder that came into his eyes was answer enough. What could it possibly matter to anyone who opened it? It would soon be ready for Divine Service and beside that, nothing else mattered ...'.

A Time to Mourn

The day before he died he expressed the wish to make his profession of faith. His task as a bishop had been to preserve, preach and defend that faith. At the end of his life, he wanted publicly and solemnly, in the presence of his chapter to declare the same faith, thereby handing down the apostolic tradition unblemished to his successor. The Vicar General and three canons of the diocese were hastily

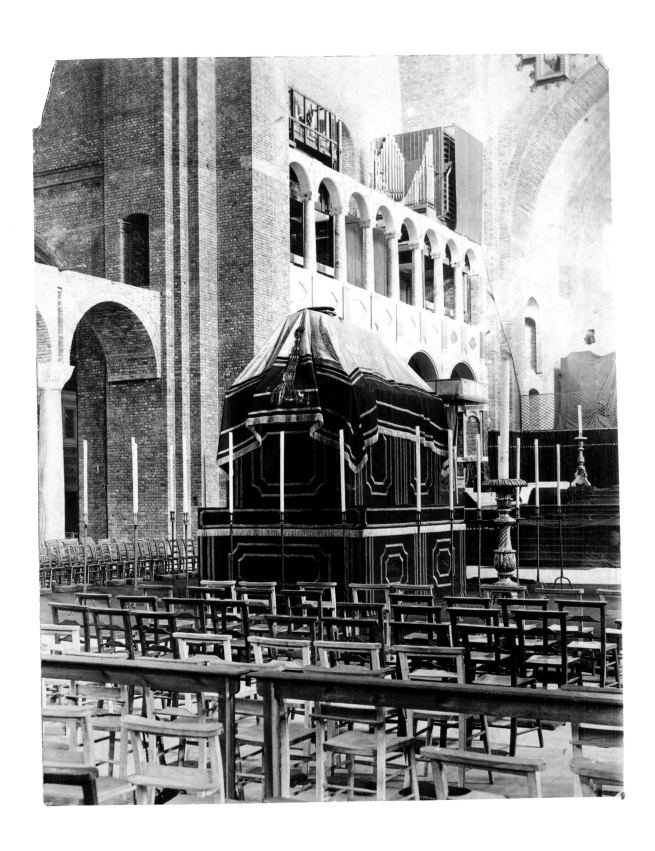

summoned from Westminster and robed in his *cappa magna* the Cardinal had himself brought down to the sanctuary of the college chapel for the short, unusual ceremony. He died a little before midnight on 19 June, the Feast of the Sacred Heart.

So it was that on 26 June 1903, a year after the death of the architect, the first public liturgy at Westminster Cathedral was the Requiem Mass for its founder, Cardinal Vaughan. A couple of months earlier he had written to his brother: 'My dear John, don't let the Vicar General or anyone else go to any expense in hanging the Cathedral in black for my funeral. I want a common elm coffin - a hearse and only two horses - to Mill Hill, where I am to be buried ...'. The night before the funeral Mass, the coffin rested in the centre of the nave. The great spaces of the interior were shrouded in darkness, lit only by eight tall candles that stood around the heavily-draped catafalque beneath the dome of the crossing. An impression of the night appeared in *The Tablet*:

'The drenching rain of the previous week had ceased on Sunday, and a thin mist hung round the domes and turrets in the chill night air. Faithful groups had been waiting patiently outside the doors for some hours when at twenty minutes to eleven the simple hearse and a single coach arrived. The doors closed on the leaden casket which was received by the cathedral clergy and the people went their way. The deep, mysterious shadows of the mighty pile closed round the body as in the tomb. The noble monument of a splendid faith; the builder raised it as a house of prayer for the living and the dead. He was not destined to intone the grand *Te Deum*, yet as he lay there in the stillness of death, up in the domes the echoes seemed to linger of Newman's *Dream of Gerontius*: 'Praise to the holiest in the height and in the depth be praise'.

Members of the religious orders had come to keep an overnight vigil and knelt in prayer. In the morning the Mass was

sung in the presence of most of the Catholic bishops of England, five hundred of the clergy and a concourse of people from all over the country.

A Time to Keep

Pope Leo XIII died a month after Cardinal Vaughan and one of the first acts of his successor, the saintly Pius X, was the appointment of Bishop Bourne, then 46, and Bishop of Southwark, to the See of Westminster. Francis Bourne was born at Clapham in 1861. He had a thoroughly Roman Catholic education, starting at Ushaw as a young boy, then Saint Edmund's College, Ware, Hertfordshire, after which he thought he might join the Dominican Order. At 19, he went instead to the diocesan seminary in Hammersmith followed by two years at Saint Sulpice in Paris, which left him with a great regard for French Catholicism. He completed his studies at Louvain and was ordained at Clapham in June 1884, the year Cardinal Manning made his final purchase of land for the building of Westminster Cathedral. He worked in parishes at Blackheath, Sheerness and Mortlake and in 1889 began the foundation of a seminary for the training of new priests. Although young when he moved to Westminster, he already had a great deal of pastoral experience. Eight years later he would be raised to the Sacred College of Cardinals with the same title as Cardinal Wiseman's, that of Saint Pudenziana. He remained Archbishop of Westminster until his death in 1935.

Bourne's installation (or enthronement) as Archbishop was the next public event of 1903, followed by the opening of the Cathedral for continuous daily use from Christmas Eve onwards. As the decade drew to a close, preparations were under way for the formal and solemn consecration of Westminster Cathedral as a building sacred to the worship of God. Canon Law forbids the dedication of any church until it is free of all debt and there was a £7,000 deficit on the general building fund. In February 1910,

the Archbishop issued a special appeal and by the end of April, the whole sum had been received. There was then nothing to stand in the way of the consecration.

(Opposite)
Catafalque for Cardinal Vaughan's funeral 26 June 1903. Organ in the tribune was installed for the first performance of Elgar's 'The Dream of Gerontius'

Dalmatic from set of Byzantine - inspired pontifical vestments made for Cardinal Bourne, 1928 (Catalogue number 138)

A Time to Bless

The Rite of the Dedication of a Church as it was found in the Roman Pontifical (the book of rites for the use of a bishop) at the start of the twentieth century was a ceremony of great length and remarkable intricacy. No other service in the liturgy could bear comparison with it. For more than a thousand years, its three main features had in various ways been combined in the pontificals of the Western Church: the burying of relics of the saints under the altar, the Solemn Mass of Dedication and the consecration itself. The burying of relics is highly reminiscent of a funeral. The consecration, with its series of exorcisms, lustrations and unctions, has several points of contact with baptism (the rite of initiation *par excellence*), and the Mass, as the crown and seal of the whole service, supplies all defects and imparts of itself a sanctification which transcends all else. All three are historical actions of the Church of extreme antiquity.

The ceremonies in 1910, carried out with the greatest formality and dignity, occupied the participants for three days. They began on Monday, 27 June at 4 pm with the Exposition of the Relics in the Cathedral Hall. Archbishop Bourne entered in procession and ascended the platform on which an altar had been erected. Here he sealed in silver caskets, together with three grains of incense and an inscribed strip of parchment, the relics of the bodies of the saints intended to be deposited under each of the thirteen altars of the Cathedral. Those for the high altar were relics of four English saints, Saint Boniface of Fulda, Saint William of York, Saint Thomas and Saint Edmund of Canterbury. Just as Cardinal Vaughan had regarded Saint Joseph as his special patron, so his successor showed a particular devotion to Saint Francis de Sales, and the relics of this saint too, were to be placed in the high altar. As the caskets were sealed, each was placed on a miniature shrine to await the ceremony of burial the next day. The Cathedral choir sang *Justorum Animae* by William Byrd during the rite, which was followed

by the singing of Matins and Lauds. According to the liturgical calendar the following day was the Vigil of the Feast of Saints Peter and Paul and in those days, a rule of fasting on the day preceding a feast day would normally have applied. Instead, the Pope gave a special dispensation from the fast for all those attending the ceremonies of the day. (Since the Second Vatican Council 1962-65, such decisions are no longer taken in Rome but by the bishop of the local diocese. By virtue of the same reforms, formal fasting obligations have been greatly reduced although Roman Catholics are still encouraged to fast as an act of self-denial.) Understandably this dispensation was much appreciated, since the clergy were on duty for seven and a half hours and the laity for three and a half, being admitted to the Cathedral at eleven in the morning, after a long and exhausting wait in hot summer sun and what Bentley's biographer describes as 'a curiously high wind'.

The rite of consecration was preceded by the office of Prime, sung in the Cathedral Hall at 7 am. At 7.30 the ceremonies began, 'full of strange and half-forgotten symbolism' (de l'Hôpital) with the recitation of the seven penitential psalms before the relics. At 8 am, the Archbishop, in golden cope and mitre and carrying his pastoral staff left the Hall, accompanied by deacon and sub-deacon vested in white albs. Preceded by cross-bearer and thurifers (bearers of thuribles containing live coals with incense, wafting fragrance) they walked in procession to the west front of the Cathedral where the outdoor rites began in the quiet early morning hours. First came litanies of the saints invoking their prayers, then the blessing of salt and water, placed on a table outside the great door. Accompanied by two acolytes bearing lighted candles the archbishop made three prescribed circuits of the building, carrying a spray of hyssop which he dipped into blessed water to sprinkle the outer walls and ground. This action symbolised the sacrament of baptism and triple immersion into its saving waters. Concluding each circuit the Archbishop,

43

standing at the threshold, claimed admission to the new church, knocking once on the door with the end of his crozier. The choir formed a wide semi-circle around him. At the third time of knocking, on the words 'Open, open, open!' he traced a cross on the threshold with the end of his staff. Immediately a solitary deacon standing within, threw open the doors. As the little procession entered the empty building, the high doors closed again excluding everyone except the stone-masons who would assist the bishops by sealing relics into each altar to be consecrated. The third stage of the rite began. In preparation for this, the floor of the nave had been painted with two broad, diagonal white paths, intersecting at the centre. At intervals of six feet there were heaps of ashes, a card being placed by each heap, inscribed with a letter of the Greek or Roman alphabet. The Archbishop took his place on a faldstool (a portable episcopal chair) placed at the point of intersection while the choir sang the ancient hymn to the Holy Spirit: 'Veni Creator Spiritus', the Litany of the Saints and the Canticle of Zachary (Luke 1:68-79). During this he set off with his attendants towards the west end. Then starting from the north-west corner he traced the twenty-three letters of the Greek alphabet in the little mounds of ashes set along the prepared path. Returning to the south-west corner, he then formed the twenty-four letters of the Latin alphabet along the second path. This ancient rite symbolised the instruction of the newly-baptised in the elements of faith and Christian doctrine, the crossing of the two lines symbolising the dominion of Christ and his redemptive cross.

There followed a procession around the interior, repeated three times to bless the walls from within. The first time, the lower parts, the second at head height, the third yet higher. The entire floor was blessed from high altar to main entrance, crosswise from side to side, then north, south, east and west. Then a great procession of all those in the building set out to bring the relics of the saints from

Dedication ceremony - the tracing of the alphabet

their temporary location in the Cathedral Hall, Ambrosden Avenue. At last the crowds in the open air were able to see and take part in the proceedings. Bright, sunlit banners and flags waved in a stiff breeze as the purple-clad mace-bearer was followed by a long line of regulars or 'religious' - Augustinians, Benedictines, Carmelites, Dominicans, Franciscans, Jesuits, Oratorians, Passionists, Redemptorists and Servites, all in their distinctive habits - then the diocesan clergy in cassocks and white surplices. Canons representing every diocese in the country walked ahead of the sacred relics. These had been laid on four biers with silk canopies, and were now carried on the shoulders of the younger priests and accompanied by thurifers. The twelve bishop-consecrators in copes and mitres came next. As the procession made its way around the exterior of the church Archbishop Bourne came into view similarly robed, staff in hand and attended by eight papal chamberlains in scarlet uniforms. As they processed around the whole building the choir sang psalms with

the four antiphons appointed for the occasion. The procession returned to the west door where the flag of the United Kingdom and the papal flag flew side by side above the Archbishop now seated on a faldstool, from which he delivered the prescribed address, exhorting all to show reverence to consecrated churches. He then anointed the door of the building with chrism (consecrated oil) in the sign of the cross. The procession with the relics entered the Cathedral where they were placed on the high altar.

The next part of the ritual was the simultaneous consecration of all the altars. The thirteen bishop-consecrators taking their respective silver caskets of relics carried them in procession to the different chapels and each began the ceremony of deposition. Meanwhile the doors were re-opened and the patient crowds were admitted to the building for the first time. During the outdoor procession, several thousand chairs had been set out inside for their use. In the centre of each marble altar top a bishop

inserted the small container of relics in a prepared cavity, closed it with an oblong piece of marble and with the help of a stone-mason, sealed it with mortar. At the high altar, under the great baldachino, Archbishop Bourne was assisted in this role by Osmond Bentley, the son of the architect.

A Time for Every Matter Under Heaven

Now the long ritual of incensing and anointing all the altars ensued, accompanied by many psalms, antiphons and prayers, then the anointing of the twelve stone crosses which are let into the walls of the church. At Westminster there are brackets at each of these points designed to hold candle sconces. Every year on the anniversary of the consecration these sconces are installed and their candles lit throughout the day. Each is shaped like a forearm with a fist bearing a candle. As Rabanus Maurus (AD 788-865) observed,
these recall the walls of the heavenly Jerusalem, on whose foundations were inscribed 'the names of the twelve apostles of the Lamb' (Revelation 21:14). Next, on every altar, the burning of five crosses of wax tapers and incense preceded a further anointing of the altar stone - the slab covering the reliquary, on which the sacred actions of the Mass would be carried out - and the dressing of the altars, after which the altar cloths, candlesticks, crucifixes and other furnishings were also blessed.

Only now did the Pontifical Mass of Dedication begin after six hours of *lustrations* (purification), blessing and anointing. It was celebrated by Doctor Cotter, Auxiliary Bishop of Portsmouth, in the presence of Archbishop Bourne and the twenty-six bishops and abbots assembled in the sanctuary. At the *elevation* the great bell (named Edward in honour of Saint Edward of England, King and Confessor) pealed out for the first time. It had been cast only ten weeks earlier at the ancient foundry of Mears and Stainbank in Whitechapel watched by the Archbishop, the Duke and Duchess of Norfolk, Mrs Elizabeth

Bentley, the architect's widow and members of her family. This bell was a gift of the Duchess but was never 'baptised'. That little ceremony had been planned for May, but was postponed indefinitely, owing to the death of King Edward VII.

Despite being in a state of near exhaustion, the choir reportedly sang the Mass beautifully. Richard Terry, Master of Music, had chosen the *Missa Quinti Toni* by Orlando di Lassus (1520-94) and the motet *Elegi abjectus esse* for five voices by Peter Philips, an English ecclesiastic of the sixteenth century. Appointed organist and choirmaster in 1901, Sir Richard Terry remained for over twenty years, as Westminster Cathedral became an influential centre of excellence in church music. A worldwide letter of guidance from the pope (*motu proprio*) dated 1903 served to confirm what Terry had already been doing at Westminster: developing the use of plainchant and polyphony in the liturgy. His successors have fostered and developed the tradition, although few occasions can have been as demanding as that midsummer day in 1910. At 2.30 pm the Archbishop gave his final blessing and the people dispersed - only to return in large numbers for Vespers and Benediction of the Blessed Sacrament at 7 pm! Their stamina was rewarded by the reading of a message from Pope Pius X. 'The Holy Father, present in spirit at today's solemn consecration of Westminster Cathedral, whilst the sweet strains of their hymns still resound in the ears of the faithful, begs God that he would ever hear their prayers from the throne of his glory on high ...'. The telegram in reply was also read out: 'The Archbishop of Westminster, together with his chapter, clergy and people and the bishops of England together with their chapters have received the message and blessing of the Holy Father with feelings of the greatest gratitude. They tender to him the expression of their most devoted attachment both to Peter and to Peter's successor.'

(Opposite)
Consecration sconce, one of twelve installed around the church and lit on the Feast of the Dedication of the Cathedral, 1 July each year

The following morning, 29 June 1910, another great feast would dawn - that of Saints Peter and Paul and the anniversary of the laying of the first stone. It would be celebrated that year in a special way, as the sixtieth anniversary of the restoration of the Catholic hierarchy in England. But for the present, it was time to adjourn and rest from ceremony. Another link in the chain of apostolic continuity had been restored that day. This long, ancient rite for the consecration of a church in 1910 was identical with that by which Westminster Abbey had been hallowed in 1065, nearly eight hundred and fifty years earlier.

The Roman Catholic Cathedral in Westminster is a Victorian building opened in 1903. For the first seventy years of its life its towering front was one of the best-kept secrets of central London. From the beginning it was hemmed in by rows of small-scale houses that had got there first. Many a Londoner over fifty is likely to have no recollection of seeing it as a child. By 1976 however, after redevelopment of the surrounding area (steel and glass office blocks by Elsom, Pack and Roberts), all was revealed. Suddenly, here was a massive yet intricate facade in light orangey-brown brick and Portland stone with domes, turrets, balconies, arches, windows, inscriptions, mosaic and a soaring campanile set back from the front. If you ascend to the viewing level at the top, the Cathedral will lay out before you all the other great buildings of London as far as the eye can see including Westminster Abbey, where the kings and queens of England have been crowned throughout the centuries. There are eight hundred and fifty years between the two churches, yet both were built by Londoners as a way of proclaiming their firm faith in the God of Jesus Christ. It was not until 300 years after the Reformation that the Roman Catholic Church was permitted to have its own bishops again. This Restoration of the Hierarchy took place in 1850 by Act of Parliament. Each new diocese started with nothing except the faith of its people. It was enough.

Guilded angel with trumpet, one of a pair at the Grand Organ above the Narthex.

Roman Catholics have a strong sense of history if only because they think in terms of a continuity that stretches back to the apostles. The history of the early Christian centuries is the foundation without which the Church would have no present and no future. But it has both and believes it has the word of Jesus Christ that this is so: *'And remember I am with you always, to the end of the age'* (Matthew 28:20b). The large numbers who attend the Cathedral's services are some indication of the faith which sustains it. The Church is no stranger to crisis, but it is rarely a crisis of identity and it survives, but only (the believer would say this) with the loving help of God.

Such a glimpse of the Catholic Church's understanding of itself is the minimum it takes to enjoy or at least understand a visit to Westminster Cathedral. There is a lot to take in. It is only a hundred years old but steeped in two thousand years of Christian experience. It is a house of prayer, because the practising Catholic believes he or she can - and must - have a personal relationship with God. It is the House of God, because that is why it was built and consecrated to his service.

And now our feet are standing within your gates, O Jerusalem.

Psalm 122, verse 2

The Greek word *narthex* means a 'small casket' and that is often what the first vestibule of a church is like. In early Christian buildings it was a long porch where people who were not fully 'at one' with the community were asked to remain for the time being - penitents for example, or catachumens who were looking forward to baptism.

When the great West Door of Westminster Cathedral is open, the visitor may enter the narthex directly. Alternative access is by way of the flanking doors and their impressive porches. The brightness and splendour of a true *propylaeum* (the entrance gate of a sacred enclosure) is achieved by the fine marble-work seen here. The wall-revetment and cornice in these entry porches are white Pentelic marble. The

The Nave seen from the Grand Organ balcony

massive door frames are cut from slabs of wavy-green Carystian marble or cipollino. It comes from the southernmost part of the island of Euboea, off the Attic coast, a favourite marble of Roman and Byzantine builders and virtually the signature of John Francis Bentley on his cathedral. The Cathedral contains many examples of patterns obtained after cutting through a block of marble and reversing the natural 'waves' in the stone. Identical opposites are placed side by side, doubling and enriching the pattern and cipollino lends itself particularly well to this technique. The side walls have huge panels of a great Italian marble known as violet breccia framed by bands of dark green verd-antique. In the apses of each porch are statuary plinths designed by Bentley which came originally from the church in Warwick Street.

These front entrances give on to the narthex, the arcaded area before the main church. To the left a basin of holy water is set into the wall which the Christian visitor will often use for a blessing. It is a symbol of the waters of

baptism and has the inscription in Latin: ASPERGES ME, DOMINE, HYSSOPO ET MUNDABOR, LAVABIS ME ET SUPER NIVEM DEALBABOR ('Purge me, with hyssop and I shall be clean. Wash me and I shall be whiter than snow'). It expresses a desire to be purified before entering the presence of God. In early basilican church buildings the narthex had associations with the waters of life as here, where the Baptistry leads off the narthex to the right. Before the Baptistry in a position matching that of the holy water stoup on the left is a small shrine of Saint Anthony.

Ahead lies the main body of the church, the nave, from the Latin *navis*, meaning a ship. The nave of a church is the place of the people, where they are carried forward in their journey towards God. The ship is the church of Christ upholding the individual soul above the stormy waters of life in a material world.

From the narthex we see the nave stretching before us towards the high altar under its elegant canopy or baldachino. Suspended between the sanctuary and nave is the great rood or crucifix. It seems to float in the dark spaces above, a brightly-lit red against the cavernous arches that soar upwards. Thirty feet high and carved in wood, the cross was made in Bruges from Bentley's designs. The wood is painted and gilt, with canvas stretched on both sides over the recessed centre. The designs for its decoration were prepared by the late William Christian Symons and submitted to the architect shortly before his death. Curiously, from some error in measurement, impossible to correct later, its proportions were not as they specified. Perhaps the Belgians were confused by feet and inches. Bentley's intention had been to suspend the rood from above the baldachino but being delivered so large, it had to be brought forward to a space of its own. The figure of Christ is about 18 feet high, on a vermilion ground, bounded along the outer edge by a line of vivid green. This touch of contrasting colour was added at the suggestion of John Singer Sargent,

Saint Peter enthroned. Bronze figure after Roman original by Arnolfo di Cambio

(Opposite)
The Sanctuary. High Altar surmounted by the baldachino with suspended crucifix by W. Christian Symons. Mosaic behind by Pownall depicts Christ in glory

Piers of the Nave

R.A., to produce a medieval jewel-like effect in the setting. The traditional emblems of the four evangelists occupy the extremities of the cross (a man's head represents Matthew, a lion suggests Mark, a bull is Luke, an eagle, John).

On the reverse side of the cross, facing the altar, Mary, the Sorrowful Mother is shown, clad in sombre garments of purple and white while texts from the hymn Stabat Mater reputedly by Jacoponi de Todi (c. 1230-c. 1306) selected by Cardinal Vaughan appear in the four outer panels. It is a view of the cross only seen by those on the sanctuary. Mary stood at the Cross of Jesus while he offered the supreme sacrifice. It is this view of Our Lady of Sorrows which now confronts the priest when he offers the sacrifice of the Mass, facing the people from a forward altar. The painting of the rood was done by Symons at floor level in the Cathedral. When complete it took eighteen hours to raise the 2 ton crucifix and suspend it in position. More than anything, the great crucifix represents the primary title of the Cathedral: the Precious Blood of Our Lord Jesus Christ.

Still in the narthex we see another powerful symbol of this dedication: two shafts of Norwegian red granite, 13 feet high and capped with white unpolished Carrara marble, supporting the central arch below the western organ gallery. They symbolise the blood of Christ poured out to save the human race.

Looking up the church we note the lighter red of the main piers clad in the marble of Middleton, near Cork. This red theme of the dedication culminates in the very dark hue of the rosso antico balustrade that divides off the sanctuary. Bentley left complete designs for the marble work of both sides of the three western doorways and the balconies over them, besides laying down the general lines of the marble revetment at this end. The floor here is paved with marble and includes elements of *opus alexandrinum*, a type of mosaic with small quadrangular tiles generally black against a pastel ground. The marbling of the floor is found elsewhere but not throughout. Bentley's plan, however, had been for a magnificent marble floor in the nave and aisles. In the nave, swimming in a sea of wave-like cipollino, were to be all the varieties of fish in Peter's net - an allusion also to the concept of the Church as a ship (*navis*), bearing her burden safely over the troubled seas of life. Bentley's designs provide for sections measuring 10 feet long by 9 feet wide, containing five waved bands with inlaid fish. (The piscean floor to be seen in Saint Andrew's Chapel may be taken as a 'pilot scheme' for the whole.) Alternate compartments were patterned with slabs of a delicate grey marble enclosed by a framing of small black and white squares. These were interspersed at regular intervals by pink or blue diamond-shaped tesserae set in a ground of golden yellow, with a dark marble border. Each panel was divided by a lighter-hued strip, 2 feet 9 inches wide, running the length of each bay. Between the bays were circles of rose-red marble, alternating with lozenges of green within similar tesserae-filled squares. All this is now academic - at least in our time. For reasons of economy and warmth in the British climate it was decided to lay a wood-block floor in the main expanse of the nave.

It is there that the tribes go up, the tribes of the Lord

Psalm 122, verse 4

Beyond the narthex and just within the nave to the left is a bronze enthroned statue of Saint Peter. It is instantly recognisable as a replica of the thirteenth century figure in Saint Peter's, Rome by Arnolfo di Cambio, with its bronze foot worn smooth by the busses of the faithful through the centuries. This figure too shows signs of the same devotion. It was given to the Cathedral by the friends of the Reverend Luke Rivington, who died in 1899, as a memorial to an eloquent preacher. Originally intended for Saint Peter's Crypt it was found to be too large for so small an area. Its present position in the nave is perhaps more appropriate, being close to the bronze wall plaque which lists the names of the popes and

archbishops of Canterbury from Saint Peter and Saint Augustine down to the present day. This statue and its pedestal were obtained from workshops in Rome through the efforts of Dudley Baxter whose correspondence with Bentley on the subject reveals some apprehension on the part of the architect. Bentley never liked craft work being ordered whose execution he would be unable to supervise. In the event, the Cathedral received a statue of high quality. The pedestal mouldings are of alabaster, the centre panels of green Polcevera marble, with a suitable inscription.

There is an enormous amount of marble in Westminster Cathedral totalling fifty-seven types by the 1990s. To make it complete the brick shell may only be veneered and this is done either in marble or mosaic. The Victorians had a tremendous respect for marble as a substance and became experts in its choice and utilisation. Bentley was fascinated by it and consulted the greatest marble expert of the day, William Brindley.

Marble columns were the first decorative feature to be placed in the Cathedral. There are twenty-nine columns in nave, aisles, and transepts coming from Greece, Norway, Italy, Switzerland and France. Each one is a monolith tapering slightly in graceful *entasis* - to carry the vaulting of the aisles and the galleries of the transepts. Looking east, eight perfect shafts of verd-antique, 13 feet high, support the galleries of the nave. All together there are 11 in the Cathedral. The source of this marble, greatly prized by the builders of classic times, was lost for centuries. Its re-discovery was due to the learning and enterprise of an Englishman, William Brindley. His attention was drawn to some lines of Paul the Silentiary, a high official and Greek poet who more than fourteen centuries earlier, in the *Ekphrasis* of the Church of Holy Wisdom, celebrated the opening of Justinian's great church in Constantinople on 24 December 563. Paul wrote of the 'fresh green stone of Thessaly', employed so abundantly by the

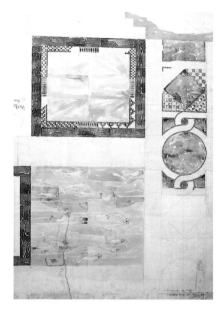

Bentley's proposed marble floor for the Nave. Design incorporates fish and sea creatures

Vert antique column from the Vale of Tempe, Thessaly

*Flagon from Bishop Fenton's plate, 1870-1
(Catalogue number 55)*

architect, as 'the marble that the land of Atrax yields, not from some upland glen, but from the local plains; in parts fresh green as the sea or emerald stone; or again like blue cornflowers in grass, with here and there a drift of fallen snow, a sweet mingled contrast on the dark shining surface.'

The redoubtable Mr Brindley sallied forth in search of this 'land of Atrax'. There, at Casamblasa, about seven miles north-east of Larissa, close to the road leading to the vale of Tempe, he located the only quarry in the world containing this green stone, this *marmor molossium.* Backbreaking labour and perseverance in excavating were necessary to uncover the ancient road in the rock, furrowed by wagon wheels of 170 BC. Then, accumulated rubble to a depth of 60 feet had to be removed before it was possible to work the quarry. Yet all this was accomplished just when this London church, working with the ancient Justinian tradition of architecture, had need of it.

The monoliths at Westminster, quarried by hand, were among the first marbles to be drawn from the re-opened source. The huge matrices from which the columns of Santa Sophia had been hewn were still to be seen. As the finished columns were being transported across the plains of Thessaly in the summer of 1897, they were seized by the Turks, at war with Greece, and held as spoils of war for many months. The withdrawal of the Turks released the marble and two years later the columns were erected in the Cathedral.

Each column stands on a moulded base of Norwegian labradorite, an inky granite whose dark surface is broken by moonlit slivers of mica. The capitals are of white statuary marble, left unpolished to avoid giving them a porcelain appearance. No two designs are the same. 'All the caps and bases,' wrote Bentley in June 1895, 'will take a new departure or rather, the carrying out of a very old one, and so with all the other details. I am not attempting a new style - that is impossible - but intend, as far as I am able, to take

the first phase of Christian architecture and develop it'.

The capitals are broadly in five groups. In those of Byzantine-Corinthian origin, the bell is entirely foliated. Pointed acanthus leaves with long flowing lines, curve upwards from the lowest moulding, while the foliation is repeated vertically on the abacus. In others of this type the abacus is moulded less elaborately but adorned with rosettes carved in relief. A second type of capital combines foliation with interlaced strapwork in very low relief on the bell of the capital, while the dosseret is sculpted with close-set leaves. Those crowning the 'grand antique' columns in the Vaughan Chantry belong to this class. They marry subtle designs with a high order of craftsmanship. A variation employed for some of the columns of the nave, is the lobed melon form, covered with lace-like tracery. A third variety, of Byzantine-Ionic style, is found in the transepts, where different forms of volute are surmounted by acanthus leaves in bas-relief curved round a conventional pineapple or a medallion displaying the sacred monogram. A fourth type, with volutes of small size and projection, is crowned by a highly-developed cushion-stone or dosseret, adorned with diagonal strapwork. This has the appearance of being overlaid with rectangular plaques foliated in very low relief. In the fifth class are the caps of pillars in the crypt, about half the height of those in the church above. Their voluting patterns are diverse, with proportions that successfully convey the sense that the columns support a low and massive subterranean weight. All the capitals of the interior were carved *in situ* by sculptors working for the Farmer & Brindley firm. Each cap occupied two men full time for three months.

In essence, Bentley's original vision for the interior was for marble decoration up to half the height of the building and all the remainder - brick walls, arches, apse and concrete domes -to be covered with coruscating mosaics. By the middle of the twentieth century progress in carrying the work forward had slowed down considerably and both the Cathedral and

53

the archbishops of Westminster had other calls on their limited resources. Decoration of the Cathedral was very low on the agenda. However, by the 1950s a lively discussion had begun as to the possibility of making renewed progress on marble-work, since nothing could be contemplated in the field of mosaic until the marble was completed. It was very far from complete at the time. There was always a strong 'leave-the-brick-alone' lobby but such views, while increasingly expressed as the 1960s approached, could not counter the obvious truth that Westminster Cathedral was erected as a shell, yet was intended to be entirely covered whenever succeeding generations could manage to do it. Another group, taking a midway position, said that Bentley's recommended scheme for marbles was too exotic, the colours too gaudy and that any veneering should be sombre and restrained and above all sourced in Britain without going overseas to find marble quarries with romantic names. In the event, the quality party won the day and work was set in motion that would complete the marble revetment to Bentley's designs. Aelred Bartlett, member of a family with a long-standing and dynamic effect on the life of the Cathedral, carried out the task of translating Bentley's coloured designs into hard stone. He and his brother Francis, later an Administrator of Westminster Cathedral, used to spend their summer holidays scouring the Mediterranean for unusual rocks. There was some rivalry between the Bartletts and the members of the Art and Architecture Committee of the day, but the enthusiasm of the brothers and their ever-deepening knowledge made it difficult for the armchair experts to prevail.

A Mr Whitehead found a long-unobtainable variety of cipollino and the rare *rosso antico* was sought out by others in Greece. A quarry of Middleton Red, the unique rose-coloured Irish marble, was located near Cork. It had last been worked in 1914 and was found where Aelred knew it to be - although now in a water-logged potato field. Help was

obtained from the Irish government to re-open the source and the Cathedral got its marble. Fine varieties of stone have been used for the lateral panels above the galleries from the splendid *brèche sanguine* of Algeria at the west end, to the dramatic black and white of the *grand antique des Alpes*, each side of the pulpit pier. Fine marble balustrades above the arcading took the place of wooden fencing. Bentley wanted his lines of perspective to run to the focal point of the sanctuary without the interruption of transept openings, characteristic of so many church vistas. Nevertheless his drawings gave added importance to the bays at the transepts by breaking the line of the balustrade with a pair of *ambones* projecting over the coupled columns.

The marble revetment of the nave which reaches as far as the semi-circular lunette windows was all but complete by 1960. With the centenary of the laying of the foundation stone due in 1995, attention turned to a series of enormous oblong panels facing into the nave above the level of the galleries - the only significant spaces still unfilled. Bentley had intended them to be filled with mosaic, manifesting an osmosis between the marble of the lower levels and the rich gold and colour in the higher reaches of the interior. It was decided that since no mosaic scheme was likely to commence in the foreseeable future it would be appropriate to complete these rectangles in carefully selected marble. Samples of marble colour and patterning were carefully examined *in situ*, among them a remarkable blue stone from Brazil named Azun McCauba. Until the discovery of this variety, the only known blue had been the legendary lapis lazuli - the Cyanus of the Romans - quarried in Central Asia. From it came the finely ground pigment that provided Renaissance painters with ultramarine, their most vivid blue. McCauba is a lighter, sky blue and somewhat startling when first encountered. The other choice for these high and spacious oblongs was *Rosso Laguna* from Verona which Bentley would have known as a further symbol of the dedication.

Chalice designed for Cardinal Nicholas Wiseman by A.W.N. Pugin, 1848 (Catalogue number 41)

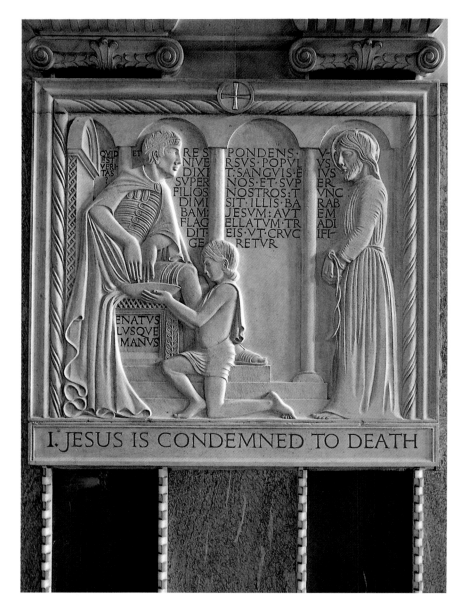

I. JESUS IS CONDEMNED TO DEATH

On the piers of the nave are the fourteen Stations of the Cross carved in low relief in Hopton-Wood stone by Eric Gill (1882-1940). Each tableau includes exquisite lines of titling by this master of letter forms. 'The Stations', also called *The Way of the Cross,* are a memorial of the Passion - the suffering and death of Christ. In each one, some incident, historical or traditional, is depicted for the person at prayer to meditate on the sufferings of Christ, from his condemnation by Pilate to his burial in the tomb. In all but two of the stations the figure of Jesus faces the nave of the Cathedral. In this he looks symbolically towards the High Altar where daily the sacrifice of the Mass is offered.

Eric Gill was invited to carve the Cathedral Stations six months after he had been received into the Catholic Church on 13 February 1913. They were not produced in chronological order. The first Station to be finished was the tenth, 'The Stripping of the Garments'. Then followed the second, and the thirteenth, in which Jesus is laid in the arms of his mother, thought by some to be the finest of all. Gill then worked on the first, in which Jesus is condemned to death. These tableaux were all in place by 1915. Significantly this great *via dolorosa* was being carved throughout the terrible years of the First World War. By March 1918 the whole series was finished and the Stations were inaugurated and blessed on Good Friday that year. After Eric Gill's death in 1940 his will was found to have a codicil which stated his wish to have his right hand interred beneath a small tablet of stone at the fourteenth station, 'Christ is laid in the Tomb'. This dramatic request was difficult to carry out. Although his full intentions were never followed the tablet is there for all to see, with the artist's initials and dates, and the single word *Lapidarius* (stone-cutter) which he preferred to the loftier title of sculptor. The Stations are arguably Gill's greatest work and a lasting memorial to his excellence as an artist.

Bentley had initially intended *opus sectile* panels but in any case the appearance of these stations was controversial at the time. Criticisms levelled at the work included terms like 'strangely crude', 'primitive', 'pseudo-Babylonian'. To the woman in the Cathedral who said she did not think them very nice Gill answered that he did not think the subject was very nice. Even among the artistic fraternity there was controversy concerning the introduction of touches of colour to the Stations. In addition to the gold and red seen today, Gill had in mind to introduce green for grass and blue for the cloaks of Roman soldiers. This is clearly indicated in the series of original designs kept at the British Museum.

The Stations of the Cross in Westminster Cathedral
by E. Rowton [Gill]
from *Westminster Cathedral Chronicle,*
March 1918

'Now that the Stations of the Cross in the Cathedral have been completed, it has been thought desirable to give a short description of the carvings and some idea of the intention of the sculptor. This is the more necessary because a good deal of misunderstanding appears to exist upon the subject, and there is danger that works which should be regarded simply as a necessary part of the furniture of the Cathedral Church - a *via dolorosa* by which the devout person retraces in spirit the holy procession to Calvary - should become not a means to devotion so much as an occasion for idle sightseeing. It would be deplorable if it became the custom in the Cathedral to 'make' the Stations in a spirit similar to that in which a person from the country goes round Westminster Abbey; and that such a possibility may be obviated we offer the following suggestions.

First, then, let us dispose of the vexed question of style. The Stations are not carved in imitation of a bygone style - Byzantine or any other. Let the would-be worshipper put any such idea resolutely away from him. A visitor in the house of a friend, being invited to sit down, does not approach the proffered chair in the state of mind of a connoisseur at a

second-hand sale. Neither should a worshipper entering a church think it 'up to him' to feel critical. In so far as the church and its furniture are works of art - that is, the work of men who are concerned for the Beauty of the things they make (and this concern is the primary concern of the artist as artist) - the worshipper should keep his mind and heart open to perceive Beauty - just as when listening to a sermon he, being in the proper frame of mind, opens his mind and heart to the perception of Goodness and does not consider whether the preacher is speaking in the manner of this or that celebrated divine - and just as one reading a work of philosophy opens his mind to the perception of Truth and does not expect the author to write in the style of this or that ancient philosopher. We are, of course, speaking of style in the merely superficial sense of outward appearance. There is a deeper sense in which it is right to use the word in connection with modern works of art. But in this deeper sense the word is so nearly allied to the word 'spirit' that we will leave it until we come to a consideration of the spirit underlying the making of things of Beauty.

The word 'Beauty' is a stumbling block, for it is so often confused with mere 'loveliness'. The lovely is that which is or represents the lovable. The lovely is lovable relatively to our love of it; but Beauty is absolute and is independent of our love. God is Beautiful whether we love Him or not; but the taste of an apple is lovely only if we taste it and love the taste. Now a work of art to be such must have this absolute quality; for it is with the Absolute Beauty that the artist, as artist, is primarily concerned. He is not primarily concerned to make representations of things which he or other people like or even love. Such making of representations is merely incidental and not necessary or inevitable. It is not as an artist that a painter makes a representation of a handsome face. As a portrait painter he is, like the photographer, the servant of his 'sitter'. As artist he is the servant of God.

The modern hankering after verisimilitude is chiefly the product of the Renaissance and the Reformation with their correlatives the paganism and agnosticism of the intellectual world and the industrialism and commercialism of the working world. The photograph and the cinema and the gramophone all help to hinder the ordinary person from a realisation of the absolute and the transcendental - of the real or substantial as opposed to the accidental and idiosyncratic. Those things are tricks, not triumphs.

It is often said, 'The old artists couldn't draw, but we can.' The implication being that the old artists - meaning, of course, pre-Renaissance artists - were inferior; and that any modern person who is negligent of photographic accuracy in drawing is drawing badly and 'on purpose', and is therefore both silly and sinful. A modern artist may, easily enough, be both silly and sinful, but the test is not either the photograph or the phonograph. A work of art is not to be judged by what it appears, nor by what it says but by what it is and what it does. Neither for the likeness rendered nor the

story told in a work of art is the artist to be held responsible as artist. These things are part of his service as craftsman. They are things given to him - things ordered by his customer. As a craftsman he may achieve a good likeness or may tell a story intelligibly and clearly, but in so doing he is not achieving more than could be done as well or better by a photographer or a journalist. A Registry Office marriage is a perfectly 'efficient' means for the legalisation of a matrimonial union, but God and the worship and praise of God are omitted. The photograph is a perfectly efficient

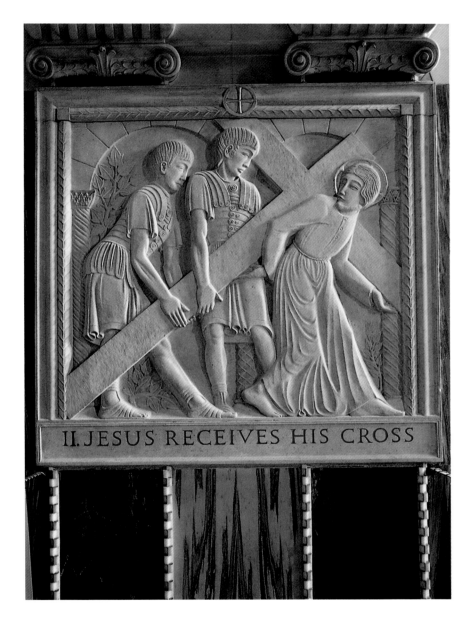

II. JESUS RECEIVES HIS CROSS

means for the rendering of a 'likeness', but God and His praise and worship are omitted. The priest brings God to the marriage. The artist brings God to the work.

Now, just as the 'contemplative' must render some service to his fellow men, if only the service of feeding and clothing himself so that he may not be a charge upon others, so the artist must as a rule earn his living by doing something useful. And just as the contemplative may often find in his service the most fruitful occasion of his worship, so generally does the artist find in his work of making what is wanted the most fruitful occasion of his praise.

Let it not be supposed, therefore, that the artist any more than the religious despises service. But let it be remembered that the primary service is that of God, that we can only serve man if we first of all serve God, and that otherwise service becomes servility and flattery.

Now we have banished from our minds, let us suppose, the question of style (the weakness of architects in that matter is no concern of ours - architects are by the nature of their work debarred from the proper attitude of mind: they are at best only artists by proxy - otherwise they cease to be architects, in the modern sense of the word, and become builders), and we have banished also the notion that the artist is primarily concerned with representation - that is, with making things like things. Let us now consider the subject of this article - the *Stations of the Cross*. First we will consider them as furniture and endeavour to decide what service is rendered by them and by the craftsman in making them, and then we will consider them as works of art - that is, as things in which Beauty, as apprehended by an artist, may be revealed.

It will be obvious that the service rendered by the Stations is a matter best known to those in authority in the Church. They, not the artist, decide upon the number and subjects to be represented. Properly also they should decide the moral and dogmatic treatment of the subjects, and that down to the smallest detail. Some people, generally women, will approach the artist (of course, while he is at work) and blandly ask him what is his idea of the Stations. That they are mystified when he replies that he is not supposed to be proclaiming *his* ideas but those of the Church, shows how completely the function of the artist is forgotten - often even by him. 'Madam,' he should reply, 'the devotion of the Stations is under the special charge of the Members of the Order of Saint Francis. Ask them'.

We will not here attempt to give a discourse upon the nature of the Devotion; we will simply describe what the artist responsible for the making of the Stations at Westminster has actually done, in so far as that is known to him and us.

The Stations of the Cross is a comparatively modern devotion, and there are in consequence no very good precedents for an artist to follow. The modern habit of allowing and paying other people to do everything for us has invaded the things of the Church; and just as the housewife now buys everything at a shop and makes little or nothing for herself, and the 'athlete' now watches other people play football instead of playing himself, and those who used to sing and dance now go to a music-hall to hear and see others sing and dance, and the parent instead of feeding his own children is now in increasing number allowing the State to do it for him - so in the Church people do not expect to discover their own emotions but must have them provided. Thus the music has become more emotional and theatrical, and hence an increasing demand in many quarters for the use of the vernacular instead of the Latin language of the liturgy. This tendency is particularly evident in ecclesiastical furniture, images and decorations, and in church architecture itself. The causes of these approaches to servility and sentimentality

are, of course, not the subject of this article. We cannot do more, therefore than note the facts - and, as the Irishman is said to have said, looking the Devil 'boldly in the face', pass on.

In the absence, then, of any good precedent, the artist attacked the problem *de novo* and endeavoured to confine himself to the bare necessities of the subjects to be represented, leaving all personal fancies as to physiognomy, costume and emotional expression on one side.

The persons of the drama are few and may be divided into two classes. They are, first, our Lord and the few faithful persons actually mentioned as being present at the various stages of the procession; and, second, Pilate and the Roman soldiers. A third class, that of the crowds of Jews and other inhabitants of Jerusalem, is unnecessary to a representation of a Passion. And its omission has the added advantage of making the worshipper himself take the part of the Jewish crowd. Too often, it may be supposed, the worshipper allows himself to hate the Jews for what they did, and forgets that he himself, had he been there, would probably have been with the crowd and not with Jesus. If then, in the Westminster Stations, there is no crowd depicted, it is because we ourselves are that crowd! In the same way it has been customary to show the Roman soldiers with every expression of cruelty and callousness. Upon them also we are inclined to throw the blame instead of upon ourselves. The soldiery was surely no more than the legal instrument; and if physical cruelty was common in that age, there is an intellectual cruelty common in our own age which is not a bit less impious. The so-called humanity of our prison system and the snobbery and pride of upper-class 'welfare' work are, we venture to think, greater blasphemies than physical torture. The Romans maimed the body, but we maim the soul. In the Westminster Stations there is no crowd shown, and the soldiers are put as passive agents, not as partisans. The costumes

are in no way to be regarded as historically accurate. They are simply garments such as anyone might wear at any time - at any rate the artist gave little or no thought to them except as more or less reasonably beautiful shapes. The expressions upon the faces are also as far as possible impassive. Any attempt to realise in stone the varying degrees suffered by our Lord has been avoided, not only because such an attempt seemed in itself sufficiently unlikely to succeed, but also because the sculptor felt it to be no part of his business to impose his notions upon others. He has confined himself to what might be called a diagrammatic treatment of the subjects. They are meant to be in stone what in words is called 'plain language' and in music 'plain chant'. They are not supposed to be either pretty or harrowing. They are, so to say, a sentence without adjectives.

The worshipper may, if he will, think of them simply as impassive reminders of the scenes of Our Lord's Passion. They do not attempt to express his feelings for him - they are like the beads of a Rosary; he must say his own Aves and make his own meditation.

Now as to the Stations as works of Art, we are less able at present to form an opinion. Some of the panels are better than others; in all there are bad things and good things. It may, however, be urged that they are at any rate stone carvings and not stone imitations of plaster models. This fact does at least make for a certain aesthetic quality which is invaluable, and would be more valuable if it were less rare. The present degradation of sculpture is largely due to the fact that the modern artist works in clay and gets his model made into stone by more or less mechanical means. The stone has therefore little of no influence upon the form of the work. In the Westminster Stations there are some passages of really good stone-carving, and the simplicity of design and absence of meretricious appeal are things to be thankful for. But in this the reader must judge for himself. Let him but approach the matter without prejudice, desirous of Beauty rather than loveliness. He will probably find himself unsatisfied and dissatisfied; but at least, if he thus approaches, he will be making his judgement from the right point of view and one from which we think judgement has not yet been given.'

The lighting pendants of the nave - or cantilevers as they were first called - were erected early in 1909. They are reminiscent of the metal circles that bear lamps in Santa Sophia as described by Paul the Silentiary. They were entirely designed by Bentley, Son & Marshall, the architect having left no record of his intentions regarding lighting fixtures. They consist of a system of plain iron rings, varying in diameter and connected by a light network of wrought iron chains painted a neutral green.

XIII. THE BODY OF JESUS IS TAKEN FROM THE CROSS AND LAID IN MARY'S BOSOM

Pulpit facing with Cosmatesque design

Lower part of Henry III's tomb Westminster Abbey in original Cosmati work. Drawing by John Marshall

With the changes in liturgical practice initiated by the Second Vatican Council, the large cosmatesque pulpit in the nave is nowadays used on great feast days. The Cathedral architect had nothing to do with the first pulpit that was erected. It had been built against the secondary pier of the south transept, where the Nottingham School alabaster of the Virgin and Child is now located. During a visit to Rome, Cardinal Vaughan commissioned Cavaliere Aristide Leonori, a Roman artist employed by the Vatican, to produce a design and carry out the work. Since he had never seen the building the result was apparently rather incongruous, as Leonori himself admitted when he saw the pulpit *in situ*. It was the gift of Ernest Kennedy. It was immediately judged too small; for one reason it was unable to accommodate the archbishop's suite in those more formal days. When the Cardinal preached he was accompanied into the pulpit by the bearer of the Metropolitan Cross, his train-bearer and master of ceremonies. Cardinal Bourne had it dismantled and replaced with the much larger pulpit seen today, his own gift to the Cathedral in thanksgiving for

his jubilee in the priesthood and the restoration of the pilgrimage to Our Lady of Walsingham. The Cathedral architect of the day, Laurence Shattock, produced a design which incorporated the Cosmati work of the original and raised the structure off the floor with pillars with the significant addition of a panel in *opus sectile* of Our Lady of Walsingham by John Trinick. There is an original Cosmati pavement in the presbytery of Westminster Abbey, the work of Pietro and Odesirio Cosmati in the second half of the thirteenth century. The craft is characterised by colourful mosaic designs in geometric patterns as seen in many Roman churches such as San Lorenzo fuori le Mura and the cloister of Saint John Lateran. The crown bosses on the pulpit stair were executed by Ernest Hawkins who had overseen restoration of mosaics in Istanbul.

In the upper central panel of the front is a carved representation of the Lamb of God, enclosed within four interlacing circles of marble and mosaic. To right and left, within niches, are figures of the four evangelists bearing their emblems.

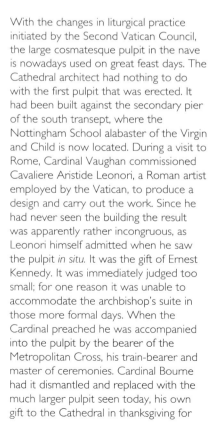

(Opposite)
Apostles. Figures from the pulpit

The Sanctuary

Set into the rosso antico balustrade, which serves as a low chancel screen, are some fine panels of yellow Italian brescia all cut from the same block. At the foot of the steps to the sanctuary is a plaque commemorating the visit of Pope John Paul II to the Cathedral on 28 May 1982. Nicolete Gray was commissioned to design the lettering. which was based on inscriptions found in the catacomb of Saint Callistus.

ECCE VESTIGIA SUMMI PASTORIS
IOANNIS PAULI II
QUI IN ANGLIA PEREGRINATOR
PRIMAM MISSAM HIC CELEBRAVIT
DIE 28 MAII 1982
IN OMNIBUS GLORIFICETUR DEUS.

(Behold the footsteps of the Supreme Pastor John Paul II who as a pilgrim to England, celebrated here his first Mass, 28 May 1982. May God be glorified in all things).

In the top right hand corner of the tablet the word PAX is surrounded by a crown of thorns reflecting the motto of Cardinal George Basil Hume OSB, 'Peace among thorns'.

The sanctuary, 62 feet deep by 50 feet wide, is enclosed north and south by two rows of columns, the raised choir beyond being narrower which has its special advantage in increasing the perspective effect of length and distance. The great piers supporting the sanctuary dome are plainly cased in slabs of dark reddish-brown Levantine, quiet in effect in order not to distract the eye from the central feature. All the lines of perspective converge and focus on the baldachino and the high altar beneath it. - a temple within a temple. It receives more light than other areas owing to the fenestration of the dome, making the sanctuary the clear focus of the whole of Westminster Cathedral.

On moulded circular bases of grey Derbyshire fossil marble, are the columns of the bold and simple arcading which carries the galleries or tribunes above. Three on either side, and dividing the sanctuary from the aisles of the Blessed Sacrament and Lady Chapels, these columns are of French jasper and a light pink Norwegian marble, each one carefully selected for delicacy of colour and pattern. The caps, of Carrara marble, have yet to be cut although Eric Gill did produce designs for the Art and Architecture Committee, but the fall of France in the Second World War put an end to all decorative work in the Cathedral and the designs were never executed. Gill was even approached to design a Paschal candlestick for the Cathedral, but Cardinal Hinsley with held his approval.

Bentley left scale drawings of the marble-work for the sanctuary, showing the marbles tinted, though not specified by name, and from these designs the work was carried out.

Bold lozenges of verd-antique and red Languedoc framed in a small inlay of black and white form the main motif of the sanctuary floor. Between these diamonds are placed small rectangular slabs of *giallo antico*. The floor immediately to right and left of the high altar, beneath the canopy-like projections of the baldachino, has circles of *rosso antico*, combined with the rich deep green of verd-antique and the more delicate hues of *campan vert*. The *predella* is floored with red Languedoc surrounded by the pale yellow of Siena, and inset with *campan vert* and verd-antique. The five steps are of white second statuary marble.

The High Altar and Baldachino

It was Bentley's determination that the high altar and baldachino should be the crown of his work, the ark within the Holy of Holies. His designs were influenced by the Church of Sant' Ambrogio in Milan. He took infinite pains and thought over their designs; and the Cardinal's decision to have a plain unadorned block of granite for the altar came as a great disappointment. However, Vaughan did have an earlier plan to collect fragments of stone from all the abbeys and priories of England which had been dissolved in the sixteenth-century and to incorporate them into the High Altar of Westminster Cathedral. It was a little fanciful perhaps. Eventually, he decided upon a single block of unpolished Cornish granite 12 feet long and weighing 12 tons, the greatest monolith in the building. This stone, the gift of the Hon. G. Saville, is furnished with a crucifix and candlesticks, each decorated with polished stone pendants. They were made from designs by Bentley, Son & Marshall, and used for the first time for the mass of consecration in 1910.

After the architect's death the Cardinal asked an M. Cantini to submit an estimate for the whole baldachino, to be prepared in Marseilles, but the idea came to nothing, and eventually the contract went to Farmer & Brindley, who began the work in 1905.

Long before this, a shipment of semi-translucent onyx columns from Africa, the choice of Cardinal Vaughan, had arrived in the Cathedral, and had to be rejected: three were found to be broken, and another was in a badly cracked condition. Two of the remaining columns may be seen in the Lady Chapel of the Birmingham Oratory. This further delay was most disappointing to the Cathedral authorities, who had already collected subscriptions of £250 each for six of the columns, but for those who wanted to see Bentley's design realised in its entirety, it was less of a blow. The order was almost immediately given for eight of the yellow Veronese monoliths which the architect had wanted. This second set arrived in July 1905, and after rapid progress had been made on the work, the baldachino was unveiled at Midnight Mass, Christmas 1906.

The eight columns which support the canopy over the altar are of honey-coloured Veronese marble. They are monoliths, as are all the columns in the Cathedral. These single stones are each 14$\frac{1}{2}$ feet high. There is in each case a white marble footing, and on this is a

solid pedestal of that old green marble from Thessaly of which there is so much at Santa Sophia in Constantinople. These verd-antique blocks are inlaid on each of their four sides with well marked oval panels of breccia and on them are placed bases of white marble from which the great yellow columns rise. Apparently growing out of them are the capitals of Carrara marble adorned with leaves: and to relieve the colour scheme small panels of pale green marble are introduced. The main arch is inlaid with breccia slabs and carries a gable of Carrara, while the ceiling is covered with mosaics of flower-like design on a gold ground designed by John Marshall. The amount of blue and silver mosaic used, as well as mother-of-pearl and lapis lazuli and porphyry, help to make it a work of supreme beauty. The complete cost of the baldachino was £7,500.

For many years the largest completed mosaic in the Cathedral has been the design above the baldachino. Its upper curve is the lower arch of the sanctuary dome and its lower curve is the archway to the apse. These two arcs define a vertical space which is crescent-shaped, posing a significant design challenge for any artist. The mosaic which has been in place since 1934 shows Christ in majesty in the heavenly sphere surrounded by the evangelists in symbolic form and contemplated by the twelve apostles in glory. Christ holds a chalice of the blood of redemption against a background of myriad faces of the just in graduated circles of blue. The whole composition is surrounded by two verses from the TE DEUM: JUDEX CREDERIS ESSE VENTURUS. TE ERGO QUAESUMUS, TUIS FAMULIS SUBVENI, QUOS PRETIOSO SANGUINE REDEMISTI (We believe you are the judge who will come. Therefore we beseech you, come to the aid of your servants whom you have redeemed by your precious blood). It was the work of Gilbert Pownall, fresh from his completion of the Lady Chapel. From some viewpoints it is partially obscured by the great rood and for this reason Cardinal Bourne had the crucifix removed to the archway near the

entrance to the tower. It was restored to its original position in 1937. This mosaic while glorious to some, has been strongly criticised through the years for a number of reasons, including perceived weaknesses of design, crudeness of colour and a failure to take account of iconographical norms for a highly stylised allegory of this type. There was trouble from the start, with the aesthetics of the piece consistently disparaged by the culturally sensitive. Cardinal Bourne was persuaded to halt work on the apse which was stripped of mosaic with the exception of the floral archway - but not until after his death. Many have been surprised to learn that for a while the apsidal curve was partially clad in tesserae, yet former choristers of the period recall the dropping of tiny tiles on their heads and sheet music as they sang.

Several artists were approached by the Art and Architecture Commitee in 1939 to suggest alternative schemes and proposals included the adoration of the Lamb on the tympanum with a vision of paradise in the apse. As controversy rumbled on, Eric Gill was approached and asked to suggest a new scheme for the crescent wall. He proposed a picture of a Palm Sunday procession, an angel holding a chalice and a way of the cross. When his tentative plans were not taken up he admitted to being greatly relieved. In 1954 Sir John Rothenstein proposed to the Art and Architecture Committee that Boris Anrep be asked to design a scheme replacing the existing mosaic in the crescent tympanum. Anrep created an interesting model avoiding the architectural faults of the existing composition. His view was that the first design had not divided up the crescent for an effective composition. A hemi-cycle of this type could only be effectively composed if a horizontal line were drawn to detach the spandrils for which separate designs would then be created. Anrep's main theme was to have been the Last Supper, but despite his prestige and well-argued case, public opinion was against taking down the Pownall work.

Proposed alternative design for the tympanum arch by Boris Anrep

At the Gospel side of the high altar stands the archbishop's throne or *cathedra*, a facsimile, though smaller, of the throne in the basilica of Saint John Lateran in Rome. It was the gift of the Catholic Bishops of England to the Cardinal Vaughan. The architect later told the story of how the Cardinal had one day surprised him by observing, as he proceeded to unroll the drawing, that he had 'ordered a throne' - as though he had ordered an armchair in Tottenham Court Road. Since it was an exact copy of the throne at the Lateran it had no

(Opposite)
Saint Paul. Detail of tympanum mosaic to the rear of the Sanctuary

canopy and was by definition a papal throne - as the architect was able to point out. But the order had already been given and the replica arrived very soon after Bentley's death. The canopy required for an episcopal throne was eventually designed by F.A. Fawkes of the Bentley firm. Constructed in fumed oak and walnut, inlaid with holly and ebony, the head is upheld by a panelled and carved backing, which stands on the floor behind the throne, and is flanked by side wings. It is composed chiefly of white statuary marble with mosaic ornament arranged in geometrical forms.

On the front, below the seat, is cut the following inscription:

HERBERTO S.R.E. CARDINALI
VAUGHAN
ARCHIEPISCOPO
WESTMONASTERIENSI
METROPOLITANAM SEDEM
TOTIUS ANGLIAE EPISCOPI
OBTULERUNT A.D. M.D.CCCC.

(To Herbert Vaughan, Cardinal of the Holy Roman Church, Archbishop of Westminster, the bishops of the whole of England gave this Metropolitan Chair, 1900 AD).

The architect was for a time under the impression that the choir stalls were provided for by the gift of the famous Dupplin carvings. He had casually mentioned to Cardinal Vaughan that these fine stalls were on the market. The carvings consisted of fifty-four superbly crafted antique stalls which originally furnished the whole chapel of the Cistercian monastery of Saint Urban, near Lucerne. The monastery was suppressed in 1841, and the carvings were sold into English hands. They were bought in 1866 and moved in forty railway trucks to Dupplin, by the 11th Earl of Kinnoull. When he died in 1897 the carvings were again to change hands.

Inquiry revealed the price to be prohibitive as far as the Cardinal's own resources were concerned; but, as usual, instant assistance was at hand. A generous benefactor came forward, bought the stalls, and presented them to the Cardinal, even promising to bear the expense of fitting them into the Cathedral. After the purchase the architect for the first time inspected them, to discover that they were absolutely unsuited, both in style and size, to the requirements of the sanctuary. Laurence Shattock later prepared a complete set of designs for stalls of Austrian oak and walnut inlaid with ivory, ebony, holly and rosewood. Provision was made for canons of the Cathedral chapter, the college of Cathedral chaplains and altar servers. The front row of benches display names of Old Testament prophets culminating with Christ.. Bronze grilles were planned to mark off the sanctuary from the ambulacra behind the canons' stalls and the beginning of this work can be seen on either side of the Archbishop's throne.

There is provision for eighteen canons, six more than the usual number as a mark of the importance of the founding of the Cathedral. In addition the canons and chaplains wear the distinctive *cappa parva* of the Roman basilicas, said to have been designed by Michelangelo. The ceremony of the installation of canons is taken from the rituals of St Paul's (London) and Lincoln Cathedrals. These rituals were chosen as being appropriate sources for Westminster representing respectively the metropolis and one of the largest dioceses in the pre-Reformation Church in England. The sources were the *Registrum* of St Paul's Cathedral AD 1294-1303, the *Liber Niger* of Lincoln which dates from 1300 and the *Registrum Novum* of Lincoln, drawn up by Bishop Alnwick in 1439.

The Apse

The wall and parapet between the sanctuary and retro-choir has four arched openings, which give light to the crypt and add variety and interest to the background of the altar. These openings are filled with grilles of bronze gilt. The surrounding wall space is covered with choice, vertically placed slabs of Greek cipollino, each bounded by a narrow strip of the fine *rouge antique* of the Pyrenees. In the centre of every panel of the green marble is set a lozenge of the red, outlined with a border of gold tesserae.

From 1923 there was a wooden reredos behind the High Altar. In 1927 this was replaced with a small painted screen with an icon representing the head of Christ. serving to cover the gestures of the Master of Music. as he conducted the choir This was replaced in 1929 by a screen of white Carrara marble set with a bas-relief of Christ holding the chalice of his redeeming blood, carved in Hopton-Wood stone by Lindsey Clark. It bears the inscription:

DOMINE JESU REX ET REDEMPTOR
PER SANGUINEM TUUM SALVA NOS
(Lord Jesus, King and Redeemer, save us by your blood)

Underneath the carving is a verse from the Te Deum:

TE ERGO QUAESUMUS TUIS FAMULIS
SUBVENI, QUOS PRETIOSO SANGUINE
REDEMISTI
(We beseech you therefore come to the aid of your servants whom you have redeemed by your precious blood).

(Opposite)
Sanctuary stalls inlaid with names of the prophets

The Baptistry

The first of the seven sacraments of the Christian Church, Baptism is frequently called 'the door of the sacraments' and 'the door of the Church'.

In commissioning Westminster Cathedral Cardinal Vaughan asked that the chapels should physically portray the Christian journey from life to death starting with the Baptistry and ending with the Chapel of the Holy Souls showing the progression from birth to death, the joy of Christmas to the agony and Resurrection and Christian hope of Easter.

The first baptisms took place in the open air. It is not clear when the first baptistries were built. In ancient times the term was applied to a bathing place or pool. The Latin word BAPTISTERIUM, also used of the vessel or tank containing water for Baptism, has both Jewish and pagan connotations. When Jesus was a guest at the wedding reception in Cana (John 2:6), the big stone water jars were there for ritual ablutions, religious observances prescribed for the Jews. For the Romans, though, bathing was entirely a matter of hygiene and relaxation. The construction of the early baptistries may well have owed something to the bathing apartments of the *thermae* - if only their plumbing. Pliny, in speaking of the public baths twice uses the word *baptisteria,* and it was applied to the tanks in the courtyard of suburban villas and the bath in the circular chambers at Pompeii. So as early as the time of the apostles, open-air baptisms were giving way to indoor ceremonies (Acts 9:18) for practical reasons as well as for privacy and solemnity. Reverence for the rite itself and for the water, which in time came to be specially blessed, gave rise to the need for a special receptacle -a basin or font (from the Latin *fons,* a spring of water) both for the ceremony and for keeping the water available. In the Western Church the oldest fonts are in the Roman catacombs, hewn from the stone floors of baptismal chapels. They are also to be seen in early Christian paintings, usually as a shallow basin, in which the neophyte (new Church member) stands up to his ankles in the water while more water is poured over him by the person doing the baptising.

In buildings erected for the offices of the Christian faith, a special chamber was set aside, often a rather large, separate structure. Generally circular or polygonal, it contained a font in the centre, a round, cross-shaped or octagonal sunken well, whose brim was level with the stone floor, or partly raised above it by a low curb of masonry. A perfectly preserved Christian font of the sixth century was excavated in 1952 in Qelibia, east of Carthage. Steps into the water came from two facing sides, so that the candidate could walk down into the water, reach the centre and, after the Baptism, walk out again by the steps on the opposite side. Baptisms were conducted at the Easter and Pentecost solemnities, when there would be large numbers receiving the sacrament. A replica of this early form of font may be seen at the Church of Saint Charles Borromeo, Ogle Street, London, near the Post Office Tower. It enables the community to administer Baptism in the 'primitive' form by total immersion, providing a powerful sign to those present.

The earliest extant 'free-standing' baptistry is to be seen alongside the Basilica of Saint John Lateran in Rome, said to have been built in its original form by the Emperor Constantine in 324. From the fourth century such round or polygonal baptistries spread through the Roman world, their design possibly derived from Roman circular temples or tombs. When separate baptistries were no longer considered necessary the immersion of candidates gradually gave way to the simpler pouring of water, for which only a small receptacle was needed. This smaller font was then placed in a separate chapel in the main church building, sometimes in an enclosure formed by a railing or open screen. It seems that from about the sixth century, baptistries were constructed as part of the church itself, though still outside the main architectural space - sometimes in a porch of some kind.

The Baptistry of Westminster Cathedral is an excellent place to start a tour of the interior because the very space itself signifies a beginning. According to Roman practice it should

Chapel of Saint Gregory and Saint Augustine seen through the Baptistry gates

be railed off and have a gate fastened by a lock. It is and it does. The Baptistry is entered through a broad and deep archway at the south side of the narthex. On the marble alongside the gates there stands a small, finely carved wooden statue of Saint Christopher. An inscription on a bronze plate on the base of the statue tells the story of how it was given by Hilaire Belloc after seeing his son set sail for the Flanders Front during the First World War. Hilaire Belloc presented the statue to the Cathedral for the protection of the troops during the hazardous Channel crossing.

The Baptistry is a square, cross-vaulted compartment enclosing Bentley's splendid octagonal, moss-green marble font raised

on a plinth of white marble and ascended by three steps. The font was made in Rome in 1901 on the instructions of Cardinal Vaughan, who had received the necessary funds from the Dowager Lady Loder and presumably saw no reason to delay its construction. So although Bentley had provided the design he was prevented from overseeing the work. All his life he had supervised the crafting of his designs and to have this perogative removed by his client clearly hurt. Early in the year, specimens of the marble to be used were submitted for his approval and at the end of December, the Cardinal announced the font was finished and had left Rome. Bentley never saw it. It remained in its packing cases until many months later when the Roman masons

came over to set it in place. The font contains a deep circular basin, 5 feet in diameter, covered by a flat, undecorated lid of oak. A projection on the western side, where the priest stands to baptise, provides him with a small, oval uncovered basin of white marble and there is therefore no suggestion here of total immersion.

The marble revetment of the Baptistry was paid for with bequests of Mrs W de l'Hôpital and Miss H.M. Bentley, the daughters of John Bentley, the architect of the Cathedral. Originally there was an altar dedicated to Saint Anne given in memory of Canadian Servicemen who fell in the Second World War.

Chapel of Saint Gregory and Saint Augustine

This chapel was built to commemorate the two great apostles of England. Gregory the Great, who became pope in 590, the first monk to do so, decided to send a papal ambassador to England and appointed Augustine to this task - a monk from his own Roman monastery.

There is evidence of Christianity during the Roman period, but from the middle of the fifth century, the Gospel came to England, with the followers of Saint Patrick, and the progress of Christianity in the north of England was led and directed by Celtic bishops and missionaries - until, that is, Rome took up the mission in the person of Gregory the Great. For the first fifty years after the arrival of Augustine as his papal legate, these Celtic Church leaders had difficulty conceding authority to the Roman Church in England, although they did so in 664 at the Synod of Whitby.

Gregory, born around 540, was a pope of rare abilities. Highly educated, a trained lawyer, he was appointed Prefect of Rome when he was only thirty. After a while he abandoned his post and possessions, turned his house into a monastery and lived there as a simple monk for three years. Pope Pelagius sent him as his representative to Constantinople. He returned six years later as abbot of his monastery of Saint Andrew on the Coelian Hill. It was during this time that he is said to have met some young Angles, offered as slaves in the Roman market. In a famous story, the English historian Bede relates how Gregory, noticing their fair hair and complexion, remarked that rather than 'Angles' they would merit the description of angels if only they were Christians.

At the entrance to the chapel the incident is shown in a picture high on the north-west pier. Along the top of the panel runs the inscription: NON ANGLI SED ANGELI SI CHRISTIANI (they are not Angles, but angels if they are Christians). The work itself was completed in October 1912 and is in opus sectile. This is a type of mosaic in which specially cut pieces of marble and other coloured stones are used to build up the main figures of the design, in order to form either uniformly coloured or variously toned areas while tesserae (tiny square tiles) are only used 'in a supporting role'.

Standing in the Roman slave market, Gregory's hand rests on the youngest of three children with the merchant and an African standing near. A young monk carries the abbot's pastoral staff. Behind the figures is a marble portico through which is glimpsed green trees, blue sky and the hills of the Roman *Campagna*. True or fanciful, the story points to a conviction in Gregory's mind that no peoples, however distant, should be kept in ignorance of the Gospel.

As pope, Gregory promoted a higher standard of public worship and encouraged liturgical music. He is the patron saint of Westminster Cathedral Choir School as well as being the patron of plainsong. In the earliest days of the school it was the boys who collected and subscribed the necessary funds for this picture as a lasting memorial to Saint Gregory and his concern for the youth of England. Along the base are the words: PATRI PATRIAE NOSTRAE ET BIS SUO PUERILI CANTORES. This means that they offered this gift to him as father of our fatherland and doubly their father, as the boys spend their lives singing the music of the Church, which, bearing his name, is called Gregorian Chant. Gregory obtained the pope's agreement to set out himself on the mission to convert England, but was brought back after three days! After the pope's death, Gregory, although keenly reluctant, was elected to succeed him and was consecrated in Saint Peter's on 3 September 590.

On the columns of Saint Gregory's Church on the Coelian Hill in Rome are inscribed the names of Augustine and his five successors in the See of Canterbury. They were among the forty monks from Pope Gregory's own monastery of Saint Andrew, whom he sent

out to evangelise England. From the Bishop of Rome, these missionaries received the *pallium*, which symbolises the character and origin of their mission and jurisdiction. Gregory exulted in the first-fruits of that mission.

His emissary, Saint Augustine, had landed in 597 at Ebbsfleet near Richborough, a Saxon fortress on the Kent coast. He had made his way to the court of King Ethelbert of Kent, whose Queen was Bertha, a Merovingian Catholic princess. Influenced both by his wife and the legate, the king was baptised a Christian and gave his support to Augustine's mission, who thus became the first Archbishop of Canterbury, looking out over a land of many tribes, princes and

beliefs. Those who had been Christians largely followed the ways of the Irish Church, from which they had received their faith. In 1940, to mark the fourteenth centenary of Gregory's birth, the fourth Archbishop of Westminster, Cardinal Hinsley, gave an address in which he said: 'Gregory's mind and intention was that no people should have an alien culture forced upon it. But races, tribes and nations were all to be made one under God and in Christ'. He died on 12 March 604 and lies buried under an altar consecrated to his name, near the entrance to the Sacristy of Saint Peter's in Rome.

We enter the chapel from the aisle through two arched openings supported

by double columns of Swiss Cipollino find one of the few fully completed chapels in Westminster Cathedral. The decoration has a strong narrative element. The theme is unmistakable - the historical evangelisation of England directly from Rome. The altar is recessed within an arch, the altarpiece occupying its whole width and continuing the line of an upper cornice. There is a central canopied representation of Saint Gregory and Saint Augustine, in *opus sectile* work, flanked in side panels by Saint Augustine's leading companions - Saint Laurence, and Saint Mellitus on the right, Saint Justus and Saint Paulinus on the left. All wear episcopal garments and stand on pedestals inscribed with their names. Pope Saint Gregory, on the left, with *pallium* and the triple crown of the papacy and holding his pastoral staff, appears to be heeding the Holy Spirit as a dove, approaching his ear. Saint Augustine, dressed as a monk, carries a picture of the face of Christ - the vernicle - as the banner of his mission to England. The upper levels of the chapel are covered in mosaics of shadowy gold. Important aspects of the story are told here pictorially, beginning with the semi-circular tympanum above the altarpiece. Here, Saint Gregory is shown, enthroned and turning with outstretched hands to Saint Augustine who kneels before him to receive his apostolic charge. Crowned and clad in white beneath a purple robe, the pope holds a scroll in his left hand which reads: COR CORAM DEO (The heart is open to God). A bishop and other clerics of the papal court look on, as Augustine and his fellow missionaries accept their mission. Around the upper border of the scene an inscription reads: S GREGORIUS MAGNUS AUGUSTINUM IN ANGLIAM MITTIT REGI ETHELBERTO EIUSQUE POPULO CHRISTI FIDEM PRAEDICATURUM (Saint Gregory the Great sent Augustine to England to preach the faith of Christ the King to Ethelbert and his people).

The great lunette at the east end is the reception of the missionaries by Ethelbert, King of Kent, with Queen Bertha. They look to their right at a group of three missionaries led by Augustine, with whom the king seems to be disputing. The queen listens, her hands joined in supplication. Below this mosaic are the words: SANCTUS AUGUSTINUS ANGLORUM REGI ETHELBERTO CHRISTI FIDEM PRAEDICAT (Saint Augustine preaches the faith of Christ to Ethelbert, King of the Angles). Portraits of Saint Peter and Saint Paul in circular medallions appear in the upper part of the spandrels. Saint Peter carries the keys of his office and a scroll with the words PETRUS APOSTOLUS JESU CHRISTI (Peter, Apostle of Jesus Christ). Saint Paul, carrying the sword with which he was martyred, holds a scroll inscribed: PAULUS SERVUS JESU CHRISTI (Paul,

servant of Jesus Christ). The crown of the ceiling barrel vault is sheathed in gold mosaic. Six full-length figures of saints occupy the ramp of the vault - three on each side - standing in tender green grass sown with spring flowers. The reference - it may safely be assumed - is to the first springtime of the Catholic Church in England, in contrast to which, John Henry Newman in a famous address on 13 July 1852, spoke of its resurgence in his own day as ' The Second Spring'. The saints represented are all historical figures, men famous for their Christian commitment in the centuries that followed Augustine's mission. Each is divided from the next by a long-stemmed blossoming tree. On the north side, nearest the altar is Saint Edmund, king and martyr, holding the arrows of his demise and a royal orb. Next is Saint Bede the Venerable, monk of Jarrow and lifelong scholar. His *Ecclesiastical History of the English People* is unique in providing us with an account of Christianity in Britain from its beginnings up to AD 731. He is shown with his book and pen. On the opposite ramp are shown Saint Wilfrid of York, bishop and martyr, and Saint Benedict of Nursia, the founder of Western monasticism (c. 480-c. 550) for whom Saint Gregory, the first pope to be a monk, had a deep admiration. Saint Benedict now shares with Saints Cyril and Methodius the Church's title Patron of Europe. Also on this side of the chapel is a representation of Saint Cuthbert of Lindisfarne, who died in 687. Each patriarch is shown holding a pastoral staff. Originally, Cardinal Vaughan's list of saints for these mosaics included Saint Alban, the proto-martyr (first of all martyrs) of England. Alban's death had taken place in one of the last persecutions before the Emperor Constantine, thus predating the Augustinian mission. His place was taken by Saint Oswald.

A screen of pavonazzo marble separates the back of this chapel from the Baptistry. Above its gates are placed the figures of Saint John the Baptist and Saint Augustine, standing shoulder to shoulder in the centre. Their work is linked at a

crucial juncture of human history. John, the last of the prophets of the Old Covenant, was charged with preparing people for the saving work of the Messiah - in their midst already but as yet unrecognised - in the person of Jesus of Nazareth. Augustine, a missionary of the New Covenant, the new apostolic age, is entrusted by the Church with the work of spreading the Gospel. The Gospel message is that Jesus Christ, by his sacrificial death, Resurrection and Ascension into heaven, has vanquished sin and death, thrown open the gates of paradise and promised to lead all who believe in him into the presence of the Eternal Father. Having passed through death and never to die again, the Risen Lord has withdrawn from human sight, one day to return in glory.

In panels flanking Saint John the Baptist and Saint Augustine there are allegorical figures in decorative circles, representing the waters of Baptism, which flow down in copious streams, into the spandrels of the arch from the tilted vessels in their hands. Four half-figures of angels hold scrolls in their hands, inscribed with the names of the four rivers of Paradise: Tigris, Pison, Gihon and Euphrates.

Bishop Challoner's Tomb

Bishop Richard Challoner is buried in this chapel. His tomb is marked by a simple slab at floor level close to the south aisle of the Cathedral. During the greater part of the eighteenth century Richard Challoner was the leading figure of the Catholic Church in England. He was the son of a Presbyterian wine-cooper of Lewes. After his father's death his mother became housekeeper to a Catholic family at Firle, Sussex. It is not known whether she was already a Catholic but her son was received into the Church at Warkworth, Northamptonshire, at about the age of 13. This was at the home of the Holmans, a well-known Catholic family. Lady Anastasia Holman was the daughter of the martyred Viscount Stafford. It was their chaplain, John Gother, who instructed Richard

Challoner in Catholic doctrine and obtained a place for him at Douai College in Northern France. The Douai seminary had been established by Cardinal Allen (1532-94) to educate students for the priesthood and train them for the English mission. (The name of the present seminary in Chelsea for the Diocese of Westminster is Allen Hall, after the same great churchman.) Richard Challoner was 14 when he went to the continent and it is not known whether he ever saw his mother again. His education was to prepare him for an uncertain role in a society where Catholics seemed destined for extinction. Yet in 1708 he took the college oath, binding himself to return and work as a priest in England, when required to do so. In 1716 at the age of 26 he was ordained by the Bishop of Tournai. He graduated Bachelor of Divinity from the University of Douai three years later and in 1720 was chosen by the college president to be his vice-president and prefect of studies. Challoner was an industrious teacher, known for his fervent piety, committed to expounding the spiritual dimensions of the Church's faith. He gained his doctorate in 1727 and was finally allowed by his superiors to return to London, making this move in 1730.

Dressed as a layman, Doctor Challoner ministered to the small number of Catholics in the capital, often celebrating Mass in secret. Catholic worship remained illegal although the penal laws were enforced with less severity than previously. He worked tirelessly in the poorest quarters of London, visiting the prisons and seeking out those in spiritual and moral need, bringing too a measure of material support. In his spare time he studied and wrote, approximately seventy titles in all, mainly devoted to instruction and spiritual guidance. His was the hand responsible for the Rheims-Douai version of the Bible. He became co-adjutor bishop to the Vicar Apostolic of the London District with the title Bishop of Debra. In 1758 when Doctor Petre died, he succeeded him as Vicar Apostolic. Nearly 70 and in poor health he applied

Tomb of Bishop Challoner. Pair of candlesticks designed by Bentley for College of Saint Stanislaus, Beaumont

for the help of a co-adjutor and was given James Talbot by the Holy See. Challoner was a fine administrator in the face of extraordinary difficulties. He opened two schools for boys and one for girls. He started conferences for London clergy and founded the Benevolent Society for the Relief of the Aged and Infirm Poor. Such activities were all the more remarkable in that Challoner spent

most of his London years in hiding, given the state of the law. He often had to change his lodgings in haste to escape the attention of informers, keen to earn the government reward of £100 for the conviction of a priest. For some years, he and his London priests were continually harassed in this way. Eventually, in 1778, the situation was remedied by the Catholic Relief Act by which Catholic

Portrait in oils of Richard Challoner. The blue of his robe honours the Mother of God, being a reference to England as 'The Dowry of Mary'

*Chasuble made in memory of Bishops Challoner and Talbot
(Catalogue number 121)*

priests were no longer liable to imprisonment for life. This concession, welcome though it must have been, caused a renewed upsurge of bigotry in some quarters and two years later the Gordon Riots - portrayed in Dickens' *Barnaby Rudge* - broke out . The chapels and houses of Catholics were attacked and wrecked. From his place of refuge, the bishop, now nearly 90, could hear the frenzied anger of the mobs. They were searching for Challoner with the intention of dragging him through the streets. When they failed to locate him, he escaped to Finchley where he remained until the riots came to an end.

Six months later Bishop Challoner died. After ceremonies in London, his body was given into the care of a Mr Bryant Barrett of Milton Manor on the Berkshire-Oxfordshire border. Mr Barrett, a friend of the bishop, had been a convert to Catholicism. The Rector, the Reverend James Warren, committed the remains to the Barrett vault and wrote in the register: *'Anno Domini 1781, January 22. Buried the Reverend Richard Challoner, a Popish Priest and Titular Bishop of London and Salisbury, a very pious and good man, of great learning and extensive abilities.'* (The mention of Salisbury seems to have been some kind of confused deference to Mr Barrett, whose Milton country seat was in the Anglican diocese of Salisbury.)

The Barrett family vault at Milton was opened and inspected in 1907. The bishop's inner coffin of lead was intact and the nameplate read: *'Right Rev'd Doctor Richard Challoner, Bishop of Debra, Died Jan. 12, 1781, Aged 90'.* In the 1940s a process was begun for the removal of the remains to Westminster Cathedral. Understandably, the people of Milton, both Catholic and Anglican, were less than pleased, but in 1946 the translation to the Chapel of Saint Gregory and Saint Augustine was carried out. This is how the body of Doctor Challoner, Vicar Apostolic of the London District, comes to be at rest in this Chapel of Saint Gregory and Saint Augustine.

Wisdom of Solomon

The *opus sectile* picture to the left of the main altarpiece makes a pair with the picture of Saint Gregory and the English slave children which it faces. This work, on the north-east pier depicts the Old Testament story of Solomon, the Just Judge (1 Kings 3:16-28). The entire cost of decorating this chapel was met by one of the founders of the Cathedral, Sir Henry Hawkins, who had been a famous judge and advocate. The picture shows King Solomon, seated on his throne of judgement. Before him stand and kneel the two mothers, rival claimants for custody of the one living child. To the right of the picture a soldier stands ready to cleave the surviving baby in two. Thus Solomon identifies the real mother, for she gives up her claim rather than see her infant die. The inscription underneath reads: TIMUER: REGEM VIDENTES SAP: DEI ESSE IN EO AD FACIEN : JUD (They stood in awe of the King, because they perceived that the wisdom of God was in him, to execute justice).

Sir Henry Hawkins - whose judicial wisdom is compared here to that of Solomon - was born at Hitchin, Hertfordshire, in 1817, the son of a solicitor. He was knighted by Queen Victoria in 1876 and at 60 was appointed judge of the High Court of Justice. Remaining on the bench for twenty-two years, Hawkins was raised to the peerage on his retirement in 1898 shortly after becoming a Catholic. For a long time there had been a warm friendship between himself and Cardinal Manning. They would meet on Sundays to discuss general topics; but 'I can truly say', said the new Lord Brampton, 'he never made the least attempt to proselytise me. My reception into the Church of Rome was my own free choice. I acted for myself or I should not have acted at all.' He was 90 when he died in October 1907. Lady Brampton died shortly after and although John Bentley, the Cathedral architect, had arranged for designs to be prepared for a double tomb with recumbent effigies in this chapel - to be placed where

Challoner's tomb is now positioned - they were not buried here but at Kensal Green. At this time it was not possible to bury bodies within the City of Westminster. The sculptor Joseph Swynnerton had been working on a model for such a tomb at his studio in Rome, with the judge to be depicted in full robes and wig.

On the Thursday after Brampton's death, his body was carried into the Cathedral and lay in state overnight in the Chapel of Saint Gregory and Saint Augustine, brought to completion by his generosity. The mosaics, begun in December 1902, had been completed in May 1904. The marble floor had then been laid - not, incidentally, to Bentley's sumptuous first design, the cost of which had seemed excessive to Lord Brampton. In addition to £2,000 given by Lady Brampton to the Cathedral Building Fund, the couple had jointly provided the £8,500 needed, with the exception of the *opus sectile* work. Here, as in the Chapel of the Holy Souls, the marbles were selected by the architect himself and are of exceptional quality. Examples of the two principal Cathedral marbles, verde antico and cipollino, are seen here at their best. It was in this chapel that the first marbles were installed; these are the light breccia panels that cover the south wall. To the right and left of the altar, panels of rouge jaspe are inset with ovals of Swiss cipollino. The altar frontal is 'straw' Siena and the top of the altar is Norwegian Pink of which there are also columns in the Sanctuary.

While Bentley had naturally retained strict control over all marble work, he had to bow to the wishes of the donor in the matter of mosaic technique and the pictorial decorations in *opus sectile*. The firm of Clayton & Bell had been selected at the express wish of Lord Brampton and appointed about a year before Bentley's death. Nevertheless, the architect's rule for Cathedral mosaics had been firmly established as: 'Byzantine style and Greek drawing'. He had always strenuously impressed this precept on

Silver Urn or Sepulchre for the Altar of Repose on Maundy Thursday. The Eucharist is contained in a gold English Chalice from the reign of Henry VIII

anyone working on the Cathedral's mosaics. Yet this was not to be the approach of Mr J.R. Clayton - secure in the donor's patronage - and this is why the nature of the mosaic decoration and *opus sectile* in this chapel is so radically different from that of the Holy Souls Chapel. The latter had been pure Bentley

in spirit, the result of a meeting of minds between himself and the artist Christian Symons, but it may be assumed that this glorious work, already in place, had left the judge unmoved. In the words of Bentley's daughter: 'The late Mr Clayton's faith in progress in art and his belief that the attempt to resuscitate the dead in styles of art is a profound mistake, are the reasons given for employing a treatment so remote from the methods of Byzantine workers .... Bentley's position was that the art of Byzantium was by no means dead but awaiting its re-awakening and call to new life.' The architect and mosaicist met initially, but once the commission had been offered and accepted they saw very little of each other and the question of technique never arose between them. The difference is that with Clayton's designs, the tesserae - tiny mosaic tiles - are regular, close-jointed and set with great precision. The resulting effect is very different from the freer, multi-angled laying down of the tesserae in the Holy Souls Chapel, emulating Byzantium. The architect made all the necessary arrangements for the surfaces to be prepared to receive the mosaics, but his influence on Mr Clayton's work extended no further than this.

From the earliest days of the Cathedral this chapel has received the special care and attention of the Knights of the Order of Saint Gregory the Great. The ornamental candelabra made by the Escaré Metal company proper to the chapel were given by the Knights in 1922. Every year on the feast of their patron saint, they attend a Mass here, offered for the repose of the souls of their deceased brethren. The late Canon Pilkington wrote the following Latin inscription for the Knights, to be seen on the west wall, beneath the gilt screen:
HOC IN SACELLO PATRONO COELESTI DICATO, EQUITES ORDINIS SANCTI GREGORII MAGNI QUOTANNIS FESTO EJUSDEM RECURRENTE SACRO ADSISTERE SOLENT ET PRO FRATRUM ANIMABIS HOSTIAE DIVINAE OBLATIONEM CURARE (In this chapel, dedicated to their heavenly patron, the Knights of the Order of Saint Gregory the Great are accustomed each year, on his feast day, to assist at Mass, and to have the Divine Victim offered for the souls of their deceased brethren).

Two of the Cathedral treasures have a particular association with the Chapel of Saint Gregory and Saint Augustine. A silver *urna* or *capsula* (sometimes questionably described as a *sepulcrum*) was designed and crafted, in the 1920s. It can best be described as a free-standing tabernacle for the Blessed Sacrament. For many years it was used on Maundy Thursday, when this altar became the Altar of Repose. The only other day it was to be seen in the Cathedral was the Feast of Corpus Christi. Within the *urna*, the Blessed Sacrament was reserved in another treasure - an important English silver-gilt chalice, with the hallmark of 1529. This was the year before the Reformation Parliament.

The *sepulchre* custom dates from the Middle Ages and it was regarded as central to the Holy Week liturgy. On Maundy Thursday the priest would consecrate three hosts, one for his communion at that Mass, one for communion on Good Friday and the third to be used in the *sepulcrum* ceremonies. After the Good Friday ceremonies came the 'burial' of Christ in the Easter Sepulchre. The priest removed his vestments and carried a pyx containing the third host consecrated on Maundy Thursday to the sepulchre where it was placed with the cross which had been used by the people during the liturgy. The host was removed before Mass on Easter morning and replaced in the hanging pyx above the high altar and the crucifix was 'raised' and carried round the church in solemn procession.

A THIRD TIME

Memorial to Oliver Plunket

In the south aisle between the Chapel of Saint Gregory and Saint Augustine and the next chapel, that of Saint Patrick and the Saints of Ireland, there is a memorial in mosaic to Saint Oliver Plunket, the martyred Archbishop of Armagh and Primate of All Ireland. The connection with Saint Patrick's Chapel is clear enough, but the link with the previous shrine is less immediately obvious. Both Pope Gregory and Augustine were monks; Saint Oliver was a member of the Third Order of Saint Benedict and willed his remains to the care of his Benedictine confessor, Dom Maurus Corker. Like Bishop Challoner, buried nearby, he suffered great hardship during a period of persecution. His execution at Tyburn was the last in the long line of martyrs for the Catholic faith who died on that scaffold in the sixteenth and seventeenth centuries.

Oliver Plunket was born near Oldcastle in County Meath in 1629. As a student at the Irish College, Rome, he was remembered for all-round brilliance. Ordained to the priesthood in 1654, he was appointed representative of the Irish bishops in Rome and lived there as a college professor until 1669 when he was appointed to the primatial see of Armagh, for which he was consecrated in Ghent. He received the *pallium* the following year. Plunket went first to London where for some time he worked to get the anti-Catholic laws in Ireland applied with less rigour. Only then did he start work in Armagh. Within three months he had administered the Sacrament of Confirmation to about 10,000 people. By December 1673 - he reveals in a letter to Rome - he had confirmed 48,655 people. To do this he had endured great hardships, seeking out homes of the faithful in woods and mountains, mainly confirming in the open air. When the persecution of the Irish Church intensified in 1673 he went to ground with the Archbishop of Cashel.

Writs for the arrest of Doctor Plunket were repeatedly issued by the

Government. Finally he was seized and imprisoned at Dublin Castle on 6 December 1679. The trial was moved to London. The preoccupation in court was that a rebellion was being organised in Ireland. If so, did it not follow that the primate would be at its head? In any case, the fact that Oliver was a Catholic bishop was bad enough. Chief Justice Pemberton, who presided at the trial, stated from the bench that there could be no greater crime than to try to promote the Catholic faith 'than which there is not anything more displeasing to God or pernicious to mankind in the world.' Plunket was condemned to death.

On 11 July 1681, a serene Doctor Plunket, under heavy guard, was led to Tyburn for execution. A vast crowd lined the route and an eye-witness declared that by his discourse from the scaffold and his heroism in death, he gave more to the glory of religion than he could have won for it by many years of fruitful apostolate.' The body was first interred at the Benedictine abbey of Lamspring in Germany, but 200 years later it was translated to Saint Gregory's College, Downside Abbey, England. The head was enshrined apart and since 1722 has been venerated at Drogheda by pilgrims from all parts of Ireland.

Westminster Cathedral's mosaic memorial to Saint Oliver (1924) is the work of Boris Anrep. Working *in situ*, the artist built up the design tile by tile from the front, whereas mosaic is normally assembled back to front and then transferred from paper sheets on to the receiving wall. An unusual feature is the inclusion of mother-of-pearl among the tesserae. The icon of the martyr represents him holding a pastoral staff in one hand and the Book of the Gospels in the other. From his left arm hangs a rope, the emblem of his martyrdom. At the base are shown the arms of the Diocese of Armagh and an inscription: Oliverius Plunket, Martyr Beatus, Armacannus Totius Hiberniae Primas Apud Tyburn AS (anno salutis) Kal. Quint. MDCLXXXI. Aureolam Meruit (Oliver Plunket, Blessed

Silver reliquary containing a relic of Saint Oliver Plunket designed by Laurence Shattock after a Celtic original discovered in 1891
(Catalogue number 107)

(Opposite)
Saint Oliver Plunket mosaic by Boris Anrep, 1924

Martyr, Archbishop of Armagh and All Ireland, won the crown at Tyburn on 1 July in the year of his salvation 1681).

In the 1920s, a relic of Oliver Plunket was given to the Cathedral by the Abbot of Downside. In order to be able to expose the relic for public veneration, a special reliquary was subscribed and commissioned - a copy of the Lough Erne Shrine, an early Irish reliquary acquired by the Royal Irish Academy. It had been discovered in 1891 when fishermen at Lough Erne near Enniskillen found it caught in their nets. It was made of bronze with an inner box of yew, whereas the Plunket reliquary, made in Dublin, is silver with jewelled bosses and an inner box of cedar. The relic, in a sealed glass tube, rests inside on silver supports. It was designed by L.H. Shattock, a former Cathedral architect at Westminster. Its decoration includes the *triquetra*, an interlaced Celtic ornament that symbolises the Trinity - a corner-stone of Irish devotion since the time of Patrick. The ebony plinth designed to support the reliquary includes these inscriptions: QUAE TE TERRA TULIT, SIMUL ET QUAE SUSTULIT, ORAT: PALMES OLIVERI NOBIS SIT PACIS OLIVA. (Pray for both the country which bore you and the country of your martyrdom: Let the palm branch of Oliver be to us the olive branch of peace.) *From the Irish and English clients of Blessed Oliver in the year of the truce, 1921.*

Chapel of Saint Patrick and the Saints of Ireland

Stepping into the Chapel of Saint Patrick it is noticeable that the east end is formed in the structure of a main pier. This enabled Bentley to provide scope for a deeply recessing arch above the altar. To right and left, this is broached with a vaulted niche. Irish marble has been incorporated in this chapel wherever possible. The altar was designed by J.A. Marshall of Bentley's firm and carried out by Farmer & Brindley in 1910. The altar frontal is of pale green Connemara with an oval of Cork red marble in the centre. This is entwined with two snakes carved in cipollino, matching a pair at each end of the altar; two more snakes have been carved into the ends of the altar's Irish black fossil marble. The reference is to the legendary expulsion of all the snakes of Ireland by Saint Patrick - an analogy for the triumph of the Gospel over the forces of evil and their very real challenge to the Church in every age. There is a dossal or background panel of the same black basalt inlaid with twenty-seven mother-of-pearl shamrocks. The altar steps are white statuary marble; the predella in the same material is inlaid with mosaic and lapis lazuli.

Irish Regimental badges are mounted within the arcading of the south wall

For many years after the completion of the altar very little further work was attempted and the chapel is said to have looked rather forlorn'. Bentley had himself prepared the designs, not only for the reredos but also for much of the marble revetment of the chapel walls. Eventually the necessary funds were raised and the marble-work continued, under the instructions of the Cathedral architect at the time, L.H. Shattock. High up on the walls are slabs of very rare stones, marble-framed as if they were paintings. They include panels of ancient Egyptian porphyry from Gebel Duchan, 23 miles from the Red Sea in the Eastern desert. The block from which these slabs were cut was brought to England by Lord Elgin, who had obtained it in Constantinople, where it was reputed to have come from the Temple of Diana at Ephesus. The marble suppliers were Farmer & Brindley who had long possessed rare examples such as these and made them available to Mr Shattock. Another of their treasures was the source of the two green panels seen in the west wall. This is Corsican smagdarit, cut from a boulder given to a convent of nuns in Corsica and intended for the decoration of their chapel. It was found too hard to work and lay abandoned for a long time on the seashore. Eventually it was bought by Farmer & Brindley and shipped to England, receiving the blessing of a Corsican priest on departure. The centre panel is a slab of *brèche universelle* from the Nile.

The floor is very fine and quite distinct from the paving in the other chapels. Where possible Irish marbles were used: Connemara marble, Irish black, and Cork red figure prominently. The chief element of the design is a Celtic cross in Cork red with an Irish sign of the Trinity in the head of the terminal. The sides have panels of Cork red and *vert d'estours*, inlaid with key patterns from Clonmacnois, and the trumpet pattern together with interlaced ornaments.

The altar is dominated by an unusual statue of Saint Patrick in gilt bronze. It was designed by Arthur Pollen and placed in the chapel in 1961, the Patrician Year, the 1,500th anniversary of Patrick's birth. When this statue was installed the necessary modifications to the reredos followed a plan of Mr Goodhart-Rendell and were the gift of Miss McHugh, a generous benefactor of the Cathedral, in memory of Lord Augustus Loftus.

Just as Saint Gregory and Saint Augustine are apostles of the English, so Saint Patrick (387-461) will always be venerated as the great apostle of Ireland. Born in Britain, possibly the son of a Roman official, Patrick was carried off into slavery as a 16-year-old by Irish marauders. For six years he tended sheep for his captors in the valley of the Braid and on the slopes of the Slemish near modern Ballymena. Roused by an inner call, he ran away from his masters and after travelling a couple of hundred miles was blessed to find a ship ready to sail for Britain. Back home and among friends he now set his heart on serving God in the priesthood. Preparation for such a ministry has always required education and Patrick is next encountered on the continent - at Saint Martin's monastery in Tours and

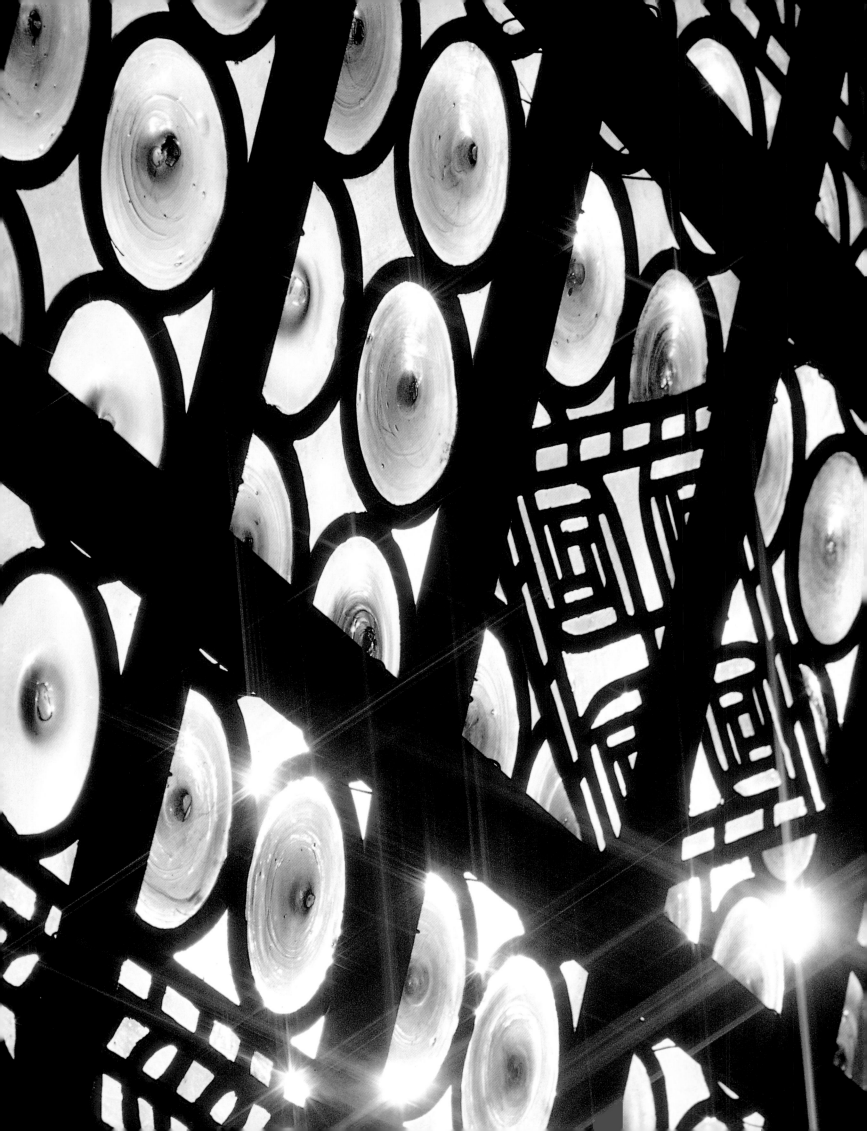

again at Lerins which was then acquiring a reputation for learning and piety. We know from a ninth-century life of Saint Germain of Auxerre that Patrick was one of his disciples. He accompanied the bishop on a mission to Britain and was later sent by him to Rome, where Pope Celestine I supported his wish to set out for Ireland and blessed his mission. Patrick was ordained a bishop at Turin by Saint Maximus and returned to Auxerre to prepare for Ireland under the guidance of Saint Germain. It was probably in the summer of 433 that Patrick and his companions landed at the mouth of the Vantry River close by Wicklow Head. The Druids were at once up in arms against him. He headed inland to seek friendlier territory. The character of his apostolate was the work of challenging the tyranny of Druidic paganism which apparently held the people in thrall. Patrick set about driving it out of the country by the conversion of chieftains, kings and the High King of Ireland himself. The work took years and many confrontations with entrenched powers but he succeeded. The day came when he was granted permission by the High King to preach the Gospel throughout Ireland. In 440 Patrick took up the task of the conversion of Ulster. The work prospered and the local chieftain invited him to select any site in his territory for the building of a church. Patrick chose the hill on which the old cathedral of Armagh was built and where again, in modern times, the new Cathedral would be erected and consecrated. In due course the whole country was won over to faith in the Christian Gospel, a legacy unparalleled in the life of any other individual in the Christian era. Patrick died in 461, on 17 March, the day his feast has been celebrated annually ever since.

As a teacher of the Christian faith Saint Patrick illustrated the central doctrine of the Trinity to the pagan Irish by means of the shamrock, the meadow plant with a three-part leaf on the one stem. Hence the recurrence in his chapel of the symbols of the Trinity, the mother-of-pearl shamrocks in the reredos, the

Marble of the altar reredos inlaid with mother-of pearl shamrocks

(Previous page)
The Fitzgerald Chalice

interlaced pattern on the floor at the foot of the altar and the central design of the pavement - a Celtic cross with its trinitarian symbol at the head of the terminal, the frieze around the walls with its white shamrock leaves set against a background of green Swedish marble. Instead of a metal grille between the chapel and the south aisle, Saint Patrick's has a pierced and carved marble screen based on one in the cathedral in Ravenna. Here the shamrock of Saint Patrick is interspersed with the oak leaves of Saint Brigid who attended his passing and prayed with him at the last.

Each year on the Feast of Saint Patrick Mass is said in this chapel, for which the priest uses a unique chalice. Known as the Fitzgerald chalice (catalogue no. 67), this is a rare example of Catholic plate made in these islands during penal times. It was given to Westminster Cathedral in the 1950s by Mr Dudley Fitzgerald. Made in Galway, c. 1719 for one of his ancestors, it had been in his family ever since. The date and origin are further attested by the maker's mark and inscription. Galway, like Youghal, is one of the old walled towns of Ireland where there were goldsmiths who marked plate with their own stamps up to the year 1783. The chalice was made in 1719 by Richard Joyes (or Joyce) and Mark Fallon.

On the front facet of the spreading octagonal foot of the chalice is an engraving of the crucifixion. On a larger scale is the Blessed Virgin and Saint Mary Magdalene (the latter bare-headed and wearing eighteenth-century costume). Behind the cross stands a little chapel from penal times which may represent the church in which the chalice was first used. Under the foot of the chalice these words are inscribed: 'Pray for the souls of Mr Patrick fiz Gerald and Mrs Cecily Darsy his wife who caused this chalice to be made for theirs and their posterity Anno Domini 1719'.

The prayers asked for on the foot of the chalice were soon needed; Cecily Fitzgerald died the year the chalice was

The golden figure of Saint Patrick above the altar provides the focus for the Irish Chapel

made, leaving to the care of their young father a little boy, John, and Elizabeth, who was deaf and dumb. Patrick Fitzgerald was the third son of John Fitzgerald of Gurtines, County Kilkenny, who had been dispossessed of his lands by Cromwell and 'planted' in the parish of Turlough, County Mayo. His son Patrick became a merchant in Galway and married a daughter of Peter Darcy, of the famous 'Thirteen Tribes of Galway'. This strange appellation was first used to describe the thirteen leading families of Galway by Cromwell's soldiers as a term of reproach, because of their extraordinary loyalty to each other during the time of their troubles and persecutions. It was afterwards adopted by the families themselves as a mark of distinction. The memory of no less than three of the famous 'tribes' is enshrined in the Fitzgerald chalice, for the names of both the goldsmiths, Joyes and Fallon, are numbered among them.

There is a story about the goldsmith, Richard Joyes, quoted by Sir Charles Jackson in *Hardiman's History of the Town and County of the Town of Galway*. In his

youth Joyes, on a voyage to the West Indies, was captured and taken to Algiers by pirates and sold as a slave to a Moorish goldsmith. He remained with the Moor for fourteen years, working at the goldsmiths' art, and appears to have been regarded as a highly skilled craftsman. On the accession of William III in England, one of the king's first acts was to send an ambassador to Algiers to demand the immediate release of every British subject held there in slavery. The demand was reluctantly complied with by the Bey and Joyes was free to leave. The Moor, however, on being ordered to release Joyes, offered his only daughter to him in marriage and half his property, as an inducement to remain, but Joyes refused the offer and returned to Galway. Back home he carried on the business of a goldsmith with great success. Having no son, Joyes bequeathed his property to his daughters. One of them was married to Andrew Ffrench, also a member of one of the Galway Tribes. Mark Fallon appears to have been taken into partnership and, after the death of Joyes, continued the business (Jackson, *English Goldsmiths and their Marks*).

Repository of the Roll of Honour to men of the Irish regiments who fell in the Great War

(Opposite)
Altar frontal includes Cork red marble entwined with snakes which Patrick 'expelled from Ireland'

Around the walls of the Chapel of Saint Patrick are the badges of Irish regiments largely now disbanded. There is also a book of remembrance enshrined here, in which the names of 50,000 Irish soldiers who died in the First World War are inscribed providing a memorial to those who fell in battle.

4th (Royal Irish) Dragoon Guards

Raised in 1685 as the Earl of Arran's Cuirassiers for service under King James II. After various changes of title it became the 4th (Royal Irish) Dragoon Guards Regiment in 1788 and was the only Dragoon Guard regiment with an Irish title. Took part in the charge of the Heavy Brigade at Balaclava in 1854. Amalgamated in 1922 with the 7th Dragoon Guards (Prince's Royals) to form the 4th/7th Royal Dragoon Guards.

5th (Royal Irish) Lancers

Raised in 1689 and disbanded in 1799. Re-instated by Queen Victoria in 1858. Fought in the Duke of Marlborough's campaigns, the Boer War and the First World War. Amalgamated with the 16th Queen's Lancers in 1922 to form the 16th/5th The Queen's Royal Lancers.

6th (Inniskilling) Dragoons

One of three regiments raised from Protestants who were besieged in Enniskillen when James II landed in Ireland in 1689, which later became the 6th (Inniskilling) Dragoons. In 1922 amalgamated with the 5th (PCW) Dragoon Guards to form the 5th Royal Inniskilling Dragoon Guards.

Irish Guards

Founded in 1900 on the command of Queen Victoria in recognition of the bravery of the Irish Regiments in the Boer War. The regiment is the only one in the Household Division to have a mascot, an Irish Wolfhound.

The Royal Irish Regiment

Formed in 1684 as the Earl of Granard's Regiment of Foot, becoming The Royal Regiment of Ireland in 1695 and in 1881 The Royal Irish Regiment. Disbanded in 1922.

The Royal Inniskilling Fusiliers

Raised in 1689 as Tiffin's Regiment of Foot, subsequently in 1854 becoming the East India Company's 3rd (Madras Infantry) Regiment and in 1861 the 108th (Madras Infantry) Regiment, after the Indian Mutiny. In 1881 its title changed to The Royal Inniskilling Fusiliers. In 1968 amalgamated with The Royal Ulster Rifles and The Royal Irish Fusiliers to form The Royal Irish Rangers.

The Royal Irish Rifles

Raised in 1793 as Fitch's Corps. Became the Royal Irish Rifles in 1881 and in 1921 The Royal Ulster Rifles. In 1968 amalgamated with the Royal Inniskilling Fusiliers and The Royal Irish Fusiliers to become The Royal Irish Rangers.

The Royal Irish Fusiliers

Raised in 1793 as the 87th (The Prince of Wales's Irish) Foot in 1866. To commemorate the presentation of colours in 1833 by Princess Victoria, the future Queen, the title changed to 89th (Princess Victoria's) Foot. In 1881 the title changed to The Royal Irish Fusiliers (Princess Victoria's). In 1968 amalgamated with The Royal Inniskilling Fusiliers and the Royal Irish Rifles to become The Royal Irish Rangers.

The Connaught Rangers

Raised in 1760 as the 88th (Royal Highland Volunteers) Foot and after many changes of title became The Connaught Rangers in 1891. Disbanded in 1922.

The (Prince of Wales's) Leinster Regiment (Royal Canadians)

Originally part of The Honourable East India Company as the 3rd (Bombay European) Regiment. Became the 109th (Bombay Infantry) Regiment in 1861 and in 1881 The Prince of Wales's Leinster Regiment (Royal Canadian), disbanding in 1922.

The Munster Fusiliers

Formed from the amalgamation of the 101st (Royal Bengal Fusiliers) and 104th Bengal Fusiliers in 1881 when it became The Royal Munster Fusiliers. Disbanded in 1922.

Royal Dublin Fusiliers

Originated from the Honourable East India Company, The Madras European Regiment (1648) and The Bombay Regiment (1661) became respectively 102nd Royal Madras Fusiliers and 103rd Royal Bombay Fusiliers and later formed The Royal Dublin Fusiliers in 1881. Disbanded in 1922.

18th (County of London) Battalion, London Regiment (London Irish Rifles)

In 1859 when the threat of French invasion roused the country to arms, The Corps of Irish Gentlemen-at-Arms' was raised in London. It was decided to organise a rifle volunteer force under the title of the London Irish Volunteers. One of the first recruits was Lord Palmerston. It served in South Africa, and in the First and Second World Wars.

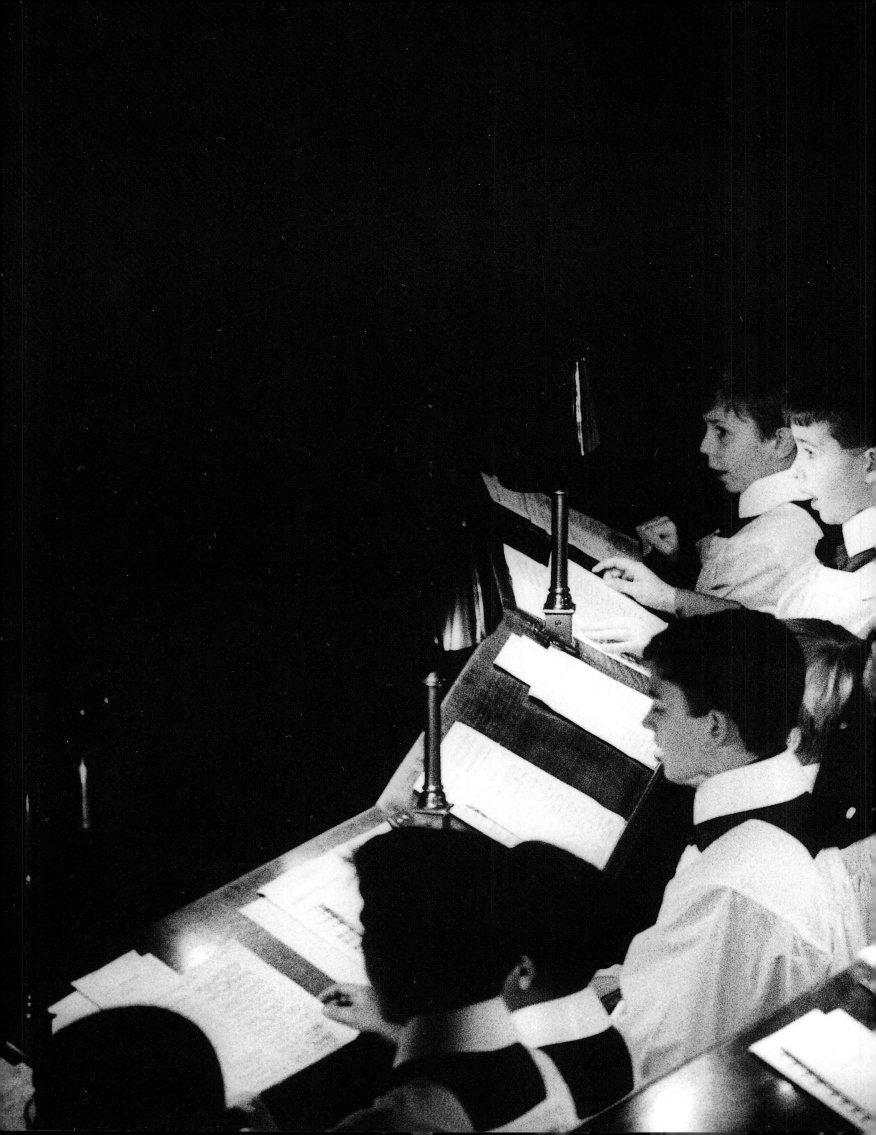

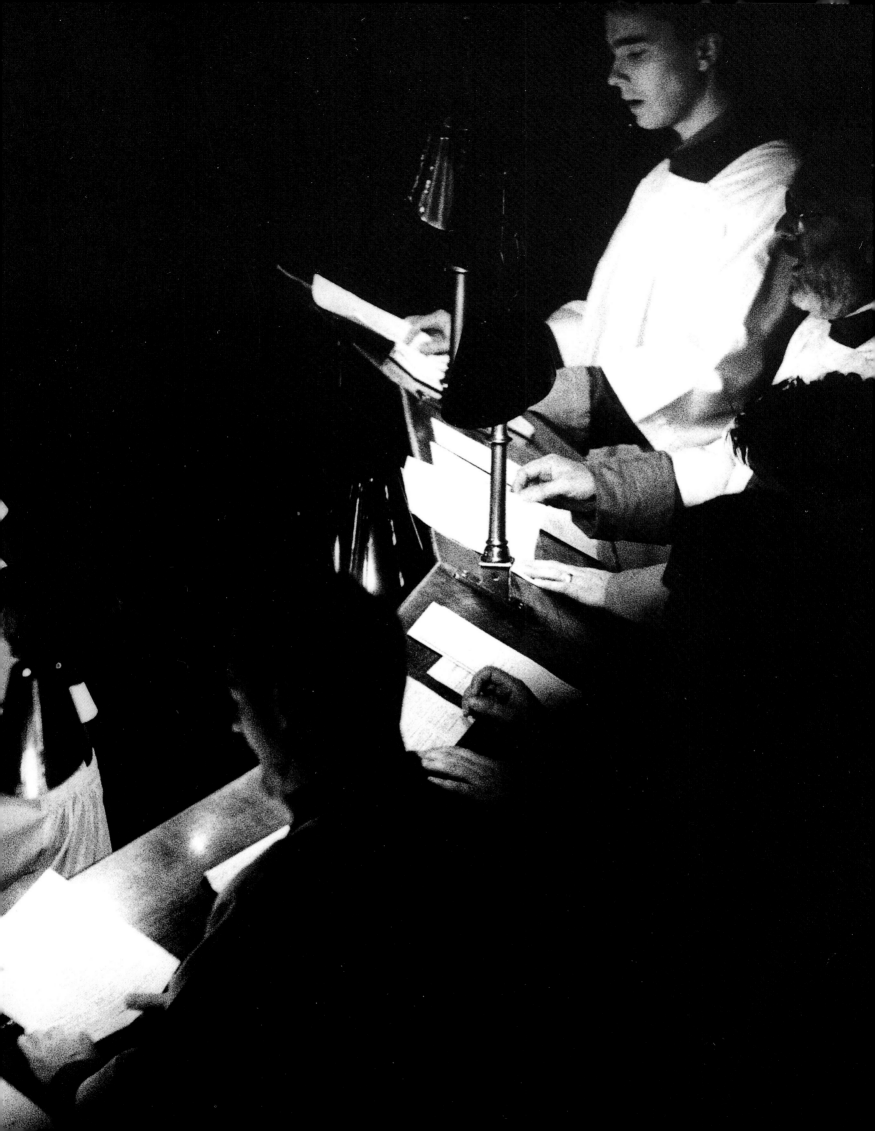

Chapel of Saint Andrew and the Scottish Saints

The reliquary of Saint Andrew is marked by a Harold Stabler bronze and enamel design

(Opposite)
Deeply incised spirals mark the columns of the baldachino

Returning to the south aisle and walking east, the next chapel is dedicated to Saint Andrew and the Saints of Scotland, for the Scots have as their chief patron one of the four closest companions of Jesus of Nazareth, one of the twelve apostles. In the fourth gospel, Andrew together with John (who was to write that gospel) had been disciples of John the Baptist, whose testimony had first led them to follow Jesus. At once, Andrew acknowledged Jesus to be the Messiah and hastened to introduce him to his brother Peter (John 1: 35-40). Together with James and John these two fishermen of Galilee became the closest companions of Jesus, his inner circle. He was present at the last supper, when Jesus instituted the Eucharist. He beheld the Risen Lord and witnessed his ascension. He shared, too, in the graces and gifts of the Holy Spirit at Pentecost. When the apostles went out to proclaim the Gospel to all nations, Andrew would have been prominent among them, but the Scriptures contain no details of his apostolate. Eusebius states that he went to Scythia and there is a tradition that he was put to death at Patras in Greece by order of Aegeas, the Roman governor; that he was bound to a cross, not nailed, in order to prolong his sufferings. His martyrdom is said to have taken place in the reign of Nero, on 30 November 60 AD, the date on which both the Latin and Greek Churches keep his feast. The tradition that the cross on which Andrew died was formed like an X (decussate) has been convenient for artists - since this shape identifies Saint Andrew in works of art - but it cannot be traced earlier than the thirteenth century. Relics of Saint Andrew were translated from Patras to Constantinople around 357. In the thirteenth century, when the city was taken by the French, these relics were brought to Italy by Cardinal Peter of Capua and placed in the Cathedral at Amalfi. Any relics of Saint Andrew to be found elsewhere and authenticated by the Church - there is one in this chapel - would have come from this source.

Stepping into Saint Andrew's Chapel it is immediately noticeable that the decoration has a unity which sets it apart from the others. The materials used are austere and the colours subdued. Nevertheless it shows the qualities of fastidious good taste and superb craftsmanship that identify the Arts and Crafts Movement, burgeoning in the early years of the twentieth century. Although the chapel was unveiled in 1915 and finally completed a year later, the altar had already been consecrated in 1910 by Doctor Keating, Bishop of Northampton. During the ceremony, attended by a stonemason, the bishop deposited a silver casket into a hollowed-out recess at the foot of the large copper crucifix. A colourful circlet of enamelled bronze by Harold Stabler marks the presence of the reliquary. Containing the relic of Saint Andrew, this was immediately sealed with marble by the stonemason. The three steps, which are Pentelic white and the soft grey marble of Mount Hymettus, lead up to the open table, a slab of dark granite surmounting five pillars of red Peterhead granite with bronze capitals and a base slab of grey Aberdeen granite. There is a fine canopy over the altar on four green columns with bronze capitals and bases. Although columns with bands of bronze around them are often to be seen in Byzantine churches, this treatment is unusual and effective, in harmony with the brown beaten copper of the dignified crucifix that fills the reredos space to the height of the baldachino. On the east wall, on either side of the baldachino are four sculpted reliefs of principal Scottish saints - Ninian, Margaret, Bride and Columba.

That Saint Andrew's Chapel was finished at an early date is due to the munificence of one man - the 4th Marquess of Bute - who promised £10,000 to bring the chapel from brick shell to completion. There was one condition - accepted by Cardinal Bourne - that the whole of the marble and mosaic work should be placed in the hands of Robert Weir Schultz. The choice was appropriate as Schultz was a pioneer in Byzantine studies. He was born in Glasgow in 1860, and came to London in 1884 where he joined the architect's office of Richard Norman Shaw (1831-1912). In the same year, Shaw's pupils founded the Art Workers' Guild. Inspired by William Morris it was to become an influential body of architectural craftspeople. Schultz was elected to membership in 1891. He worked at the

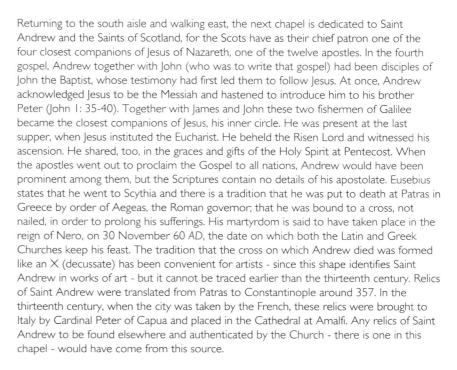

offices of Ernest George and Peto, two firms responsible for the flourishing of British Arts and Crafts in the 1890s. His Byzantine studies led to close friendship with W.R. Lethaby who wrote the standard work of the time -read by Bentley when his cathedral project was beginning - The Church of Santa Sophia, Constantinople, a Study of Byzantine Building (1894). Schultz gained a travelling scholarship (1887-88) which took him to Italy, Greece and Turkey in the company of Ernest Gimson, a significant designer-craftsman whom Schultz would later bring in for the furnishing of the Chapel of Saint Andrew. Gimson was perhaps the most talented furniture designer in what would later be known as the Cotswold School. Between autumn 1892 when Cardinal Vaughan became Archbishop of Westminster and July 1894 when John Bentley was appointed, as many as twelve architects were considered for the work of designing the Cathedral. Bentley had become a Roman Catholic some years earlier and Schultz, a Scots Protestant, once claimed to A.B. Waters that had he become a member of the Catholic Church, he would have got the job of designing Westminster Cathedral. At all events, he had two first-rate clients in the 3rd and 4th Marquesses of Bute, Scots patrons of the arts and, like the Dukes of Norfolk, Catholic laymen of the highest distinction and influence. Schultz worked for the 3rd Marquess until the latter's death in 1900. The Chapel of the Scots was unveiled on the Feast of Saint Andrew in 1915, when at 8.30 am Cardinal Bourne celebrated Mass at its altar. His altar-server, appropriately, was the Marquesss of Bute, who had made the work possible.

The knowledge of Byzantine style and technique which Schultz had brought to the project made a considerable impression. In 1916, a reviewer in *Country Life* wrote: 'here is no mere archaeological exercise, no dead copy of the churches of Rome or Ravenna or the East, but a live piece of design, wrought out in valuable materials, with mature knowledge of design and method'

The quiet dignity of an integrated chapel design

The Gimson stalls

Scotland's colours - the blue and white windows

Saint Andrew the Fisherman depicted in the west wall mosaics by Gaetano Meo

(*Country Life*, 8.1.1916, p.2). Not everyone was charmed. The correspondent of *The Times* declared that 'the marble casing of the walls under the mosaics is positively freezing in its colourless coldness ... colour blindness could not have led to a more deplorable result.' This is a little harsh since the scheme gains great dignity and a look of antiquity from its severe colouring.

Although Bentley's firm had produced designs based on the founder's drawings, they did not form the basis of the work of Schultz. According to Bentley's daughter and biographer, these drawings disappeared without trace. Had they been succeeded by unworthy designs the shortcoming would have been serious. As it was, Robert Weir Schultz was ideally suited to the project. (His surname became a liability with the anti-German hysteria of the pre-war period and in 1914 Schultz changed his name to R.W.S. Weir.)

Schultz had his coloured designs approved by the Cardinal in 1910. When drawings of the completed work were shown at the Royal Academy in 1915 their differences from the original were only a matter of detail. Many artists and craftspeople worked under Schultz's direction to realise the concept. With the brick shell as their canvas, the members of the Art Workers' Guild were able to demonstrate their skills. The common unity of their efforts had its source in the belief that architecture was chief among the arts and other creative activities were in service to it.

With Lord Bute's £10,000 to spend, it is interesting to see what the money was able to purchase in 1910. £3,450 went on marble bought and cut by Farmer & Brindley. £1,130 bought the screen separating the chapel from the aisle. Made of stainless tin, it is surmounted by electric lights in pale sea-green glass, part of the set made for this chapel by W. Bainbridge Reynolds. The chandelier, which is in the shape of a Byzantine 'polycandelon', contains an ostrich egg, which was highly symbolic in Eastern art, but was also a device for stopping church mice from climbing down the chains to drink the oil of the lamps! J. Sterling Lee was paid £1,290 for the sculpted copper crucifix. The remarkable bronze candlesticks for the altar, modest in size and with their strongly coloured enamel in harlequin patterning, appeared on Harold Stabler's bill for £189 0s 7d. Close inspection reveals that their feet are in the form of little fish. The £477 spent on stalls for the chapel produced the most notable result. Superbly crafted in ebony and ivory they are the work of Ernest Gimson, in close collaboration with Schultz. The kneelers are the product of another close collaborator, Sidney Barnsley. Ian Nairn, while critical of the Cathedral as a whole, wrote in 1966: 'Here, in the choir stalls and kneelers, is a real work of being, style and expression pounding together. Ernest Gimson designed them in 1912, without self-conscious doubts. He knew his style and his compound of rectilinear shapes and

Flat fish, eels and other sea creatures in Saint Andrew's floor

(Previous page)
(Left) The chapel, completed in 1915 at the behest of the Marquess of Bute, has a screen of stainless tin. The stalls are 'Cotswold School', by Ernest Gimson
(Right) A fisherman's floor with the contents of a net, inlaid in the marble pavement

rich inlay burns away in - liturgically speaking - a fairly unimportant part of the building' (*Nairn's London*). (A prototype for the stalls is Cheltenham Art Museum: English walnut inlaid with bone; the ones in the chapel are in brown ebony inlaid with bone.) The final bill for the chapel came to £10,537 5s 2d including a frugal £1 8s 6d for a pair of silvered candlesticks obtained from Constantinople and still in use. Dom Michael Barrett OSB received 12 guineas (£12 12s) to compile a list of Scottish saints. These names can be seen incised on the wall marble - round the upper part of the blue slabs forming the high dado - and continuing right round the east and south walls. (Father Barrett had written *The Kalendar of Saints of Scotland*, published by the Benedictine Abbey of Fort Augustus.)

Together with his close supervision of the craftwork throughout the chapel, Schultz designed the mosaics which cover the upper part of the walls, arches and vaults.

His patron Lord Bute took a close interest in the progress of the work which he inspected at regular intervals. Indeed, although the chapel was ready for its opening in 1915, work was still going on a year later. Architect and client had conferred over the work from 1910 until 1916. By 1923 it was necessary for cleaning and repairs to be carried out and additional work including the installation of a confessional in the outer wall. Schultz's supervision was his last job for the Marquess.

The mosaics are conventional and straightforward in the manner of early Byzantine work. They were carried out by Signor Gaetano Meo who had worked under Sir William Richmond on the mosaics in Saint Paul's Cathedral, together with two of his team of six mosaicists. Signor Meo had studied mosaic in Sicily, Ravenna, Rome and Venice and one of his craftsmen was a Venetian. The tesserae were brought from Venice; the *intonaco* (plaster) was the same composition as that used in Saint Paul's, with ingredients which,

slightly modified, matched those used in the fifteenth century to restore the mosaics of the Baptistry in Florence.

On the west wall is the figure of Saint Andrew in blue cloak and white tunic, his hands raised in acceptance of his martyrdom by crucifixion. His cross faces him across the chapel in the east wall mosaic above the altar. He is surrounded by nature including deer, rose bushes and olives. An inscription in English begins: Saint Andrew, Our Lord's first apostle, a fisherman of Bethsaida in Galilee, whom with his brother Simon Peter, Jesus saw fishing and called them to him ....'. High on the west wall are vividly patterned slabs of bright yellow and brown from the island of Skyros in Greece. On the east wall there are sheep rather than deer - the flock tended by an apostle of Christ. Golden rays emanate from Saint Andrew's cross with the white dove hovering above, symbolising the blessing of the Holy Spirit. On either side is a prayer for the Feast of Saint Andrew in Latin and English, the latter coming from a translation of the Roman Breviary by the 4th Marquess: O Precious Cross, which the members of my Lord have made so fair and goodly, welcome me from among men, and join me again to my Master, that, as by thee He redeemed me, so by thee also He may take me unto Himself.' The ceiling vault was designed to shimmer, with mosaic patterned like the scales of a fish. At the sides of the ceiling, places associated with Saint Andrew are represented. In the centre above the windows is Constantinople showing Hagia Sophia, the Church of Holy Wisdom, the mother of all Byzantine churches - although long since turned into a mosque. On either side are Bethsaida, Andrew's birthplace, and Patras, his place of exile. On the opposite side of the ceiling, looking towards the nave is St Andrews in Scotland (the medieval city based on contemporary drawings). On its left is Milan, chosen for its association with the relics of the saint - showing not the cathedral but the Byzantine church of Saint Ambrose. On the right is Amalfi on the Mediterranean coast where the body

Fish scale patterning of the ceiling mosaics

of Saint Andrew is said to have been brought. The fisherman motif seen in the mosaic patterns of scales is taken up again in the marble floor. With its wave patterns and inlaid marble fishes and crab it also provides an echo of a Bentley idea - never realised (in fact opposed, in view of its physical coldness) - that the entire floor of the Cathedral should be a sea of marble, populated with sea creatures, fish and crustacea, representing the great net cast into the sea which is the Church.

Chapel of Saint Paul

Austrian oak bench ends carved to a design by Shattock

Walking eastwards, the next chapel is dedicated to Saint Paul, the Apostle of the Gentiles' who together with Saint Peter, founded the Church at Rome. He was the great missionary apostle of the earliest years of the young Church, whose journeys, work and hardships are described in the Acts of the Apostles, and to some extent also, in the great letters of instruction Paul wrote to new Christian communities burgeoning around the Mediterranean. Clearly he was not one of 'The Twelve', yet insisted on the right to be called an apostle.

Paul was a Pharisee, with the Hebrew name Saul, and was highly educated unlike Peter and the other fishermen among the apostles. He spoke of his home town with pride: 'I am a Jew, from Tarsus in Cilicia, a citizen of no mean city.' He also claimed Roman citizenship which helped him out of trouble on a number of occasions on his travels. As a young man Saul had persecuted the young Church as ruthlessly as any military officer. On the road to Damascus, however, a light from heaven' flashed around him, he was thrown from his horse and temporarily blinded while hearing a voice: Saul, Saul, why do you persecute me?' It was the moment of his conversion, an experience he would refer to again and again in later years. After accepting baptism a few days later, he embarked on a radically new life, teaching what he had understood in that mystical encounter on the Damascus road. Paul spent the remainder of his life establishing communities and facing opposition with heroic courage, as zealous in proclaiming the risen Christ as he had once been in opposing him.

Against this background the subject of the mosaic on the south side of the chapel becomes clear. Above the windows and framed with a triumphal arch motif is the scene of the shipwreck on Malta (in Latin, MELITA). The name is said to refer to the island's honey-coloured stone, here seen in the rocks. The ship has been run aground at the place where two seas meet and Paul, thrown into the sea, clambers ashore. In the mosaic on the north side, runs the inscription DE FORTI EGRESSA EST DULCEDO (Out of the strong came something sweet) which is the riddle of Samson (Judges 14:14). There is a large medallion showing the head of a fierce lion, a reminder of Saul's belligerence towards the Christian Church before his dramatic conversion. 'Something sweet' is represented by bees which seem also to connect with the reference to honey on the Malta tableau opposite.

Thus Saint Paul is the foremost patron of those who convert to Christian belief and seek membership of the Church. In the early days of the Cathedral it was thought that the decoration of this chapel might be funded by the thank-offerings of those who, like Paul, were converts. A box was placed in the chapel but progress in collecting was slow. Then in 1913 Mrs Caroline Sambourne-Palmer approached Cardinal Bourne with an offer of funds if the chapel could be made a memorial to her parents, John and Anna-Maria Anstey. The marble wall-linings were soon put in hand and the chapel was opened in the autumn of 1917 although it was not until much later that work on the pavement and mosaics was begun.

Returning to the mosaics of the north side - in the space between the arches there is a basket with ropes attached, an allusion to Paul's escape from Damascus when he was lowered over the city wall in a basket (Acts 9:25). Not surprisingly Paul is by tradition the protector of basket-weavers and rope-makers! Above the inscription a group of churches is depicted against a wide expanse of open sky. Paul's last known voyage, during which the Malta shipwreck occurred, brought him eventually to Rome where he was put under house arrest whilst awaiting trial. His execution is believed to have taken place during the

...ET INGREDERE CIVITATEM ET ... ...TIBI QVID TE OPORTEAT FACERE   JERVSALEM

ESSE QVAM VIDERI

Cosmatesque pavement, 1940

(Opposite page)
Roof of the Anstey Chantry (Saint Paul's Chapel)

reign of Emperor Nero in about AD 64-5 and tradition has it that at the place of execution, on a site known as *Aquae Salviae (*the modern Abbey of the Three Fountains) his severed head bounced three times and in each place a spring of water began to flow. At all events, three churches were later built there. These are the little churches represented in this north mosaic.

Paul's faithful followers carried his body for burial at the vineyard of a wealthy Christian lady called Lucina, a mile outside the city wall. As with Saint Peter's grave on the Vatican Hill a *cella memoriae* was erected over his tomb. The Emperor Constantine transformed these two *cella memoriae* of the founding apostles into basilicas. Throughout the Christian centuries the basilica built over the tomb of the great apostle has been a place of pilgrimage -it remains so today - while the title and dedication spread to churches all over European Christendom. When London's own first cathedral church was founded in *AD* 604 it was dedicated to Saint Paul. Before the Reformation, the kings of England were honorary canons and protectors of Saint Paul's Basilica in Rome (a larger one, begun in 386 by Valentinian II and Theodosius the Great), and in return, the abbots of its monastery were Knights of the Garter. This chapel may therefore be regarded as one of the most important dedications in the building. It is certainly one of the best architecturally. Together with its twin, Saint Joseph's Chapel on the south side, it has a deep apse cut into the massive buttress wall of the transept.

The Conversion of Paul on the Damascus road is depicted on the west wall of the chapel. Paul, brought to his knees, surrounded by a strange nimbus of light and temporarily blinded is addressed by Christ. The inscription below reads: SURGE ET INGREDERE CIVITATEM, ET IBI DICETUR TIBI QUID TE OPORTEAT FACERE (Get up and enter the city and you will be told what you are to do)(Acts 9:6). A sword lies at Paul's side and the red and blue of his garments are the

colours traditionally associated with him. The sword is both the emblem of his struggle (1 Timothy 6:12) and the instrument of his martyrdom. The cities of Damascus and Jerusalem are shown left and right. Among the buildings of the Holy City some twisted columns are seen, which iconographic tradition suggests stood at the gate of the Temple. The high wall is an evocation of what is now known as the Wailing Wall, the only visible remains of Herod's Temple as it was in the time of Jesus. The walls of Damascus are shown with a city gate of Roman type below an arched entablature and propylaeum.

Covering most of the chapel vault and apparently billowing upwards to the sky is a mosaic tent of iridescent colours in the form of a *velarium*, which in antiquity would have been woven by a tent-maker. Like many Pharisees of his time, Paul, although a scholar and teacher of the Hebrew Law, also worked with his hands. His trade was tent-making, weaving and stitching goat's-hair cloth, and he made a point of economic self-reliance. Here on this ceiling there is a Star of David motif and a Byzantine Christogram (the Greek Chi-Ro) which can also be seen as combining the initial P of the saint's name with the palm, emblem of martyrdom. Interestingly, the Chi-Ro itself can fit precisely into a Star of David.

The mosaics date from 1963. Boris Anrep, the Russian mosaicist, had completed a major work in Westminster Cathedral's Chapel of the Blessed Sacrament but was now too old to attempt another commission. Instead he agreed to supervise Justin Vulliamy, his long-term artistic and technical associate, in the design and realisation of the work. Anrep was responsible for the detailing of the principal figures but became unhappy with the final results. Before his death he dissociated himself from the totality, feeling unable to regard it as his own work. The manufacture and preparation of the mosaic *smalti* was the work of Orsini in Venice, and the task of fixing *in situ* was done by Peter Indri with the help of Hussey Brothers and the firm of Zanelli Ltd.

To the east, the domed surface of the apse has a grey-blue sky sprinkled with stars. On the arch is the inscription DOMINUS LEGEM DAT (The Lord gives us the Law), interspersed with four little books signifying the Gospels. In the tympanum above the arch are head and shoulders depictions of Christ and the apostles Peter and Paul (because of Saint Peter's usual prominence Anrep was anxious that here they should be portrayed as equal). Christ is giving his law of love, shown as a scroll. The subject occurs on a number of early Christian sarcophagi, and (with the inscription) in mosaics of the fourth and fifth centuries. The portrait' of Paul has been taken from that in the Capella Palatina at Palermo which although late, is one in which the earliest reported characteristics of the man are portrayed. There is no description of Paul in the New Testament, yet a tradition does exist that he was a 'man of moderate stature, with curly hair and scanty, crooked legs, with blue eyes, large-knit eyebrows, long nose; and full of the grace and pity of the Lord ...'.

On each side the water of life flows through green slopes and a rocky landscape. The triptych above the altar is gilt bronze and shows a figure of Saint Paul in bold relief, surmounted by a representation of the saint's martyrdom. An enamelled shield bearing the arms of Saint Paul is centred on the lower part of the triptych. On the doors is inscribed: VAS ELECTIONIS EST MIHI ISTE UT PORTET NOMEN MEUM CORAM GENTIBUS ET REGIBUS ET FILIIS ISRAEL (This man is my chosen instrument to bring my name before gentiles and kings and before the people of Israel)(Acts 9:15). This text is used as the second antiphon for the Office of Readings for the Feast of the Conversion of Saint Paul. On either side of the altar a *piscina* is set into the apsidal wall, of buff-coloured stone with decorative inlays. The Latin word *piscina* means a fish pond

Canopy of a piscina

of Tinos flanked by panels of porphyry. The altar steps are Pentelic. The sombre but satisfying marble-work is predominantly grey-green. The apse of the chapel is lined with white and grey Proconnesian marble, divided by strips of *verte Campagne*. This Proconnesian is drawn from extensive quarries which were known as early as the fourth century *BC*, on the island of Proconnesus, in the Propontis or Sea of Marmora. The marble was also called Cyzican, a reference to the nearby peninsula. There are several columns in Santa Sophia which came from the Temple of Cybele in Cyzicum. It was used a great deal in Constantinople, not much in Rome, but frequently in Ravenna. Columns of Proconnesian are to be seen in the church of Sant' Apollinare Nuovo, and there were others in the Basilica Ursiana before its final destruction in the eighteenth century.

On the wall facing the altar the lower parts are lined with cipollino and *verd-antique*, and the upper parts with Hymettan. The arms of the donor are set into this wall in *opus sectile* together with a dedicatory inscription. Between the chapel and the aisle there is a fine column of Greek cipollino, and the smaller pillar between the windows is barbillo. The arcading of the window wall is done with small columns of pavonazzo.

A striking feature of this chapel is the floor. It was the fifth Archbishop of Westminster, Cardinal Hinsley (1935-43), who decided that the flooring in the side chapels should be completed by laying a special pavement for this 'Anstey Chantry'.

A design was prepared and approved, on a par with the pavement laid earlier in the Chapel of Saint Joseph. The result is a magnificent example of Cosmatesque craftsmanship. The Cosmati, whose work has endured in so many great churches, were a family of Roman stonemasons in the twelfth and thirteenth centuries. They developed their technique (which included using slices of porphyry columns

to make the flat red circles in their patterns) as a means of using the myriad fragments that lay around a despoiled Rome. Their fame was such that they were invited to London to build the tomb of Henry III and to lay the floor of Westminster Abbey. The Cosmatesque pavement seen here was assembled just before the Second World War under the direction of Edward Hutton and completed in June 1940. It is based on a design taken from the Capella Palatina with a bold pattern of Pentelic inlaid with verd-antique and porphyry. The colours harmonise with the mosaics of the vault, where instead of a gold ground as in other chapels, the clear pastels of the

tent complement the pavement geometry below.

Cardinal Heenan (1963-75), eighth Archbishop of Westminster, is buried at the foot of the twelfth Station of the Cross opposite this chapel. The plain slab of marble is inlaid with fine lettering designed and carved by Nicolete Gray. The script of the title of the Cardinal's church in Rome is modelled on the fourth century inscriptions of Pope Saint Damasus I and that used for 'Cardinal Priest' is a triumphant Roman style invented for the same Pope after the conversion of Constantine, to honour the tombs of the martyrs.

Mary's Domain
from South Transept to Lady Chapel

The altar under the apse of the Lady Chapel

(Opposite)
The word AVE meaning 'Hail!' is the first word of the angel Gabriel's greeting to Mary

Leaving the Chapel of Saint Paul and continuing east, the visitor enters an area which is devoted to Mary, the Virgin Mother of God. Of all the saints, no human person in the story of mankind is accorded greater reverence by the Catholic Church than Mary the mother of Jesus. This devotion is by no means unique to Roman Catholics, of course. Many Anglicans hold her in the same high esteem while the entire spectrum of Eastern Churches manifests profound reverence for the *Theotokos* - Bearer of the Divine. The many titles accorded her underpin all the iconography to be seen here. Most importantly, Mary is seen as the new Eve, no more than human yet a unique creation, untainted by original sin, that source and cause of the fall of humanity. Her acceptance of the divine will at a crucial juncture in the story of humankind's dealings with God is recorded in the simplest terms in Saint Luke's gospel. The angel Gabriel has appeared to Mary and explained that she has been chosen to bear the son of the Most High by the power of the Holy Spirit: *'Then Mary said, ' Here am I the servant of the Lord; let it be with me according to your word'* (Luke 1:38). With these words, spoken in the town of Nazareth by a young girl engaged to be married, the redemption of the human race is set on course. To the Church's way of thinking, Mary is *that* important. She becomes mother of the Divine Redeemer and is revered for her absolute readiness to accept the will of God in her life - the perfect exemplar of the Christian ideal. In the inspired words of her Magnificat:

'My soul magnifies the Lord,
and my spirit rejoices in God my Saviour;
for he has looked with favour on the lowliness of his servant,
surely from now on all generations will call me blessed.' (Luke 1:46-48)

At Westminster Cathedral, the whole area at the eastern end on the right, beginning just before the south transept and culminating at the altar of the Lady Chapel, may be regarded as Mary's domain. Moving from the Chapel of Saint Paul to the south transept, we pass two recesses with brightly coloured apsidal mosaics in recognition of Mary's parents. Already we are walking into the family home. By tradition, Mary's father and mother are known as Saint Joachim and Saint Anne. They are not named in the Scriptures, nevertheless theirs is a strong tradition based on one of the most famous of the apocryphal writings, the *Protoevangelium Jacobi (c. AD 170-80)*. This work was translated into many languages and from very early days Joachim and Anne were taken as a model of Christian married life. Given that Mary is the mother of Jesus, her parents are grandparents of Christ, and so themselves belong to the Holy Family. Joachim and Anne are seen as fitting symbols for the messianic expectations of the Old Testament, whilst forming a bridge to the new dispensation.

As the south transept is entered it is seen to function as an extended nave for the Lady Chapel ahead. Passing the steps of the cosmatesque pulpit a seated figure of the Virgin Mother is encountered, set against the wall of one of the main piers of the nave. The question arises: what is an English medieval image of the Virgin doing in a nineteenth-century Cathedral for which nearly every item of decoration has been custom-made? A clue lies in the title given to this seated figure in 1955 - Our Lady of Westminster.

In the fourteenth century Westminster possessed two notable shrines of the Blessed Virgin. The more famous of the two was annexed to the Royal Chapel of Saint Stephen where the Houses of Parliament now stand. The other was in Westminster Abbey. The first mention of the Abbey shrine of Our Lady of the Pewe occurs in the Sacrist's Roll for 1379-80. The shrine is now the entry to the Chapel of Saint John. There was a common link between them since at both, the Mother of God was invoked under the title of Our Lady of the Pewe, often called *Le Puy*. Scholars have given many possible explanations for the meaning and significance of this title. In medieval documents the King is often referred

The letters IHS inscribed on this capital show the original intention for the Blessed Sacrament Chapel to be on the south side of the Cathedral

Basil Carey-Elwes and 'Josie' completing the mosaic in a confessional alcove

to as His Most Puissant - powerful - Majesty. It may be that Mary was invoked here, in the heart of government, as the Most Puissant Queen of Heaven. Those overseeing the life of Westminster Cathedral had long wanted to revive this local devotion to the Mother of God.

The serene alabaster figure seen here is a carving of the Nottingham School and belongs to the first quarter of the fifteenth century. Little is known of its history. In the mid-1950s, during Monsignor William Gordon Wheeler's time as Cathedral Administrator, the statue was seen at the Grosvenor Antiques Fair, newly arrived from a dealer in France. In 1954 it had been displayed at the Paris Exhibition of the Chef d'Oeuvres de la Curiosité du Monde. Little was known of its provenance or where it had spent the preceding centuries. It was purchased on the advice of John Pope-Hennessy, Director of the Victoria and Albert Museum. Monsignor Wheeler, later Bishop of Leeds, wrote: It had been bought from a French family by the ecclesiastical art dealer, Wolsey. Cardinal Griffin [1943-56] was very keen that the Cathedral should have the statue and gave me a cheque to go along and buy it. When I got there, Wolsey told me that, alas, he couldn't let me have it because the Dean of York had bespoken it for York Minster and had started a fund for the purpose. I said: "But if the arrangement were to fall through, I would be very grateful if you would let me know." Some months later I went into Wolsey's place again and he said: "Oh, I was about to let you know that the Dean of York has written to say that he has had no further donations apart from one given by Sir William Milner, and if Westminster Cathedral still wants it, he thinks you should have it." So the alabaster was installed and when it was inaugurated by Archbishop Edward Myers (Cardinal Griffin was ill at the time) the Dean of York was represented, appropriately, by Sir William Milner.' This dedication took place on 8 December 1955, the Feast of the Immaculate Conception of the Blessed Virgin.

It was decided to erect the statue in its present position, close to the Lady Chapel and under the thirteenth of the Eric Gill Stations of the Cross, the title of this bas-relief being particulary apt: *The body of Jesus is taken down from the cross and laid in his mother's bosom.* Years earlier, as an Anglican curate in St Bartholomew's, Bournemouth, Gordon Wheeler had known a fine altar made of silver and something similar seemed to him appropriate here. The silversmith Dunstan Pruden was approached but the estimated cost was prohibitive. Nevertheless, to delineate a shrine, the floor was relaid by Aelred Bartlett, marble expert and brother of Francis Bartlett who would be one of Gordon Wheeler's successors. Two wrought iron candle-holders complete the shrine and many come to pray before the statue.

The statue is worthy of close inspection. Mary is depicted as Queen of Heaven, enthroned and crowned. The folds of her garment trail over the flowers of a heavenly field. She is the 'Seat of Wisdom', SEDES SAPIENTIAE. In her left hand she holds a lily sceptre as the 'Virgin most powerful', VIRGO POTENS. Yet another of her many titles, it is a reference to her God-given sway in heaven and on earth. On her arm Mary supports the Logos, the Word-made-flesh, Eternal Wisdom. With his right hand the child blesses an orb, symbol of the earth, his possession. It is an echo of many biblical texts including Psalm 24:

*The earth is the Lord's
and all that is in it,
the world and those who live in it;
for he has founded it
on the seas and established
it on the rivers.*

In the transept itself and to the right are the main confessionals of the Cathedral parish, occupying the space between interior buttresses. Here the Cathedral chaplains administer the sacrament of reconciliation for several hours each day. The arch above the furthest space is finished with mosaic showing on one side

Saint Peter with the inscription 'And he went out and wept bitterly' (Luke 22:62) and on the other, Saint Mary Magdalene with the words 'Her sins which were many have been forgiven' (Luke 7:47).This alcove is the earliest example of mosaic work in the building after Bentley's death. Cardinal Bourne (1903-35) employed two mosaicists, Basil Carey-Elwes and 'Josie' to start a school of mosaicworkers. It is appropriate that confessions are heard in this part of the Cathedral since it is traditional for priests (who see themselves as dispensing the sacrament of Christ's mercy) to place their lives and ministry under Mary's protection. She is described as 'Refuge of Sinners' and a favourite prayer adverts to this role of the Mother of God with the words: 'I come to you, Mother, and stand in your presence, unhappy sinner that I am. Despise not my poor words, O Mother of the Word incarnate, but graciously hear and heed my prayer ...'. Another feature of Mary's 'domain' is the outside door at the back of the transept which provides access for those entering the Cathedral on wheelchairs. Her title 'Health of the Sick' is a reminder that those suffering in mind or body are placed under Mary's care by the Church. Anonymous donors provided £30,000 to have the entrance and ramp specially designed and constructed. They were formally opened by Cardinal Basil Hume in 1982 to mark the International Year for the Disabled.

Like the Nottingham alabaster, another remarkable work of art was acquired in the 1950s. This is the figure of Saint Thérèse of Lisieux, by Giacomo Manzù, located high on the same massive pier as the alabaster but on the side facing into the transept. Manzù's bronze is a plaque in low relief and of great simplicity. The top of the oblong frame is empty; Saint Thérèse is dressed in her habit as a nun of the Order of Carmelites. There is no trace of a conventional halo. Instead the strong, not beautiful, face is slightly shadowed by the cowl or hood of her religious habit.

Thérèse was born in France in 1873, into a large, rather intense family. At the age of 10 she contracted a strange illness that brought three months of convulsions, hallucinations and comas. Finally while praying before a statue of Our Lady of Victories the illness passed from her - a cure she always maintained was miraculous. From her earliest years Thérèse had been extraordinarily religious. As a child she was bright and retentive but also shy and often withdrawn. She was devastated by the loss of her mother at an early age. In 1886 she experienced a mystical change of heart which effected a visible transformation; a new maturity and a radical, more focused commitment to serve God to the utmost. Two years later at 15, she entered the cloistered convent at Lisieux where she spent the remaining nine years of her life. In the last four of these, as acting Mistress of Novices she articulated her 'Little Way', a fresh and lively restatement of basic Christian truths. Her autobiography, published posthumously, enjoyed enormous success and brought a knowledge of her spiritual courage to millions. She was canonised as a saint in 1925 when Pope Pius XI said 'she achieved sanctity without going beyond the common order of things'. It is the key to understanding Saint Thérèse.

In Manzù's sculpture, she looks back over her shoulder yet her whole body, and the position of the feet, indicate she is moving swiftly forward - someone hurrying to heaven, yet remembering with love those still in the world. The long cloak sweeps down to the ground with minimal drapery. The roses she holds are irregular spiky stalks, cut from garden bushes, not the usual prim blossoms from mawkish portraits of the 'Little Flower' as she was once unhelpfully known. The composition is as forceful as it is austere with the emphasis on strength of purpose.

This work was put in hand at the suggestion of Sir John Rothenstein in 1958. It took the place of an unsatisfactory representation of the same saint by John Trinick. (It seems Mr Trinick arrived one day to join the line of those waiting to make their confession. To his dismay, he found workmen with chisels, chipping away at the mosaic he had created a few years earlier! Whether he continued to wait his turn in the queue for the sacrament of reconciliation is not recorded.)

Giacomo Manzù (1908-91), the sculptor of the present work, was one of Italy's leading post-war artists. He was a communist from the same home town as Pope John XXIII. They became close friends and there are significant bronzes of the pope by this sculptor.

To maintain a commitment to fine art, Elizabeth Frink was approached to make two bronzes for this same part of the Cathedral. The Society of Saint Vincent de Paul, a quiet but highly effective support group for the disadvantaged, was ready to subscribe to a sculpture representing Saint Vincent, its patron. The schools of the English Benedictine Congregation were to fund the other - a representation of Saint Benedict, Patron of Europe and father of western monasticism. Frink prepared some initial sketches for Saint Vincent but took them no further before her death in 1993. The spaces remain to be addressed by others. Also in this transept is a war memorial to Catholic members of the Royal Canadian Air Force by David Partridge. It is in the form of the Chi-Rho - Greek monogram for Christ - made from hundreds of flat-headed nails. The X of the Chi-Ro is meant to recall the runway of a wartime airfield. This is above the triple circles commemorating the roundels (or bull's-eyes') on all wings and fuselages of the R.C.A.F. Partridge, himself a Canadian who had served in the R.C.A.F. created one of his 'Configurations' or 'Three-Dimensional Mosaics'. The nails represent the sacrifice of men of the R.C.A.F. Below there is an inscription by Edward Wright.

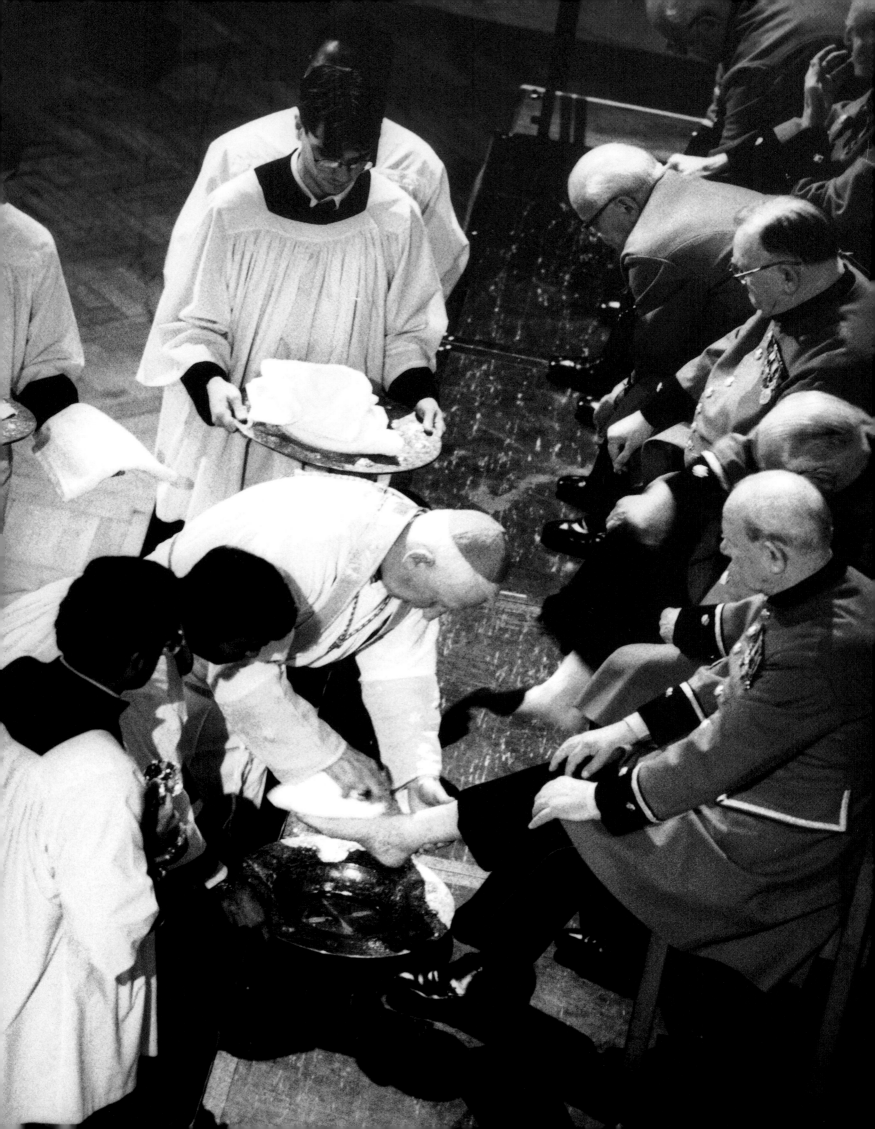

Chapel of the Blessed Virgin Mary

Mosaic of Madonna and Child by R. Anning Bell

(Opposite)
In the Pownall mosaic from the chapel roof an angel
holds a garland symbolic of the Rosary

As the Lady Chapel is approached the vista is framed by two heroic columns of *rose de Languedoc* supporting an arch. Surprisingly, the carving of one of the capitals includes the letters IHS, the monogram for Jesus. Originally, the space for the Lady Chapel was intended for the Chapel of the Blessed Sacrament, whereas the latter occupies the matching area on the north side of the building. For the same reason, the words *Ave Maria* appear on the exterior over the door from Ambrosden Avenue into the north transept - the wrong side of the building! The reason for the switch was ceremonial. At an early date, difficulties were foreseen for liturgical processions leading out of the Sacristy.

The chapel is 70 feet long, 21 feet wide and 38 feet high to the crown of the barrel vault. The nave has three bays open to the aisles except for a low parapet wall. The north aisle or *ambulacrum* divides the chapel from the main sanctuary, the one on the south provides the start of a processional way into the church from the Sacristy. Looking towards the front of the chapel two niches are seen on either side of the altar. A third, in the centre of the apsidal wall and now completely covered by the mosaic altarpiece, was part of an original plan for the sanctuary which included a circular baldachino. The added floor space provided by the niches was intended to facilitate movement around the altar.

Planning for the Lady Chapel began very early. On the death of Baroness Weld in 1879 it was learnt she had bequeathed £11,333 in memory of her son, Gordon Samuel Weld, for the building and decoration of a Lady Chapel in the future Cathedral. In the thirty-five years that elapsed before it could be used for its intended purpose the sum almost doubled. Cardinal Vaughan allocated the bequest and from the earliest discussions conveyed his wish that the chapel should express the devotion of the people of England to the Mother of God. From the start of the discussion, Bentley was deeply involved. His suggestions were published anonymously in the *Westminster Cathedral Record* of February 1899 and reprinted with a plan in an edition of *The Tablet* dated 29 December 1900. The liturgical life of the Cathedral began here, when the first Mass took place on Lady Day (25 March) in 1903. In that year, the old parish church of Saint Mary in Horseferry Road, served then by the Jesuits, was given up and closed. It was then that this location became the centre of parish worship. Although the contract for the marble decoration to designs by Marshall was signed in 1907, the chapel could not be handed over to the workmen until the new tabernacle for the Blessed Sacrament Chapel was finished and placed in its final position. That accomplished, the work of fixing the marble began just after Easter 1908 and proceeded at speed in order to be ready in time for the Eucharistic Congress to be held at Westminster from 9 to 13 September that year. The nineteenth of such congresses, it was the first to be held in an English-speaking country and brought to London many of the leading figures in the Catholic world of the time, headed by a legate of Pope Pius X. Already the new Cathedral was providing the needed setting for great occasions, as a contemporary description shows:

'The impressions left by the scene of that evening [the inauguration of the congress] will never be effaced from the minds of those present. The dense crowd, which not only filled every corner of the building but blocked each avenue of approach, the dim vastness of gaunt brickwork and vaulted roof overhead, the brilliantly lighted sanctuary, the purple robes of innumerable prelates, the subdued roar of cheers and the blare of trumpets from outside, the thrill that swept through the church as the Legate passed up the aisle ... all these things are memories which will be handed down amongst English Catholics as long as Westminster Cathedral stands.' We can imagine the crowds, after the ceremony, flocking to the Lady Chapel to inspect the newly completed marble decoration.

The general colour scheme is light, the variegated marbles being framed with white, of a superior quality, from Italy. The piers of the arcades are panelled with a delicately tinted variety of *giallo antico* from ancient Roman quarries in Africa. The slabs are opened out, paired and quartered, so that the veining forms a symmetrical arrangement. At the sides

A section of the arch into the Lady Chapel and part of the narrative frieze

these piers are panelled with slabs of *verd-antique* - a serpentine marble from the ancient quarries of Thessaly. The walls of the apse are lined in the lower part with a variety of Greek red marble that accentuates the delicate tinting of the others. Above the springing level of the arches the detail is more ornate, and the colouring of the marbles more varied. The brecciated purple panels in the nave, and the unique specimens of pink pavonazzo in the apse are from Italy. Over the small doorways on each side of the apse is a panel of black-and-white antique, a marble much used by the Romans. The niches and spandrels of the arches are lined with vertical strips of green and white. The soffits of the arches are enriched with a delicate interfacing

pattern in gold-and-blue mosaic. The altar is of white marble, with a central panel of Greek cipollino.

In 1908, space was reserved for a mosaic representation of the Immaculate Conception of the Virgin, set in a white marble reredos. This Lady Chapel altarpiece is the work of Robert Anning Bell, RA (1863-1933) who also designed the mosaic tympanum on the west front, over the main entrance to the Cathedral. He is responsible too for the four portraits of Old Testament prophets in the apsidal niches, which were executed by Gertrude Martin and her team of women mosaicists who had worked extensively on the Chapel of the Holy Souls. The Latin text around this standing

figure of Mary with her divine child reads: SUB TUUM PRAESIDIUM CONFUGIMUS SANCTA DEI GENITRIX NOSTRAS DEPRECATIONES NE DESPICIAS IN NECESSITATIBUS NOSTRIS (We flee under your protection, Holy Mother of God, Do not reject our prayers in our hour of need).

Before this mosaic was put in place there was a painting of the Blessed Virgin after Murillo which was later removed to the Throne Room of Archbishop's House.

The background colour of the mosaic is blue, Mary's colour, and the whole is enclosed in a frame of white marble enhanced by her monogram, crowned, deeply carved and repeating eight times.

At the top of this frame is a crowned fleur-de-lis, a Marian symbol associated with the Annunciation.

All the higher mosaics are the work of Gilbert A. Pownall and are acknowledged to be a great deal more successful than his enormous vertical mosaic on the archway of the main apse to the rear of the Cathedral sanctuary. It was in 1930 that three English mosaic workers began pushing into the cement-coated brickwork of Westminster's Lady Chapel the one million or so tesserae which now cover the roof and apse. As we have said, Cardinal Bourne wanted to set up a permanent school of mosaicists to carry forward the decoration of the Cathedral and eventually to maintain all surfaces in good condition. He arranged for Shattock, the Cathedral architect at the time, to visit Venice with the artists involved. In 1931, two Venetian workers were engaged under the supervision of Shattock and the artist responsible for the designs and cartoons, Gilbert Pownall. Their first work of decorating a south transept alcove was followed by a start being made on the apse. On the Vigil of the Purification 1932, the curtains were removed and about one third of the new mosaics were seen to be completed. By 1935 the decoration was finished. It represents the life of the Blessed Virgin, the Rosary (a traditional prayer system) and some subjects and figures connected with Mary.

In the chapel apse, looking upward to the centre of the concave, the Holy Redeemer sits enthroned. This chapel may be dedicated to Mary but the central position of Christ affirms that as a creature of God she, like all humanity, owes everything to the eternal Word, 'through whom all things were made'. Theologically she is described as 'immaculate' because in the words of Bossuet, 'Mary was the first of those whom the Precious Blood has purified'. There is an echo here of the Cathedral's primary title and dedication. While the mosaic shows Christ in glory, this

Redeemer REGNAT DE LIGNO CRUCIS (reigns from the wood of the cross), but the cross here is very different from the stark gibbet of Calvary. It is a life cross - its wood being that of an ARBOR NOBILIS, a noble Tree of Life; from it gush fountains of living water. Above, its branches spread out, covering the whole crown of the vault. It bears grapes and while birds nestle in its foliage, butterflies flutter in and out. There are even ladybirds and a stag beetle to be seen. On the right of the Tree of Life stands the Blessed Virgin in prayer, crushing the Serpent of Evil under her feet. She is shown as patroness of London, with the Tower of London, Tower Bridge and even a Thameside warehouse beside her. Given that Saint Peter has been honoured for more than a thousand years as Patron of Westminster he stands here on the left of the tree with the exterior of Westminster Cathedral behind him. Behind Mary is Saint Gabriel, archangel of the Annunciation and behind Saint Peter stands the archangel Michael, protector of Christians against attack from spiritual enemies. The south side of the apse contains a medallion of David the ideal king of Hebrew history.

Drawing back from the curved depth of the apse, the upper mosaics are filled with smaller figures. Behind Saint Gabriel are three angels, together with nine saints renowned for their devotion to the Blessed Virgin: Saint Philip Benizi, Fifth General of the Servites or Friar Servants of Mary; Blessed Crispin of Viterbo, the Franciscan Capuchin and Saint Juliana Falconieri, another pivotal Servite saint and foundress of the 'Mantellate'. The Servite Order had come to England from Italy in 1864 and from 1873 to 1899 established an English province. 1888 was the year in which their Seven Founders (early thirteenth century) were canonised as saints. The impression the Servites were making in London at the time probably accounts for their strong representation in these designs. The group also includes Saint Gregory the Wonder-Worker, Saint Ildephonsus, Saint

Barrel roof and apse mosaics

Marble archways in the wall by the ambulacrum

Hyacinth, Saint Casimir, who refused the crown of Poland in devotion to Mary, Blessed Herman Joseph, and finally Saint Brigid, the close associate of Saint Patrick. As these nine Marian saints are scattered through a millennium of Catholic life and history, their costumes vary but not incongruously. In the wreath surrounding the vault at the entrance to the sanctuary are medallions commemorating Our Lady's three places of sojourn. A star stands for Bethlehem, a cross for Jerusalem and a little house for Nazareth. In other medallions are portrait-heads of the first four Archbishops of Westminster - Cardinals Wiseman, Manning, Vaughan and Bourne. On the face of the arch, necessarily contracted, is the whole 'Hail, Mary' prayer in Latin.

The life of Mary forms a frieze round the whole chapel, starting at the north-west corner with King David enthroned (Mary being of the house of David) between her parents, Saints Joachim and Anne. Then follows her birth, her presentation in the Temple, her espousal to Saint Joseph, the Annunciation, the Visitation to her cousin Elizabeth and the scene in the stable at Bethlehem, with the three kings present. The story of Mary's life is continued round the apse. We see the Presentation of the child Jesus in the Temple (the Circumcision), the Flight into Egypt, the Finding in the Temple, the home and workshop at Nazareth and the Marriage Feast at Cana. After Cana, the band of figures is broken by the white marble reredos above the altar although the monogram of the Blessed Virgin bridges the gap. Next comes a scene in which Mary bids farewell to her son Jesus at the start of his public ministry. She gives him the seamless robe over which during his baleful Passion, Roman soldiers would cast lots. The Way of the Cross comes next, followed by a glimpse of the Crucifixion - this in the form of a *Stabat Mater*, showing only the foot of the Cross and the sorrowing mother beside it. The sequence ends with hope and joy as news of the Resurrection is brought to Mary by Saint John and Saint Peter.

Moving again towards the back of the chapel, the Descent of the Holy Spirit at Pentecost on the Blessed Virgin and the apostles is depicted on the south side. Then comes the appearance of the Risen Lord to his mother and a picture reflecting a tradition according to which Saint Gabriel intimated to Mary at Ephesus that her passing was imminent. In the next scene - the death or Dormition of the Blessed Virgin - Saint Thomas is shown arriving late and there are lilies in the tomb, both details from legend rather than Scripture. In the window recess we see the apostles who constantly drew strength from Mary's devoted motherhood and finally, Saint Luke writing about Mary as part of his gospel.

Above the frieze on the north wall, beginning again at the north-west corner, the papal promulgation and definition of the doctrine of the Immaculate Conception are represented. In the first 'blind' window Our Lady of Perpetual Help is shown as a full-length figure. Between the two blind windows the appearance of the Virgin to Saint Dominic is seen, as she gives him the Rosary, a form of prayer she requests of the Church. In the second blind window is the *Pietà* (Mary with the body of her dead son in her arms) and between this and the apse, Saint John the Evangelist, to whose care she was entrusted by Jesus in his dying moments (John 19:26). Opposite Saint John, above the frieze on the south wall is Saint Joseph, Mary's husband and the foster-father of Jesus. Between the first two windows Saint Simon Stock receives a vision of Mary, said to have taken place at Cambridge in 1216. She offers him the Scapular of Mount Carmel, a pious devotion with which his name would become associated. Between the second and third windows the Blessed Virgin is shown with Saint Bernadette of Lourdes and beyond the third window stands the figure of Saint Edmund Rich, Archbishop of Canterbury. In the barrel vault over all these subjects are decorative canopies, surmounted by a garland representing the fifteen mysteries of the Rosary. This

chaplet of spoken prayer consists of three sets of five repetitions of the Lord's Prayer, each followed by ten Hail Marys, symbolised here by a chain of red and blue flowers, meandering through the vault and held by six angels with outspread wings. The tops of the window recesses are adorned with portraits of very early women martyrs, Saints Lucy, Agatha and Justina, and in the blind windows opposite, Saints Cecilia and Katherine. There are four alcoves in the chapel, each with an apsidal mosaic by Robert Anning Bell showing one of the figures who foretold the coming of the Messiah - the prophets Daniel, Ezekiel, Jeremiah and Isaiah.

Over the entry to the whole chapel is a Latin inscription: TOTA PULCHRA ES MARIA ET MACULA ORIGINALIS NON EST IN TE (Mary, you are utterly beautiful and original sin is not in you). On the tympanum over the arch at the west end - facing into the chapel - the Coronation of the Blessed Virgin as Queen of Heaven by Christ her son takes pride of place. A six-winged seraph attends on each side. Centred in the blue underside of this arch is the *Stella Maris*, Star of the Sea, another of Mary's titles. Just as the sailor relies on the stars to navigate, so the steady light of Mary's love guides the Christian pilgrim towards his or her journey's end. Minor details include richly elaborated designs of fruits and flowers in the soffits of the windows and a small panel under Our Lady of Perpetual Help, containing two orange blossom trees, for Mary's espousal. Under the *Pietà* are two young pigeons - the offerings of the poor which Mary and Joseph brought to the Temple at the Presentation of Jesus (Luke 2:24). In the same section camels are seen in the caravan of the wise men while the central boss of the Rosary vault contains a crown of twelve stars. The observant will also notice a beehive and an alert little rabbit tucked away in Pownall's elaborate design.

The floor marbles are carefully worked. Bentley had left a detailed, coloured

Marble floor designed by Bentley carried out in the 1950's

drawing of the floor of this chapel which was completed in the 1950s. Attractive features include garlands and green leaves and a slab of rare green marble - *brèche universelle* - containing a remarkable flash of dark red jasper.

Above a gate of wrought brass that leads from the Lady Chapel into the *ambulacrum* a circular golden plaque is mounted on the wall. This medallion of Ostra Brama was presented to Westminster Cathedral by the Polish Fighter Squadron of Vilna, on 15 March 1944. The plaque represents a picture of Mary famous throughout Poland, known as the Ostra Brama of Vilna (Vilna is no longer in Poland).

NOMINE AVIATIONIS POLONIAE ACIES
EXPLORATORIA VILNENSIS TIBI
BEATISSIMA MATER HOC VOTUM
DEDICAT DEPRECANS GRATIAM
VILNAM REDEUNDI UBI SORTI
PATRIAE SEMPER VIGIL FAVES.
D 15 MART 1944

In the name of Polish Aviation
the Exploratory Force of Vilnus
dedicates this offering
to you, most holy Mother,
beseeching you to restore Vilnus
when, ever watchful,
you bestow your favour upon the destiny
of our homeland.
15 March 1944

Crypt Chapel of Saint Peter

Detail of Edward Pugin's design for the tomb of Cardinal Wiseman

(Opposite)
The tomb of Cardinal Godfrey

The first two Cardinal Archbishops of Westminster are laid to rest beneath the high altar of Westminster Cathedral. Their tombs are approached by descending to the crypt, dedicated to Saint Peter, which occupies the whole of the space under the retro-choir. The tombs of Nicholas Wiseman, first Archbishop of Westminster (1850-65) and his successor Henry Edward Manning (1865-92) dominate the mortuary chapel of Saint Edmund, Archbishop of Canterbury, within the crypt. An altar dedicated to Saint Edmund of Canterbury occupies the recess on the south side. Built of grey Derbyshire marble it has a gated space beneath in which the relics of the saint are kept. In the space above the altar is a mosaic by W. Christian Symons dating from 1912. The mosaic workers built it up from the front rather than reversing on to paper before fixing. It shows Saint Edmund with his attendants by the River Thames, blessing London before leaving England. London Bridge, the Tower and Old Saint Paul's are seen in the background with the inscription *SNP Edmunde ora pro nobis*. In the opposite recess stands the tomb of Cardinal Manning in red and white marble surmounted by a bronze effigy, a work of superior quality by John Adams-Acton. The arch (archivolt) above is decorated in mosaic with the heads of angels and a book, a work by Boris Anrep done before 1914 when he was called up for service in a Russian regiment where he served as an officer in Galicia. After the war the work was not resumed and finally the design was lost. In the centre of the little chapel lie the remains of Cardinal Wiseman below a monument of gothic design by Edward Pugin, looking somewhat out-of-character with its Byzantine surroundings. It was designed for the original tomb in Kensal Green Cemetery where it stood for forty-two years until 1907 when Cardinal Bourne obtained the Home Secretary's permission to move the remains of the first two archbishops to their resting-place here at Westminster.

In the main crypt two other cardinals are buried. Cardinal Bernard Griffin, sixth Archbishop of Westminster (1943-56) lies under a simple slab at the centre of the apsidal curve. The inscription reminds us that each cardinal takes his title from one of the more ancient churches in Rome. Cardinal Griffin's titular church had been Saint Pudenziana in the Via Urbana, converted from a second-century building in the reign of Pope Siricius (384-99). Incidentally, the remarkable fifth-century mosaic in Saint Pudenziana's was among the sources of influence for Boris Anrep in his work on the Blessed Sacrament Chapel. The large sarcophagus on the north curve of the crypt is the tomb of Cardinal Godfrey, seventh Archbishop of Westminster (1956-63). From the inscription we learn that his titular church was that of Saints Nereus and Achilleus also called *titulus fasciolae*, after a legendary incident in the life of Saint Peter. This story, already current in the fourth century, suggested that escaping from the Mamertine Prison, the apostle Peter had bandaged his legs which had developed sores from the chains. As he hurried away from Rome one of the bandages (*fasciolae*) dropped off. A pious lady picked it up and later had an oratory built where it had fallen. In 524 the first Pope John had the relics of Saints Nereus and Achilleus brought to this church. Reginald Pole, the last English cardinal to be created before the Reformation (1537), was also given the title of Saints Nereus and Achilleus. Both Pole and Godfrey were Vatican diplomats.

Formerly there was a backfacing altar that had come from the old church of Saint Mary's, Horseferry Road, which had been closed when the Cathedral was built.

Another of the tombs in the crypt is that of a distinguished diplomatic representative at the Court of Saint James's. Count Alexander Benckendorff was the last ambassador to be accredited to Britain by a Russian sovereign. He was appointed by the unfortunate Tsar Nicholas II, and while in this country died, in January 1917. By special request of the Government and with the permission of Cardinal Bourne, the remains were interred here in accordance with the late ambassador's wishes. His daughter, the Honourable Mrs Ridley, had a memorial slab placed over the grave with an inscription in Latin and Russian designed and carved by Eric Gill (his last work for the Cathedral) although a letter to John

Cardinal Manning's crozier
(Catalogue number 48)

Marshall, the Cathedral architect, suggests that a Mr Méstrovitch from Rome was first asked to do the work.

The Latin version of the inscription was provided by the Monsignor Ronald Knox:

COMES ALEXANDER PHILLIPUS
CONSTANTINUS LUDOVICUS
BENCKENDORFF AB IMPERATORE
RUSSIAE AD CURIAM REGIS
BRITANNICA PLENARIA PROTESTATE
EXTRA ORDINEM LEGATUS KAL AUG
MDCCCXLIX A D III ID JAN MCMXVII
REQUIESCAT IN PACE.

(Count Alexander Philip Constantin Ludwig Benckendorff, Ambassador Extraordinary and Plenipotentiary for Russia to the Court of St. James's. Aug. 1, 1849 : Jan 11, 1917.' Requiescat in Pace.)

The Requiem Mass four days later was an occasion of state ceremonial, unusual for a Roman Catholic church in Britain, albeit a Cathedral. A military escort with bands was drawn up outside to salute the King's representative, the Duke of Connaught

and the Grand Duke Michael on their arrival and departure, when the British and Russian national anthems were played. The Queen, the Prince of Wales and five royal princesses were each represented. Among others present were the Grand Duke Michael of Russia, the Grand Duchess George of Russia, the entire diplomatic corps, Mrs Lloyd George representing the Prime Minister, Mr Balfour, Mr Austen Chamberlain, the Earl of Derby, the Speaker, Mr and Mrs Asquith, the Lord Chamberlain, the Master of the King's Household and the Lord Mayor and Sheriff of the City of London. Eighteen months after the ambassador's burial in this crypt, the Tsar and Tsarina and other members of the Russian royal family had been put to death by the revolutionaries.

The tympanum, above the three arches facing the apsidal wall, displays a large mosaic by Gilbert Pownall in honour of Saint Peter. The dedication of this chapel and its location are an echo of Saint Peter's in Rome where the tomb of the Prince of Apostles is considered to be the foundation stone for the whole church - a material analogy for an ecclesiological principle: 'You are Peter and upon this Rock I will build my Church' (Matthew 16:18). Here, in the crypt, the positioning of the tombs of Wiseman and Manning, the two founding archbishops, under the high altar, is another conscious parallel with Rome.

In the centre of the mosaic tableau, Saint Peter is shown enthroned as the holder of heaven's keys (Matthew 16:19). On the left, the Lord is seen inviting Peter to walk to him on the water. Those still in the boat watch as Peter sinks up to his waist. On the right, he is shown receiving the keys from Jesus, with his fellow apostles grouped behind him.

For many years the crypt chapel had a marble altar built against a wall in the central arch under the Petrine mosaic. With the reforms of the Second Vatican Council, priests no longer said Mass with their backs to the congregation. The

result was that many such altars were considered unusable and removed. When Mass is said here nowadays, a small portable altar is used, although a better long-term solution to a seemingly intractable problem is needed for locations such as this.

The crypt is lit by eight round-headed windows on its eastern and northern sides while six robust columns of Norwegian granite with voluted caps of pale grey marble support the vaulting. The four piers at the western end are sheeted with the same red granite, compounding an impression of great strength and durability. By 1907, the curved wall of the ambulatory beyond the pillars was largely clad with its marble. Slabs of Greek cipollino of a fresh green colour are skillfully arranged to allow their markings to suggest the folds of drapery. They are enclosed in bands and mouldings of Hopton-Wood stone. Three reliquary cases have been let into the south wall, cedar-lined and enclosed by gilded and glazed metal grilles. Bentley left complete designs for the marble-work of the crypt including the entrances, yet a great deal of exposed brickwork remains to be clad in marble and mosaic. The domed ceiling for instance, remains an inviting canvas awaiting a new mosaic composition. It will be interesting to see how the chapel is finally completed.

(Previous page)
Entrance to Saint Edmund's Chapel from Saint Peter's Crypt

The Wiseman tomb with Cardinal Manning's resting place beyond

(Opposite)
The altar of Saint Edmund of Abingdon furnished with Cardinal Manning's Celtic crucifix and candlesticks by Bentley. Mosaic by W. Christian Symons. Beneath the altar are relics of Saint Edmund

*Mitre and gloves by Augustus Welby Northmore Pugin, 1845.
The mitre was first worn at the consecration of Saint George's
Cathedral, Southwark on 4 July 1848, by Cardinal Wiseman
(Catalogue numbers 136 and 137)*

Monstrance made in London and given to the Cathedral by Charles Weld-Blundell in 1908. Stem set with carbuncle in the shape of a heart which, in turn, is inlaid with a diamond 'wound'
(Catalogue number 98)

Chapel of the Blessed Sacrament

The north transept with the Vaughan Chantry on the left and the Blessed Sacrament Chapel beyond

(Opposite)
Christ in his glory from the Anrep mosaics

The chapel beyond the north transept to the left of the main sanctuary is the heart of Westminster Cathedral - the Chapel of the Blessed Sacrament. At all times of the day visitors are to be seen within its gates engaged in private prayer. Votive candles flicker in the half-light while from the *lampadarium* suspended before the altar, three oil lamps glow on the marble sanctuary with its silk-shrouded tabernacle. Candles, once essential for lighting after dusk, remain a powerful symbol for prayer and the primacy of spirit over matter. Curiously, although the chapel is late Victorian, with mosaics completed as late as 1962, there is a timeless quality about this space reminiscent of hallowed sanctuaries such as the Church of the Holy Sepulchre in Jerusalem, or the chapel of the apostle's tomb beneath Saint Peter's, Rome.

Only in this primary chapel is the Blessed Sacrament 'reserved' - kept in the tabernacle - after consecration at the various Masses which occur day by day. In the early centuries, the sacrament was reserved so that people confined by sickness could be visited at home or in hospital and given participation in the communion which those in church had received. That is still one of the reasons for the tabernacle. Gradually the place of reservation became a place of prayer or vigil, and 'devotion to the Blessed Sacrament' remains a characteristic of Roman Catholic life and practice. By virtue of what is understood of the Mass - that bread and wine, brought to the altar as gifts to God, become the Body and Blood of Christ at the priest's words of consecration - the presence here of the consecrated Host (sacramental bread) is believed to be the presence of the Risen Lord himself. It is not surprising therefore, that of all the places in the Cathedral available for private prayer, the Blessed Sacrament Chapel is the first choice of those who seek such a haven. There is a stillness here which if nothing else, is conducive to reflection. Also the manner in which the chapel is decorated demonstrates a sensitivity on the part of architect and artist to the purpose of this sanctuary and the faith of those who worship here. At the time when detailed planning was being discussed, Canon Pilkington wondered whether such a chapel should be dedicated to the Holy Trinity rather than 'The Blessed Sacrament' or The Eucharist, since where the Risen Christ is there is the one God of three persons - Father, Son and Holy Spirit. As we will see when looking at the mosaics that cover apse and ceiling, the subject matter is taken from both Old and New Testaments, on themes connected with Trinity, sacrifice and the Holy Eucharist, all leading to the triumph of the Cross and the glory of the Resurrection.

The architect's original plans show that he had placed this Chapel of the Blessed Sacrament on the south side of the main sanctuary, near the Sacristy, whilst the Chapel of the Blessed Virgin Mary was to be here on the north side. The ground plans of both are virtually identical, but because Bentley intended to raise a baldachino above the altar, he had prepared three large niches in the apse of the southern chapel, to give an appearance of spaciousness behind the pillared canopy, and provision for a *piscina* or wall-mounted basin. Yet no sooner had the main parts of the fabric been completed at the turn of the century, than it was realised that every member of every procession leaving the Sacristy would have to genuflect (bend the knee) when passing before the Blessed Sacrament, since it is customary to show this mark of respect in front of the tabernacle. For a liturgical procession, moving sometimes quite swiftly in or out of church, this would simply not be practical. Cardinal Vaughan was in no doubt; the two chapels would have to be interchanged. Although Bentley accepted his client's instructions he knew that the altered conditions would prevent his design being carried out in its integrity. After Bentley died, the completion of the chapel was taken in hand by the Cardinal. (Understandably, since his younger brother, the ascetic Father Kenelm Vaughan, had been travelling the world since 1896 collecting funds to pay for it all!) The difficulty of accommodating the baldachino in an apse that was not designed for it did not trouble the Cardinal unduly since he had decided to abandon it anyway. This was no whim, he simply objected to the idea of another baldachino on columns in addition to the one over the high altar of the main sanctuary. Cardinal Vaughan preferred that it should be a shrine enclosed by grilles and gates, and with a simple canopy suspended over the altar. When he was succeeded by Cardinal Bourne (1903-35) there was some talk of reverting to Bentley's original intention, but the work of completion was so far advanced that any further change would have caused chaos.

In addition to the triple broaching of the apse by alcoves in the matching south chapel, there are a few other differences with this north one. The vault of this apse has two windows, providing much-needed illumination on the dark side of the building and considering the amount of daylight blocked out by the tall buildings in Ambrosden Avenue which were already there in Bentley's day. (By contrast, the Lady Chapel gets plenty of afternoon sunlight from the side.) This chapel is enclosed in the customary manner by grilles and gates, shutting it off as a Holy of Holies from the transept, which serves it as a nave, and from its northern aisle which is the chapel of the Sacred Heart. Both aisles have pavonazzo-lined arches opening into the chapel. The aim achieved in the marble decoration is lightness of tone, the marbles being combined in a rather severe manner when compared to the richly varied surfaces of the Lady Chapel. The need for a plain setting derives from the splendour of the metal screens with their gilding and enamel. The marble sheeting begins at the niched eastern piers of the transept. These niches are outlined with white mouldings and lined with alternate strips of pavonazzo and verd-antique up to the springing of the conch where they are headed with a black and white chevron banding. Each was later completed in the 1960s with a concave mosaic by Boris Anrep showing a colourful bird - on the north side a peacock, symbol of immortality and in the opposite recess a phoenix rising from the flames, symbolising the Resurrection.

The floor of the nave (within the gates) displays the dark green marble of

Thessaly, the paler tones of Varallo and cipollino, with Siena gold and the brown-to-pink of Languedoc. West of the gates the floor is laid with large hexagonal slabs of *bleu fleuri*, interspersed with Carrara marble which also forms the single step into the chapel. The marble hues of the sanctuary floor are green and rose: squares of Greek cipollino with pointed ovals of Languedoc in a white setting. A simple white cornice is carried round the chapel. Below it the piers are faced by a horizontal scheme of opened-out *rose de Numidie* slabs (deep yellow with a pink flush) divided by narrow bands of greyish *verte Campagne*. The inner sides of the piers and the soffits of the arches are lined with very lightly marked pavonazzo, which also fills the square-headed recesses right and left of the sanctuary. The opening on the north side of the apse contains an aumbry or wall cupboard for sacred oils, its copper door having a central panel of repoussé brass with *Olea sacra* inscribed above. The oils inside, stored in silver containers, are consecrated each year by the Cardinal Archbishop at the diocesan Chrism Mass in Holy Week. They are reserved for anointing the sick, for baptism, confirmation and the ordination of priests and deacons. The corresponding space on the south side provides access to this sanctuary from the *ambulacrum* - the aisle that separates the chapel from the main sanctuary of Westminster Cathedral.

To right and left of the altar the continuity of the Numidian marble banding (*rose de Numidie*) is interrupted by a pair of 3-foot breadths of pavonazzo, framed with mouldings; the recess on the right, at the start of the apsidal curve, contains a white piscina. The marble conch of this recess is carved with a fine pattern of overlapping leaves. Behind the altar three upright panels of Siena form a kind of reredos rising from the topmost step of the double flight behind to the line of the upper cornice. The altar itself, of cipollino and Carrara, is approached by three steps of white marble. Its forward surface (almost invariably concealed by silk frontals, in the

Lampadarium in the sanctuary of the Blessed Sacrament Chapel

liturgical colour of the day it is viewed) is composed of dark coral-brown Languedoc with scattered markings of white, framed by a moulding of deep yellow Siena with strong patterning. The white dossal which rises two feet above the *gradine* (step for candlesticks) contains a fine panel of cipollino with the usual golden edging. The altar crucifix and candlesticks given in 1909 are of a primitive Byzantine design in bronze mercurial-gilt. The lower halves of the candlesticks are set with three circles of natural stones, cornelian-red in colour. Their knops are chased with a fruit and vine-leaf pattern. The crucifix has two cross-pieces, and behind the tabernacle the throne for carrying a eucharistic monstrance takes the form of an oval plinth borne by two kneeling angels with upcurving wings. Engraved on the plinth is a chalice with the sacred host and an inscription taken from the words of consecration: HOC EST CORPUS MEUM, HIC EST CALIX SANGUINIS MEI. This gilt artefact was first intended for the high altar.

In place of Bentley's notional baldachino a flat hexagonal canopy, or *celatura,* of gilded wood, is suspended above the altar by a chain and pierced bulb of silvered bronze. Winged heads of angelic cherubim look down from the six corners of the canopy. Although suitable enough, there is nothing Byzantine about it and had Bentley lived, we may be sure that the concept would have been very different. His successor Marshall designed this, the tabernacle below it and all the grillework, metalwork - including the altar rails - and light-fittings in the chapel. These works lend a particular unity to the chapel and testify to a fine sensibility and fastidious attention to detail. They were all made very shortly after Bentley's death, approved by Cardinal Vaughan and begun during his lifetime. The light-fittings are bronze, cast and chased, enriched with much delicate ornament in gilt and blue and white enamel. The designs are based on Roman detail, strongly suggestive of Pompeian work, and reminiscent of the classical style which

Open door of an aumbry in the chapel reveals the Sacred Oils for the diocese, consecrated each year during Holy Week. The silver bowl is for the mixing of oil and balsam

Peacock mosaic in the apsidal recesses at the entrance to the Blessed Sacrament Chapel

inspired artists of the First Empire in France. It may be that Marshall, released from the constraints of mannered Byzantinism, relished the opportunity presented by direct access to the Cardinal, to work in a style to which he was more attuned.

On the steps of the sanctuary, the cast bronze communion rails are chased and gilt; the rail itself, fire-gilded for durability, is surmounted by a cushion of wood with a raised boxwood pattern of vine leaves. Between fluted railings are eight oval wreaths, enclosing red and white enamel plaques. Objects associated with the Passion of Christ are depicted on six of these, the two gate plaques containing the symbols Alpha and Omega, first and last letters of the Greek alphabet. Wherever they appear in Christian iconography they signify the beginning and the end of the cosmic creative process with which Christ is identified in the Book of Revelation (22:13). Within the sanctuary, three hexagonal lamps hang from a bar of silvered bronze

by chains strung with small enamel lozenges in blue and yellow, and with globes and pendants of carved rock crystal. Similar drops of crystal form a fringe along the bar which, in the centre, has the enamelled monogram of Christ (Chi-Ro). The hexagonal silver lamps, two of which hang low over the altar rails are set with onyx, crystal and enamels in dark blue and apple-green. Marshall's magnificent silver-gilt tabernacle, like the altar itself, is usually veiled with damask; 4 feet 6 inches high and 24 inches in diameter, the exterior is enriched with repoussé work. The interior is lined with cedar of Lebanon and white silk. In the early years of the Cathedral these silk curtains were suspended by a number of gold wedding rings, each inscribed with the name of its widowed donor. The beaten panels of each door incorporate a design of wheat and small bunches of grapes, symbolic of the offertory gifts of the Mass. Tiny amethysts make up the bunches of black grapes and these contrast with clusters of milky green chrysoprases representing white grapes. A figure of the divine pelican with wings outstretched broods over the tabernacle

dome. This same bird crowns the arch of Marshall's bronze gateway. A traditional fable suggested that when the mother pelican was unable to find food, she wounded her own breast in order to feed the young chicks with her life's blood. For the visual arts, this became an analogy for Christ's sacrificial act on the cross. Although natural history disproves the pelican story, the disgorging of food by certain birds to feed their young is common enough and may explain the legend. At all events, the symbolic bird, gilt and chased, stands on the summit of the arched gateway to the chapel. The soffit of the arch is enriched with a design in blue and white enamel continued along the frieze of the two corniced wings each side of the entrance gates. The screen has a lower latticed section containing three panels interspersed with four fluted pilasters - slender shafts of bronze, entwined with golden foliage and linked by swags of laurel leaves - that contine up to the cornice. There are similar grilles filling the arched openings on either side of the chapel. The screen with its gates took over three years to make, at a cost of £2,350. The grilles were finished by

June 1907 at a further cost of £1,500. All the decorative metalwork in this chapel is the work of Messrs J.W. Singer of Frome. Two small lecterns stand in the nave of the chapel. The wrought iron bookstand belonged to the late Canon Pilkington - it had been in his room at Clergy House. The priest's lectern is made from a small porphyry pillar given by the artist, Augustus John, in memory of his mother. It is thought to have come from one of the pagan temples of antiquity.

The funding of work on the Blessed Sacrament Chapel was largely accomplished overseas. When Father Kenelm Vaughan, younger brother of the Cardinal Founder, obtained his permission to collect money he left England for Spain in 1896. Within two years he had built up a subscription list to the value of £4,000 headed by King Alfonso XIII and the Queen Mother, Queen Maria Cristina. With the outbreak of hostilities between the United States and Spain in 1898, Father Vaughan sailed for South America where he continued his fund-raising efforts. By 1907 he had raised £18,634 and on his return to England, had the satisfaction of seeing his dream largely realised. The decoration of the chapel had begun in 1904 and was virtually completed by 1908. The following year Father Kenelm died. His devotion to the Blessed Sacrament had been profound, a commitment to prayer and expiation carried on to this day by the Guild of the Blessed Sacrament which was founded in those early years of the Cathedral's existence.

The Anrep Mosaics

The mosaics of the chapel were designed as a meditation on its special purpose and its dedication to the Blessed Trinity. In 1953, Cardinal Bernard Griffin, sixth Archbishop of Westminster (1943-56) appointed an art commission and it was agreed that the decoration of the Blessed Sacrament Chapel must have priority over all other projects. Many people had thought highly of the south aisle mosaic of Blessed Oliver Plunket, done many

years earlier by Boris Anrep (1883-1969). Born in Saint Petersburg, Anrep travelled widely before settling in Paris in 1908 where he studied at the l'Académie Julian. For two years after 1910 he was at the College of Art, Edinburgh, under F. Morley Fletcher. He served with the Russian Army in Galicia but came to London in 1916 where he was associated with the Bloomsbury Group. He returned to Paris in 1926. Anrep exhibited paintings and gained commissions for mosaics which in Britain include the Royal Military Chapel, Sandhurst, the National and Tate Galleries, the Bank of England, the Greek Cathedral, London, and a design for stone mosaics at the National Gallery. He also created mosaics for Mullingar Cathedral, Eire, and the chapel at Keir, Scotland. It was the Honourable Mrs Stirling of Keir who brought together the then Cathedral Administrator at Westminster, Monsignor Gordon Wheeler, and the artist, then living in Paris. It was recalled that in 1937 he had been asked to produce mosaic designs for Saint Patrick's Chapel and later a design for a replacement mosaic for the tympanum above the High Altar. There had always been dissatisfaction regarding the quality of the existing mosaic by Pownall. Neither project had come to fruition and the authorities welcomed a new opportunity to incorporate his work. In due course he presented a model of his proposal and the Cardinal and his committee accepted it. On 3 August 1956, Sir John Rothenstein, one of the committee members, wrote in *The Times* that Anrep's chapel promised to rank high in the artistic creations of the time.

The mosaic decoration covers all the surfaces of the Blessed Sacrament Chapel above the marble revetments. Gold tesserae are used sparingly and to subtle effect. Instead of the more usual golden background the unifying colour is a rose pink, modified with other pastel hues, deepening towards the apse. Clearly the artist was responding to the colour of the marble already in place, taking his cue from the pink revetment of the sanctuary and drawing the hue upwards to suffuse

the whole of the vault. For Anrep, drawing on his Russian traditions, this was a colour that spoke of serenity. (He had also wanted to include the scene of the Miraculous Feeding of Our Lady in the Temple until it was pointed out to him that this was an Eastern rather than a Western tradition.) The many scenes are based on biblical landmarks that lead from Abel to Christ. Naturally, the first view of the chapel is from outside the entrance arch, where the light and colour within seem to illumine the blue of the mosaic that lines the inner surface of the arch. Against this, two heavenly spirits stand guard, the Archangels Michael and Gabriel, their presence indicating the supreme importance of this chapel. In the crown of the arch above them is a three-domed Byzantine church surmounted by a chalice, a trinitarian and eucharistic emblem of all that lies inside. We have already noted the apsidal niches on either side of the arch with their lively mosaics of the phoenix and the peacock. In Christian art the peacock is used as a symbol of immortality, the 'hundred eyes' of its tail-fan symbolising the omniscient God 'to whom all desires are known, and from whom no secrets are hidden'. The phoenix was first introduced into Christian symbolism by Saint Clement of Rome, as early as the first century. This mythical bird was said to renew its life every few hundred years by burning itself on a funeral pyre. It was often put on gravestones to represent the resurrection of the dead and belief in the life to come.

The Anrep mosaics are primarily an expression of faith, with themes that reflect the unity and eloquence of the Word of God. Unveiled in December 1962 at the time of the Second Vatican Council (1962-65) and pre-dating by several years the conciliar document *Dei Verbum* (Dogmatic Constitution on Divine Revelation) they are nevertherless a vigorous reflection of some of the ideas it contains.

The nave and its vault represent the Old Testament, the sanctuary and apse celebrate the New. Along the vault of the

chapel the trinitarian theme begins in the arch and sweeps down to the apse. It is first expressed in the crown of the arch which shows the hospitality of Abraham, when he receives a visit from three angels in human form.

'He looked up and there he saw three men standing near him. When he saw them he ran from the tent entrance to meet them and bowed down to the ground ...'. Food was brought *'then he took curds, and milk and the calf that he had prepared, and set it before them'* (Genesis 18:2, 8a).

This is the subject of the tympanum facing the altar. Both Abraham and his wife Sarah are seen serving their three visitors although in the text (Genesis 18:6-10) she remains within their tent at a discreet distance. Some of the Fathers of the Church saw in this mysterious visitation by three angels the future revelation of the Trinity. The vault medallion nearest the entrance arch represents Shadrach, Meshach and Abednego, another trinitarian analogy, with a protecting angel in the fiery furnace (Daniel 3:23). The flames are turning cold blue, unable to harm the fearless young men. The next medallion, in the centre of the vault, is centred on the circle of green marble in the floor below. It shows the Lamb of God attended by angels with censers. Christ, the sacrificial Lamb of God is at the centre of history. He is prefigured in the Lamb of the Hebrew Pasch and recognised in the last pages of the Bible as the Lamb of the Apocalypse.

Finally the Trinity is clearly expressed in the crown of the apse where the figure of Christ appears flanked by its Greek letters ('I am the Alpha and the Omega, the First and the Last, the Beginning and the End', Revelation 22:13). He is centred between the Hand of God and the Dove, representing the Father and the Holy Spirit. The Father and the Spirit cannot be depicted, so the artist relies on established symbols.

Another theme is christological and concerns redemption. Christ, the pivot of

The pelican wounding its own breast to nourish its young surmounting the arch above the Blessed Sacrament gates. It symbolises the selflessness of Christ

(Opposite)
The chapel is screened and gated to designs by Marshall

(Overleaf)
Ministering angel encourages Elijah to eat in preparation for his journey

human history, is shown at the centre of this chapel. The Old Testament leads up to him, the New flows from him. The people of the Old Testament were saved through the action of Christ as much as those of the New.

The unity of the faith that binds the two Testaments into the one economy of salvation is another important concept in these mosaics. They provide a visual commentary on the Letter to the Hebrews, chapter 11. *'By faith Abel offered to God a more acceptable sacrifice than Cain's .... By faith Noah warned by God about events as yet unseen, built an ark to save his household. By faith Abraham obeyed when he was called to set out for a place that he was to receive as an inheritance. It was equally by faith that Sarah, in spite of being past the age, was made able to conceive. By faith that Abraham, when put to the test, offered up Isaac.'* Everything is centred on Christ. *'Yet all these though they were commended for their faith did not receive what was promised, since God had provided something better so that they would not, apart from us, be made perfect.'* (Hebrews 11:4,7,8,11,17a,39,40).

The apse is dominated by a jewelled cross, the symbol of Christ's triumphal sacrifice on Calvary. This triumph is the promise fulfilled of everything that the Old Testament prophets dimly understood yet urgently proclaimed.

Appropriately, for a chapel of the Blessed Sacrament, the Eucharist figures prominently in the mosaics, in the form of bread and wine. The bread motif is seen at the springing of the interior face of the entrance arch. On each side are great ears of wheat on single stalks, the note being taken up in the broad sweep of 'Abraham's tympanum', already described. It is featured again on the right-hand side, in the manna, provided by God and gathered up in the wilderness by the children of Israel (Exodus 16:13-36). This Old Testament scene is interpreted as a symbol of the Bread of Life. Jesus says: *'I am the living bread that came down from heaven'* (John 6:51). It is repeated in the scene of Elijah at Horeb. He is weary and sleeps beneath a furze bush, having fled from the threats of Jezebel. Roused by an angel, he is urged to eat. He eats and sleeps again. In the mosaic, the angel comes a second time urging Elijah to eat more ... *'otherwise the journey will be too much for you'* (1 Kings 19:7). The bread Elijah ate, which gave him strength for forty days' survival, is a *type* or foreshadowing of the eucharistic nourishment which was to be spiritual. On the right of the sanctuary the theme of bread is carried over into the New Testament and the multiplication of the loaves and fishes by Jesus (Matthew 14:19; Mark 6:41; Luke 9:16; John 6:11). Again, this miraculous feeding of the multitude foreshadows the Eucharist to be instituted by Christ at the Last Supper.

Echoes of the nourishment theme are to be found in panels beneath the three windows on the left and the two blind windows on the right. On the left wall there is a fish on either side of the word ΙΧΘΥΣ. This Greek word (icthyus) for 'fish' is made up of the initial letters for the phrase Jesus Christ, Son of God, Saviour. The symbol of a fish was used in the Roman catacombs by the early Christians. The disciples were known as *'fishers of men'* and some of the early Fathers are said to have referred to those in their care as *'pisciculi'* (little fishes). Below the lettering is a cross entwined with a symbol of eternity and in the window openings, the fruitful vine.

Both bread and wine are prominent in the standing figures of Melchizedek, in royal apparel, and Abraham dressed as a warrior, which fill the two blind windows on the right (Genesis 14:18). Both men carry a vessel filled with wine and they are further united by the left and right 'hands of God' above their heads. The panel below Melchizedek is decorated with the offerings of bread and wine brought out to the Valley of the King by this priest-king of Salem (which both Jewish and Christian commentators identify with Jerusalem). The valley lay within a quarter of a mile of Jerusalem so the walls of the city are seen at a distance behind the two men.

The sacrificial offerings of Abraham and Melchizedek were recognised by Clement of Alexandria as prefiguring the eucharistic meal. Some of the Fathers of the Church even suggested that Melchizedek was a manifestation of none other than the Son of God. Both patriarchs are recalled in the most ancient prayers of the Mass, known as the Roman Canon: *'Look with favour on these offerings'* says the priest, *' and accept them as once you accepted the gifts of your servant Abel, the sacrifice of Abraham our father in faith, and the bread and wine offered by your priest Melchizedek.'* The wine motif is woven throughout in the reveals of the window spaces at the top of which are symbols of eucharistic loaves. In the Old Testament windows of the nave, the strong, heavily laden vines are still green while the New Testament vines by the two apse windows have a red, autumnal maturity. Only with the coming of Christ and his sacrificial death, Resurrection and Ascension into heaven does the plan of God come to fruition. In the panel beneath Abraham, the brazen serpent appears, recalling those who, in the words of the Letter to the Hebrews, tried the patience of God during the desert wanderings of the Israelites (Numbers 21:9). This sign of their healing by looking upon the bronze serpent which Moses made and had set up in obedience to God, prefigures the healing power of the cross of Jesus. The sacrifice of Christ, which in the apse is represented by the blood-red cross, is foreshadowed in the Old Testament nave by the sacrifices of Abel, Noah, Melchizedek, Abraham, Samuel and Malachi. The treatment of the haloes of the Almighty in the Old Testament subjects shows them adorned with a cross, in accord with medieval precedents.

'Abel offered to God a more acceptable sacrifice than Cain, through this he received approval as righteous by God himself giving

approval to his gifts' (Hebrews 11:4). This attempt to offer sacrifice occupies the first place after the arch on the left-hand side of the chapel. On the right-hand wall, Noah's sacrifice after the Flood is shown in a highly condensed scene. The ark is there and the Lord God above with the rainbow that betokens his Covenant (Genesis 9:12-15). Noah's responsibility for the survival of the natural world is represented by a pair of hoopoe birds in a basket. Emerging from the ark with his dependents he builds an altar on which he burns a sacrificial offering to God on the first dry land they encounter (Genesis 8:20). Overhead, the dove - slate grey, like a London pigeon - still hovers with an olive branch in its beak (Genesis 8:10). This emblem of peace restored between God and people foreshadows the peace of the Christian soul released from sin and the finality of death by the waters of baptism, of which the Flood is a powerful symbol. In Christian iconography the dove would come to represent the presence of the Holy Spirit. Returning to the left-hand wall, Abraham is shown on the point of offering up his only son in sacrifice - a terrified Isaac - although an angel of God, reversing the divine command, stays his hand (Genesis 22:9). In the foreground is the ram, caught by its horns in a bush, which Abraham would offer as a substitute victim for his sacrifice (Genesis 22:13). Next comes Malachi, last of the prophets, bearing a censer and seven-branched candlestick kneeling before the angel of the Covenant. Wherever a scroll in hand is seen in this chapel it signifies the Covenant or `sacred contract' which God is constantly seeking to establish in his dealings with human beings. This composition, with the sun and moon in the background, illustrates the text: *'For from the rising of the sun to its setting my name is great among the nations and in every place incense is offered to my name, and a pure offering'* (Malachi 1:11). It is taken as a prophecy of the universality of the Eucharist - the sacrifice of Christ which will take the place of all others. In the fourth space on this side, Samuel, who had been the last of the Judges, is shown listening to the voice of

the Lord, his sacrificial knife lying on the ground beside an empty altar. *`Surely to obey is better than sacrifice, and to heed than the fat of rams'* (1 Samuel 15:22). The experience of Samuel represents another preparatory stage along the way that leads to the one perfect sacrifice of Jesus Christ.

The sanctuary mosaics have subjects taken from the New Testament. A shallow arch marks off the apse from the body of the chapel, its facing surface decorated with two supporting pillars. Above them are twelve doves, separated by sprigs of olive, signifying the apostles, the whole set against a rainbow of colour that is pure Anrep. In the sanctuary vault, Christ, blessing the world, dominates a representation of the Holy Trinity. On the left side of the sanctuary the Marriage Feast at Cana is shown (John 2:1-11). This is the occasion of the first miracle of Jesus and he is standing before the seated figure of his mother. The newly-weds, seen under a bridal canopy, look self-conscious in their wedding crowns. A servant, directed by Jesus, fills a jar with water which is already turning into wine. The impression of a tiled floor in this scene exemplifies the delicacy of Anrep's technique. Anrep apparently even asked Monsignor Francis Bartlett if the mouth of Christ might be allowed to seem to smile as the water is changed into wine. On the opposite wall is the feeding of the five thousand with five loaves and two fishes (John 6:1-15; Matthew 14:13-21). The young boy of John's gospel presents Jesus with the fish in a basket. The loaves are already in front of him. Behind Jesus, watching intently are the Twelve who also represent the multitude. A rocky rise in the background is a reminder of the gospel description of the scene as 'a lonely place' (Mark 6:35). The multiplication of the loaves and fishes prefigures the Eucharist. *`And Jesus said to them, I am the bread of Life. Whoever comes to me shall never be hungry; and whoever believes in me shall never be thirsty'* (John 6:35). In order to separate the two eucharistic miracles of Jesus from scenes in the curvature of the apse itself,

blue pillars with twin angels above them are included in the design.

All themes come together in the apse with the dominant elements of Christ and his cross. This is a triumphant cross (*crux gemmata*), a jewelled sign of the glorious victory of Christ. It also represents the Transfiguration of Jesus (Matthew 17:2; Mark 9:2). Set over the globe it is embedded in the rock from which the four rivers of Paradise flow out abundantly. In front of the globe and founded on the rock is the basilica of Saint Peter in Rome, itself a familiar analogy of the Church in the modern world, although Anrep wanted to suggest Michelangelo's original design rather than the final version that exists today. The cross is supported by two further mosaics - on the left, the Resurrection on Easter Day and on the right, the Liberation of Captive Souls by the Risen Lord. This scene, which recurs in Russian icons, rarely appears in Western art. It is as if the Western Church is so mesmerised by the happenings of Easter Day that the descent into hell by the Risen One is barely given a thought. Not so in the East. This scene, also known as the Harrowing of Hell, shows Christ newly risen from the dead, leading Adam and Eve out of their captivity from the gates of the underworld, their chains burst apart by his victory over sin and death. Christ has taken them firmly by the arm while Abel (in the same fleecy garment he wore for his sacrifice!) hangs on to his Saviour like a survivor at sea. These represent, in turn, all who died in peace before the redemption of mankind took place. Christ's haloes sparkle in this apse.

Thus a historical development that began before Abraham and ends in Christ is emblazoned on these chapel walls. The altar of sacrifice itself and the tabernacle of the Real Presence are the focal point on which all lines of the chapel converge. They are seen as a culmination of that historical process of interaction between God and human beings, shaped and nurtured by divine love, which here enters our own time and place. From the entrance arch down to the sanctuary and its apse, Boris Anrep compressed the message of the Bible in terms of a family album of the People of God.

It remains to recall some of the impressions gained at the time the mosaics were made. The artist was nearly 80 when he undertook the commission. For inspiration he had gone back a long way, virtually ignoring eleventh-century Byzantine mosaics, reaching back instead to Roman work, especially to floor mosaics with their light background. The figures are not elongated nor sharply highlighted, the eyes do not stare but instead are very natural and human. Using clouds to indicate space is a device found in such mosaics as Saint Pudenziana and Saints Cosmas and Damian in Rome. This space, endless like the sky, is contrived by covering the vault and apse with a delicate glow, largely pink but a composite of many colours in which the stars move and sparkle. The numinous firmament of the vault flies outwards in a roseate `Big Bang', reaching right down to embrace the incidental scenes on the walls, while clouds in the deeper-toned apse glint with a minimal underlining of gold tesserae.

The making of the mosaics went through various stages. Following his initial sketches, Anrep prepared full-size colour cartoons in Paris which formed the basis for the choice of mosaic *smalti*. These are the traditional glass mosaic cubes or tesserae. They are hand-cut to size, irregular in shape but generally about half an inch square. The assembling of the material on full-sized working drawings was carried out in Venice at Professor Antonio Orsoni's workshop as a preliminary to a complete revision later in London by Anrep and his artistic and technical associate, Justin Vulliamy. The mosaics were then crated and sent to a London studio. Fixing them was entrusted to Peter Indri who began work in November 1960, although alterations and adjustment went on continuously, even after the fixing was completed in December 1961. For this purpose an

enormous table was constructed in the transept. The artist continually went up to the galleries to check the work from a distance and at different angles. The two archangels of the entrance arch had to be elongated for proportion. The yellow flowers on Elijah's furze bush could not be seen, so Anrep gave them their own background of grey. Bringing the work to a final shape continued to the very last.

Monsignor Francis Bartlett recounted that when finally finished, Anrep decided that something was radically wrong and wanted to put it right at his own expense. That would have put the chapel out of commission for several more months and he was dissuaded from doing so. Maybe the thought of another three months of Boris Anrep's relentless chain-smoking in the Cathedral failed to recommend the idea to the clergy. All that Monsignor Wheeler would say was that 'for the past year the Blessed Sacrament Chapel has been walled off from the nave and Mr Anrep has been here, constantly supervising a transformation. It has been an experience and an inspiration to all of us to see the artist at work, reminiscent of another age ...'.

The question remains - what was the great 'fault' which troubled him so much? On close inspection it seems possible that it was not a matter of technique or some artistic weakness but a biblical inaccuracy. It is clear that in weaving his theological themes Anrep pondered specialist advice, taking immense care with scriptural texts and details of biblical narrative. Yet maybe, when it was all finished, someone pointed out to him that the scene on the inward facing tympanum was not strictly faithful to the text. In Anrep's mosaic, Sarah and Abraham together serve their three visitors at table. In the Bible, however, Abraham first gets his wife baking and has his servant prepare meat, but the impression is given that Sarah was never presented to the guests and therefore did not help serve the meal. *They said to him 'Where is your wife Sarah?' and he said 'there in the tent.' Sara was listening at the*

Guild of the Blessed Sacrament mace, uppermost section. Crafted in silver and enamel to a design by Harold Stabler (Catalogue number 94)

tent entrance behind him ... (Genesis 18:9, 10). On the other hand, it is not *certain* from the text that Sarah remained out of sight for the whole episode. Maybe she helped serve the food, *then* retired to the tent, leaving the men to their discussions .... It is a matter for scholars to determine.

There is a certain difficulty for the visitor wishing to examine the chapel. As a sacred place in constant use for private prayer it would be inappropriate for the peace of the chapel to be compromised by tourists, even scholarly ones. However the middle to late afternoon is usually the best time to view the decoration. When first revealed, the mosaics of the Blessed Sacrament Chapel were not particularly well-received. For many at the time they seemed too Russian, too difficult to understand and far too *pink*. Probably people were expecting ceilings ablaze with gold. Today they are easier to assess dispassionately. In many ways the Anrep mosaics are a remarkable and unique exercise in Christian iconography.

Shrine of the Sacred Heart and Saint Michael

This shrine is a tiny chapel occupying the north aisle of the Blessed Sacrament Chapel. Very narrow in proportion to its length, it terminates eastward in a small apse. On the altar is a large statue of the Sacred Heart of Jesus given by the Sisters of the Sacred Heart, an order of nuns, and those educated in their convent schools. Devotion to the Sacred Heart of Jesus is rooted in Catholic theology and the Church's understanding of Christ's love for humanity. It might best be understood in the words of the *Catechism of the Catholic Church* which says: *'The prayer of the Church venerates and honours the Heart of Jesus. It adores the incarnate Word and his heart which, out of love for men, he allowed to be pierced by our sins.'* The early Christian perception of the Sacred Heart (although pious rather than directly scriptural) is based on an interpretation of John 7:37-39 and 19:33-37. It is a concept of the heart of Jesus as the fountain dispensing the Spirit - living water (John 4:14) - from the Saviour's wounded side. As such, it is seen as a proper object of love for the Christian believer. It follows that any shrine with this dedication is intended as a place for prayer.

On the frontal of the altar is a sculpted bas-relief of Saint Michael slaying a dragon, which symbolises all spiritual enemies of the Kingdom of Christ. Scripture speaks of seven pure spirits before the throne of God. The three which have names are Saint Michael, Saint Gabriel and Saint Raphael. Incidentally, the three bells which peal daily from the exterior of the south transept are cast with these names. They were blessed in 1903 by Cardinal Vaughan shortly before he died. Tradition presents the Archangel Michael as 'Prince of the Heavenly Host', worthy of veneration for his fearless loyalty and closeness to God.

The marble-work, begun early in 1910, was finished by June of that year. On the south side the arcading of the Blessed Sacrament Chapel, with its enclosing grilles, has pier pilasters of verd-antique surmounted by an entablature of pavonazzo. This is moulded and relieved by the introduction of diamond shapes of *rosso antico*, which carry the eye up to the springing of the arcading, where the mosaic of the vault begins. This note of red, emphasised strongly in the mosaics themselves, is repeated in the altar slab of Cork marble, and the sculpture of Saint Michael in the altar frontal is flanked by panels of strongly figured cipollino. The whole is enclosed in a broad pavonazzo framing. The retable carries a pedestal of *campan vert* on which stands the life-size statue of the Sacred Heart carved in the studios of Farmer & Brindley Co. The recess behind this decidedly over-sized figure is lined with vertical strips of black panderma, an extremely rare marble, brought from Asia Minor by Farmer & Brindley in the 1880s. Alternate strips of pavonazzo terminate in a simply moulded cornice beneath the mosaics of the apse vault. To right and left of the statue at about waist height, white-framed medallions of red Languedoc break the monotony of the vertical wall treatment. There are three circular windows in the north wall, and the general effect of the marble wall-lining, which on this side ceases about 2 feet below these openings, is green and white. Here, a dado of opened-out vertical cipollino slabs is headed by two equal bands of Irish fossil and pavonazzo. This banding is repeated beneath a cornice of simple Carrara. The intervening wall space displays a light breccia panel within a larger one of verd-antique centrally between the piers. Both are edged with narrow white mouldings and they alternate with plain slabs of cipollino.

The electric light pendants in this chapel are related to some ancient lamps - light crosses - in the church of Santa Sophia at Constantinople, described in Lethaby and Swainson's book in quotations from an account of its treasures by Paul the Silentiary, the Greek poet of the sixth century. In the Westminster shrine two silvered bronze beams, with hammered ornament, are thrown across the chapel, above the cornice level. From each hangs a pair of cruciform pendants with three electric bulbs. The silver lamp suspended from the vault before the statue is less Byzantine in character. It was designed by Osmond Bentley working with Marshall who also designed the electric pendants. The lamp is

A small, narrow chapel but a quiet place for solitude

(Opposite)
Bas-relief of the Archangel Michael on the front of the altar of the Sacred Heart

inscribed as being the gift of Sir Charles Paston-Cooper, Bt, and dated 25 September 1910.

The areas covered by mosaic are the four compartments of the cross-vaulted roof, the lunette of the west end, the vault of the apse, and the upper part of the north wall above the marble dado. Because all these areas are small-scale, subject-matter was avoided in favour of conventional motifs including symbolic hearts, foliation and geometric figures in a colour scheme of red and gold, relieved with a little green and white. Not for the first time, the dedication of the Cathedral to the Most Precious Blood of Christ is recalled in decorative symbolism. The only pictorial element occurs at the west end above the narrow oak door into the galleries where, in a small tympanum, the face of Christ gazes out from a ground of plain gold mosaic. This representation, supposedly based on the last work of William Christian Symons, was completed shortly before his death in 1911. It was given by Mrs Evelyn Murray but not without a sharp difference of opinion with the artist.

Christian Symons had been a close friend of John Bentley and collaborated with the architect on the mosaic decoration of the Holy Souls Chapel. He had also created the enormous and imposing rood that hangs over the nave of Westminster Cathedral. He was an artist of national repute and when commissioned to paint a representation of the Holy Face of Christ would have had no inkling of difficulties in store. But Bentley was dead and so was Cardinal Vaughan and those left to transact the day-to-day business of innumerable projects were perhaps less sure-footed than the original visionaries. In July 1910, Osmond Bentley, son of the architect and now a director of the Bentley firm, wrote to Symons briefing him on the need for a picture of the face of Christ from which mosaicists could work. He wrote that the picture had been intended for the Blessed Sacrament Chapel entrance facing westwards but the position had now changed. Nor was it to have a white marble frame with inlaid border of coloured stone as originally planned. The picture should be set on a gold background and show the face of Christ in his agony, his head

crowned with thorns. The donor was to be a Mrs Evelyn Murray of Eaton Square. She had been impressed by representations of the Holy Face in the Church of Saint Mary, Chelsea, the Jesuit Church at Farm Street and also one in Antwerp. Christian Symons set to work. He was nearing the end of his life and it is clear from the finished painting that it was for him a meditation on the mystery of suffering. The painting arrived at the Cathedral and the storm broke. Mrs Murray's letter says a great deal about the time-honoured freedom of donors to disparage the creative work they have promised to pay for.

15 Eaton Square,
SW,
November 25th 1910

Dear Sir,

I visited this morning the Archbishop's
House to see the picture of the sacred
face which is to be copied for the
Cathedral in mosaic. I confess I do not
admire it. The face is a hard cruel face
and the colouring is wrong. The face
should not be 'so white' and the eyes are
dreadful. A person who was with me said
'they thought it positively objectionable'. I
have here a print of the bust that 'Michael
Angelo' made of the sacred face. It has
the right expression. Could your artist
come and see it or I would send you this
print to show to your artist. I am so
anxious that this 'medallion of the Sacred
Face' should be beautiful.

Yours truly,
Evelyn Murray

In a letter of 3 December to Osmond
Bentley the painter was unmoved. 'I
cannot entertain your idea of altering the
drawing of the cartoon of the Sacred
Face. Agony is, as the lady says, dreadful. I
have chosen the moment of greatest
agony that attends the words "I thirst"
[John 19:28]. It is the pictorial expression
of all my thoughts and meditations on the
subject for months. To attempt to depict
in the features anything like benignity or
sweetness would be wrong. Everything
has been fully considered. As to my
conception of the subject, the work is
finished and perfect. Nothing would
induce me to alter it.
Have the cartoon put up.'

Not only was the cartoon put up, the
mosaic was executed. It bears little
resemblance to the Symons, but perhaps
that is hardly surprising.

*"I thirst". Words of the dying Christ on the cross,
depicted by Symons near the end of his own life*

PRAY FOR THE SOUL OF ... ERT VAUGHAN
CARDINAL ... IEST OF THE ...
THIRD ARC ... SHOP ...
AND FOU ... ER OF ... DIE ...
BORN APR ...

Chapel of Saint Thomas of Canterbury

The small chapel dedicated to Saint Thomas in the north transept, and wholly enclosed by grilles of gilt bronze, is Cardinal Vaughan's chantry. Within its gates the monument to the Cardinal Founder is positioned, although by his own wish, Herbert Vaughan's body rests, not within these walls but in the grounds of the Missionary College of Saint Joseph at Mill Hill, the project closest to his heart during his prime. He suffered his last illness there and died in the summer of 1903, just two weeks after the first London performance in Westminster Cathedral of Elgar's setting of Cardinal Newman's poem on the passing of a Christian soul from this world to the next - *The Dream of Gerontius*. For four days the body lay in state at Westminster Cathedral, during which an estimated 50,000 people came to pay their respects. After the Requiem Mass the body of Herbert Vaughan was taken back to Mill Hill for burial. The recumbent effigy seen here was designed by J.A. Marshall and carved by Henry McCarthy, a sculptor who had worked for Bentley for many years. It is hewn from pure white Pentelic and the Cardinal faces the altar, his head resting on a pair of tasselled cushions. Clad in lace rochet and the characteristic skull-cap of prelates, the body is more slender than this imposing figure had been in life. His cardinal's hat rests between knees and feet, its tassels hanging on either side to the lower edge of the white marble monument which is inscribed as follows:

Pray for the soul of Herbert Vaughan
Cardinal Priest of the Holy Roman Church
Third Archbishop of Westminster
and founder of this Cathedral
born April 15, 1832; died June 19, 1903. RIP

The base of verd-antique rests on a platform of red Greek marble with circular projections at each corner to receive four candlesticks of cast bronze. These were the gift of the Dowager Duchess of Newcastle and were designed by the Bentley firm. The surrounding floor is composed of green and black marble inlaid in white.
The suggestion had been made in 1900 by Francis Bourne - then Bishop of Southwark, but later to be the fourth Archbishop of Westminster - that the decoration of a chapel of Saint Thomas of Canterbury in Westminster Cathedral might be undertaken by the Catholic clergy of whom Thomas Becket is patron saint. Becket, Archbishop of Canterbury (1162-70), had angered King Henry II by his defence of the rights of the Church against the civil power and was murdered in his own cathedral on 29 December 1170. His tomb had been one of the glories of Canterbury Cathedral until it was despoiled by Henry VIII. Bishop Bourne then of Southwark said the chapel would be a fitting testimony to the clergy's reverence for the martyr's sacrifice - a view that was readily accepted.

Shortly after Cardinal Vaughan's death the chapel was set apart as his chantry, and on 19 June 1907, the fourth anniversary of his death, this marble effigy was solemnly unveiled by his successor in the See of Westminster. That summer, as funds had accumulated for the decoration it was decided to begin the marble wall-lining. £650 was paid for the monument, and the marble altar and dado cost £350.

The chapel is entered through an arcading carried on a central pier and two columns of a rare black and white breccia known as grand antique. This pier and the lateral ones are sheeted with porphyry-coloured *rosso*, whilst high on the wall between the arches a white marble tablet displays the carved and coloured arms of the Cardinal Founder. The very characteristic Bentley capitals are in white statuary marble and the inner sides of the piers have verd-antique pilasters. The gates and grilles enclosing the chantry were designed by Marshall and made by Singer & Co of Frome at a cost of £850 - the gift of the secular clergy nationwide. Extending from the floor to the base of the capitals, they consist of slender balusters supporting a frieze, and bearing the letters 'HV', the Cardinal's initials, on

Effigy of the Cardinal Founder lies in the Chapel of Saint Thomas of Canterbury

(Opposite)
The initials HV denote Cardinal Herbert Vaughan, founder of Westminster Cathedral

either side of a mitre and beneath a patriarchal cross, the whole set in scrolled framing. These scrolls and the frieze are hand-crafted, the remainder being cast. The material is solid bronze, but gilded and chased. Inside, the chapel is veneered with marble to the level of the window-sills, above which a pair of arched openings contain four rectangular lights filled with greenish tinted glazing in decorative leading. The marble dado consists of broad slabs of heavily figured pavonazzo with vertical divisions of verd-antique. The altar, without retable, is also verd-antique, with a wreath-adorned frontal. Bentley's people designed the crucifix particular to this altar. With a base of bronze inlaid with silver, the cross accommodates an antique ivory figure of Christ. Above the head and crafted in ivory marquetry, a hand holds a wreath surrounding a dove - standard iconography for the acquiescence of the three Persons of the Holy Trinity in the

sacrifice on Calvary. This crucifix, the gift of Lady Alice Fitzwilliam, was crafted and assembled by the Bromsgrove Guild of Metal Workers.

Bentley left no details for the decoration of the Chapel of Saint Thomas, partly it seems, in deference to an intervention by Cardinal Vaughan. By 1900 the Cardinal was anxious to accelerate the completion of the Cathedral and seemed to think that the architect would be happy to receive help with various decorative schemes. Certainly, Bentley had never intended to produce all his mosaic work unaided and with the Cardinal's approval invited others to contribute their skills. But he was determined to retain all marble-work designs in his own hands - a subject about which he cared passionately. Cardinal Vaughan may not have appreciated this distinction for he invited the architect Thomas Garner to undertake the marble decoration of Saint

Thomas's Chapel. Garner, who died in 1906, was a friend of the Cardinal, and for a long period (1869-97) had been in distinguished partnership with G.F. Bodley, RA. Together they had produced ecclesiastical architecture of a high order throughout England. The former, though personally unknown to Bentley, was a friend of Vaughan's, and as a co-religionist was probably well-received among those aspiring to work on Cathedral projects. On receiving the Cardinal's invitation, Garner sought a meeting with Bentley, yet despite an encouraging exchange of letters there was to be no practical outcome. Garner eventually proceeded to make the drawings for the chapel of his name saint, but the designs were never accepted. The work reverted to the Bentley firm, which was asked to undertake it four or five years after John Bentley's death.

North Transept

Joan of Arc mosaic crafted by George Bridge after a design by W. Christian Symons

(Opposite)
Window grille near the doorway from Ambrosden Avenue

There is an important entrance from Ambrosden Avenue into the north transept. The exterior door gives on to a porch vaulted with a dome and projecting into the church. Bentley left full details for the completion of the doorway between the transept and this porch, which was later crafted in teak. The lobby is lit by a pair of small windows and also receives some light from the Cathedral itself through a small opening filled with a glazed and gilded grille. Inside the transept and above this opening is a mosaic panel of Saint Joan of Arc, the Maid of Orleans (c. 1412-31). Joan, a peasant girl from Domremy in Lorraine, 'heard voices' telling her to liberate France from the English. She inspired a small force put under her command and won a victory at Orleans in 1429 but was later tried for heresy by churchmen who sympathised with the English and was burnt at the stake. The verdict was repudiated in 1456 and she was canonised in 1920.

In May 1909, the Catholic Women's League organised a penny collection from the Catholic women and girls of England to create this memorial as an expression of reparation for a wrong done to Joan and to France. The collection raised £408 14s 11d. Christian Symons designed the panel showing Joan, the holy warrior maiden, clad in shining armour. In her left hand she holds a long sword and wears a flowing cope-like mantle. In her right she bears aloft the lilied Oriflamme of France. The mosaic itself was done by George Bridge but Osmond Bentley was far from happy with the result. He wrote to Symons on 7 September 1910 that he considered the banner and white drapery much too dark and wondered whether the panel should be reworked. This was done and it was completed by 16 November. The panel is 3 feet by 7 feet in a white marble frame surrounded by a mural revetment of very pale cipollino footed with a projecting ledge intended for flower vases. There is a plaque under the mosaic which reads:

SAPIENTIA VENDITAM JUSTAM NON DERELINQUIT SED A PECCATORIBUS
LIBERAVIT EAM DESCENDITQUE CUM ILLA IN FOVEAM ET IN VINCULIS NON
DERELINQUIT ILLAM DONEC AFFERET ILLI SCEPTRUM REGNI ET POTENTIAM
ADVERSUS EOS QUI EAM DEPRIMEBANT ET MENDACES OSTENDIT QUI
MACULAVERUNT ILLAM.

MULIERES CATHOLICAE PUELLAEQUE ANGLIAE FEMINARUM CATHOLICARUM
FOEDERATIONE CURANTE PONENDO MONUMENTO STIPEM CONTULERE

(Wisdom has not abandoned the betrayed just one, but has liberated her from sinners and has descended with her into the pit, and has not abandoned her in her chains, right up to the time it bestowed on her the sceptre of the kingdom and power against those who were oppressing her, and it has shown up the lies of those who slandered her. The Catholic wives and daughters of England in the Catholic Women's League collected the sum for the erection of this monument.)

(NB 'venditam justam' is a pun, both on Joan of Arc, and the Christian soul, with references to their fate and redemption.)

As an architect of churches with many years experience, Bentley was knowledgeable about liturgical requirements and gave a great deal of thought to this aspect of his brief - the use to which church space would be put during religious ceremonies, processions and other activities. Within this transept he had placed a single column of verd-antique to carry the bridge-like gallery that links the gallery of the crossing with that above the porch and the Vaughan Chantry. The casual observer might imagine that it would impede a procession moving through the transept; in practice there is no difficulty or hindrance. Not everyone has thought so in the past, however. The column that now looks so immobile was once removed and disposed of by a former Administrator of the

Flower vases for Joan of Arc in polished alluminium and enamel

Cathedral, Monsignor Collingwood, who was under the impression that Cardinal Griffin was in agreement with him. He simply ordered a reinforced horizontal beam to be installed in its place with decorative marble infilling above. There was an immediate public outcry, with a number of very influential artists writing to *The Times.*

17 November 1953

Westminster Cathedral
Work of the Internal Decoration

To the Editor of the Times

Sir,
We the undersigned venture to ask for the hospitality of your columns in the following matter. We have come to view with a growing disquietude the recent work of decoration in Westminster Cathedral. The mosaic work recently carried out seems to us to be consciously lacking in the fine qualities of the art. Again, the lining of the walls with various marbles in the galleries over the Presbytery seems to us to have ruined the effect of Bentley's beautiful colonnade with its columns of pavonazzetto marble.

Even more disquieting is the destruction of Bentley's arcaded screen in front of the Blessed Sacrament Chapel which has stood there for 40 years, and the removal of the monolithic column of verde Antico there which was the sister of those in Santa Sophia, for it was hewn from the same quarry discovered by the late William Brindley in the latter years of the last century after being lost since the time of Justinian.

We appeal to you, Sir, not only because money is now being asked of the public to continue this work but because of the importance of this great building, which is not only the chief Roman Catholic church in the country but one of London's most significant achievements in architecture and must be considered, we think, as a national monument. And we very respectfully suggest that the whole problem of the interior decoration calls for the most careful reconsideration at this juncture in order to achieve the grandeur of conception in its decoration which is inherent in Bentley's magnificent design and which the beauty of the building demands.

It is recorded in the official *Life* of the late Cardinal Vaughan, the builder of the cathedral, that in his last letter 'he begs his Vicar General to try to see that the future of the Cathedral is not left to whim or the taste of any one man. He takes blame to himself because he has sometimes acted without consulting others. He expresses the hope that his successor will consult laymen as well as priests upon questions concerning the decoration of the Cathedral and the adornment of its fabric.' (vol. 2 pp 482-3)

In view of this and realizing the immense difficulties confronting him in this matter the late Cardinal Hinsley formed a small committee of distinguished architects and authorities in decoration in whom he had every confidence to advise him in this matter, but we understand that this advisory committee is no longer advising the Cathedral authorities.

Yours faithfully,
Giles Gilbert Scott *former President Royal Institute of British Architects*
Kenneth Clark *Chairman Arts Council of Great Britain*
Philip Hendy *Director National Gallery*
John Rothenstein *Director Tate Gallery*
John Pope-Hennessy
Henry Moore *Member Royal Fine Art Commission*
Graham Greene
Edward Hutton

Cardinal Griffin had the Cathedral architect reinstate the column and as a result of the controversy a new Art and Architecture Committee was established.

An apsidal mosaic of Saint Nicholas
by Aelred Bartlett, 1961

Leaving the north transept and moving
westward into the north aisle, the visitor
passes two alcoves in a matching position
to those of Saint Joachim and Saint Anne
on the other side of the Cathedral. These
have apsidal mosaics representing Saint
Nicholas and Saint Christopher. The
mosaic of Saint Nicholas was carried out
by Aelred Bartlett in 1961 and represents
the saint as patron of seafarers. It shows a
young, unbearded man in the style of
Roman, pre-Christian portraits. It was
donated by the family and friends of
Dame Vera Laughton Matthews of the
WRNS and a little wren can be seen
perched on an anchor in the design. Saint
Christopher is shown as patron of
travellers by land and sea..

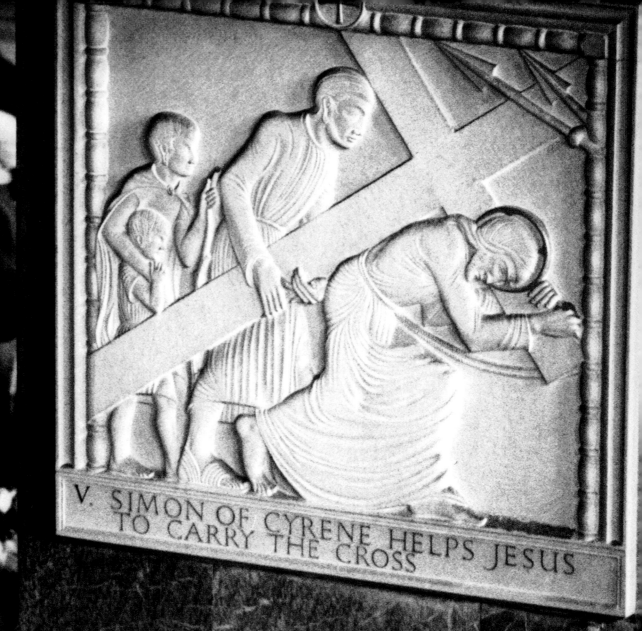

V. SIMON OF CYRENE HELPS JESUS
TO CARRY THE CROSS

Chapel of Saint Joseph

Symbol of Christ from the chapel pavement

(Opposite)
North wall arcading with rare Fior di Persico
marble column

The plan of this chapel dedicated to the husband of Mary is entirely similar to that of Saint Paul having an apsidal east wall. It remains unfinished and progress in the decoration has always been slow. In 1899 Cardinal Vaughan was under the impression that Saint Joseph's would be the gift and chantry of the Weld-Blundells, one of the old Catholic families, but in the early years of the century the Catholic public was being urged to subscribe £6,000 to cover the cost of the marbles, mosaic work, *opus sectile* and the bronze screen required to complete the chapel. This appeal received a boost from Mrs Ada Watney who in 1913 undertook responsibility for all the marble-work at a cost of £2,615. Bentley had left his designs, it was a matter of carrying them out.

The altar, consecrated in 1910 was designed by Bentley's firm. It has a frontal of Siena with an inlay of lapis lazuli and gold mosaic, inset with a lozenge of wavy Irish green marble with borders of lapis and pearl. The mensa is a fine slab of pavonazzo, typically Bentley, with his use of inlaid tesserae. The tabernacle bears an inscription refering to the Old Testament Joseph, beloved son of Jacob and Rachel:

ET ALEBAT EOS OMNEMQUE DOMUM PATRIS SUI PRAEBENS CIBARIA SINGULIS

(And Joseph provided his father, his brothers and all his father's household with food according to the number of their dependants (Gen 47:12)).

The triptych is cast bronze with a central panel depicting Saint Joseph and the Child Jesus (the upper part of the triptych is a circular panel with emblems of the carpenter's trade), modelled by H.C. Fehr. The doors are of beaten metal, laid on wood. In Scripture, Joseph is identified as the husband of Mary and foster-father of Jesus Christ. At the time of Christ's birth Mary was 'betrothed' to Joseph (Luke 1:27; 2:5) so a formal contract existed between them that was rather more than being engaged. After an angel told him in a dream that Mary had conceived a child, he carried out the command to 'take Mary as his wife' and acted in every way as the dutiful parent. Joseph looked after Mary at Bethlehem and set up home for their little family in Nazareth (Matthew 2:22). There Jesus was subject to Joseph as well as to Mary (Luke 2:51). This chapel is important in that the life of Joseph is seen by the Church as pivotal to the divine economy of salvation. Although so little is known about the man, what is understood about him from the gospels puts him at the heart of the mystery of redemption. In modern times he has been declared Patron of the Universal Church and as recently as 1962 Pope John XXIII surprised the Catholic world by adding Saint Joseph's name to the Roman Canon, the most venerable part of the Mass. Until then, it had been assumed that the words of the first Eucharistic Prayer could never be altered or added to in any way.

The work was carried out by Messrs Blunt and Wray. In 1939, the generosity of an anonymous donor enabled Cardinal Hinsley, fifth Archbishop of Westminster, to proceed with stalled work on this chapel. The idea governing the scheme was to obtain a unity of decoration. The column of Greek cipollino already in place, perhaps the finest in the Cathedral, gave the keynote, so the vacant wall facing the altar and the abutment walls on either side of the altar were lined with cipollino from Euboea, showing comparable markings. These panels, some 9 feet by 5 feet, are among the largest known monoliths - single slabs in one piece - of a marble much used in Rome in Imperial times: the great columns in the portico of the Temple of Antoninus and Faustina in the Roman Forum are of this Greek marble variety. Above, the walls have been lined with a warm breccia from Tuscany, each monolithic panel being divided by a narrow strip of Fior di Persico, also Tuscan, to match the remarkable column between the windows. This *fleur de pêche* column is suffused with violet and surmounted by a capital of doves in a basket, modelled on an original found in the 'priests' entrance' on the south side of Hagia Sophia in

Constantinople. The doves recall the Presentation of Jesus in the Temple by Mary and Joseph. In 1939 the opportunity was taken to deepen the carving on the capitals of the small columns in the arcaded wall under the windows. The colonnettes are of Algerian onyx, and above the arches is a rare onyx variety from Canada with pale, grey-blue hues, clouded and blotched with darker, stormier greys. The two large corbel-capitals that carry the arches between the chapel and the aisle were cut, following a drawing by Bentley.

As for the pavement of the chapel, a Byzantine design was prepared by Professor E.W. Tristram (1882-1952), an expert on English medieval wall-painting. The seven discs are of Egyptian porphyry, purple and green. All this marble is antique since no porphyry has been quarried since the time of the Roman Empire. Indeed the quarries, lost for the better part of two thousand years, were only discovered at the end of the last century by William Brindley. There is very little purple porphyry to be seen in England, less green, and none of either sort of any size. Probably the finest panel of purple is that in the tomb of King Richard II in Westminster Abbey. The strappings of the Joseph pavement are of porphyry, *rosso antico* and *brèche universelle*, with white bands of Hopton-Wood stone. In the centre of the design are four symbols of Christ the Lamb, the peacock (an emblem of eternity), the fish and the Chi-Rho sign or Monogram. of Jesus Christ.

The grille which was made before the Second World War according to the design of William Seymour Lindsay was erected in 1947. This chapel still awaits its mosaic decoration, which should cover the upper walls and the vault. The original idea was that the Chapel of Saint Joseph might be used for the reservation of the sacrament when the Blessed Sacrament Chapel itself was out of use. It should have a canopy, or baldachino, of beaten and cast bronze over the altar, for which a drawing was prepared by Bentley.

Detailed Bentley drawing for an altar canopy, yet to be carried out

(Opposite)
Antique Egyptian porphyry (none has been quarried in modern times) is included in a Byzantine pavement design by Professor E. W. Tristram

Cardinal Hinsley died in 1943 and is buried in this chapel. As with most cardinals' tombs, the distinctive red hat hangs over his place of rest and is allowed to decay as a reminder of the mortality common to all. Chroniclers suggest that it was Innocent IV (1243-54) who first insisted that a red hat should be the special headgear of his senior councillors. Another contemporary writer gives the exact occasion of the Pope's instruction. It was 1254 at the Abbey of Cluny where Pope Innocent with his cardinals held a conference with King Louis of France. The inscription on the tomb of Innocent IV in the Cathedral at Naples records the institution of the red hat as one of the notable achievements of his pontificate! The colour of a cardinal's dress is bright red to signify the willingness of these princes of the Church to shed their blood in defence of their faith in Jesus Christ. One notable cardinal martyr was Saint John Fisher, commemorated in the next chapel to the west of this one. When his hat arrived at Calais from Rome in June 1535, English officials stopped it going any further until the wishes of the king, Henry VIII, could be ascertained. They were wise to be cautious. Henry threatened that if the hat crossed the Channel, Fisher would wear it on his shoulders, 'for head he would have none to set it on'.

When John Fisher and Thomas More were canonised saints on 20 May 1935, Pope Pius XI addressed 3,000 English pilgrims in Saint Peter's Basilica. The Pope referred to a recent sermon on the two martyrs in which Cardinal Hinsley had used the expression *Tales ambio defensores* (I gird myself with such defenders), words traditionally attributed to Saint Ambrose on discerning the bodies of the martyrs Gervase and Protase. Hinsley adopted the expression as the motto for his coat of arms invoking the spirit of Saints John Fisher and Thomas More on his work at Westminster. Interestingly, the cockatrice on his coat of arms comes from the arms of the See of Rochester - that of Saint

Jewelled morse (cope clasp) by Omar Ramsden, 1935. Presented to Cardinal Hinsley

(Opposite)
The traditional red hat of a cardinal, suspended over the tomb of Cardinal Hinsley

John Fisher. The first archbishop of Canterbury to be created a cardinal was Stephen Langton (1207-28) and the last was Reginald Pole (1556-58) whose tomb in Canterbury Cathedral was restored by Cardinal Vaughan. When an archbishop of Westminster arrives back in London from Rome after being created a cardinal, he is solemnly received into his Cathedral while the choir sings the *Veni, Sancte Spiritus,* written by Stephen Langton.

Chapel of Saint George and the English Martyrs

Marble walls and pavement were completed in 1931

(Opposite)
The shield of Saint George in marble and the rose of mother-of-pearl mark this as a chapel for England

On the threshold of the next chapel stands a column of Swiss cipollino, more yellow in tone and waxy in texture than the primary Greek variety from Euboea.

Saint George is the patron of England, but the history of the saint is lost in the mists of early Church tradition. It seems he may have been the noble soldier who confessed Christ and was put to death at Nicomedia during the reign of Diocletian as related by Eusebius of Caesarea (c. 322). His tomb at Lydda, near Jaffa, is mentioned by the deacon Theodosius (c. 530). In the Canon of Pope Gelasius (late fifth century), Saint George is mentioned with others 'whose names are justly reverenced among men, but whose acts are known only to God.'

Saint George has always been popular in the East and the Crusaders revived his cult in Europe. At the Synod of Oxford in 1222 his feast day was ordered to be kept as a national festival, but it was only in Edward III's reign that he was made patron of England. For centuries English armies went into battle with the cry Saint George for England!' but he is also patron of Portugal, Aragon, Catalonia, Georgia, Lithuania and several cities.

For this chapel it was decided to combine the primary dedication with that of the martyrs, known to history, who played such a critical role in the survival of Catholicism in England, enabling the faith to be passed down as a living tradition from generation to generation. Added to this, a suggestion was made in 1915 in *The Tablet* - the English Catholic weekly journal - and supported by the then Duke of Norfolk that Saint George's Chapel should be made a permanent and abiding memorial to Catholics who had given their lives in the First World War. Against the north wall, therefore, marble tablets were erected to the fallen. They have wreaths and lettering incised in red on pale cream marble, surmounted by a frieze of grey-green, adorned with panels of dark red, inlaid in white with a rose, emblem of Saint George and of England.

The altar is made from a design prepared in the Bentley office and executed by a firm used here for the first time in the Cathedral - Arthur Lee & Co of Hayes. It was consecrated on 26 June 1910 by Doctor Mostyn, Bishop of Menevia, and contains relics of the saints in a silver casket set in a small sepulchre on the top, sealed in at the same time by a mason. The altar and mensa are carried out in light pavonazzo marble while the three contrasting panels of the frontal combine verd-antique with *rouge sanguine de Klaber* in the centre. The low dossal is of red Greek marble inlaid with stylised English roses in mother-of-pearl and framed in white, with the shield of Saint George carved on the terminal pilasters. Brick dados faced with red marble, capped and based with white, support the two columns which carry the canopy over the altar. The white marble altar steps of Greek Pentelic came from the quarries which provided the marble for the Parthenon at Athens. Set into the left-hand side of these steps is the inscription acknowledging the donors of the chapel (Alice Callaghan and her parents George and Elizabeth Arnold).

The Chapel of Saint George and the English Martyrs is dominated by an Eric Gill relief, placed above the altar, depicting the crucifixion. Entering the chapel we are drawn to this central work and find it to be an unusual and intriguing concept. The martyrs from the reign of King Henry VIII, Sir Thomas More, Lord Chancellor of England, and John Fisher, Bishop of Rochester, stand on either side of the cross. In the spring of 1534, both More and Fisher refused to take an oath subscribing to Henry VIII's Act of Succession. They were willing to accept the line of succession laid down by the Act, since it was a matter for Parliament, but they protested against King and Parliament setting aside the authority of the Pope in matters of Christian marriage. Sir Thomas would later say at his trial that one country cannot legislate for the universal Church. For their refusal, More and Fisher were condemned to imprisonment for life. John Fisher was executed on 22 June and Thomas More on 6 July 1535. Both men were canonised on 20 May 1935.

On the left an inscription reads: TE MARTYRUM CANDIDATUS LAUDAT EXERCITUS (The white-robed army of martyrs praises you). On the right: TU REX GLORIAE CHRISTE (You are the King of Glory, O Christ). On the book which Saint Thomas More is holding is inscribed: CAESARIS CAESARI ET QUAE SUNT DEI DEO (to Caesar the things that are Caesar's and to God, those that are God's). The panel is carved in Hopton-Wood stone finished with a low polish. It was given in memory of Mrs Boland of the Catholic Truth Society, whose little pamphlets are usually available at the entrance to Catholic churches in Britain. After her death in 1937 Eric Gill was approached to carry out the work in her memory and he later wrote (1947) of his approach to the project:

'As this is the chapel of the English Martyrs, it seemed appropriate that the altar panel should have a crucifix, and figures of Saint John Fisher and Saint Thomas More, and to portray Our Lord reigning from the Cross as Priest and King. The Cross is held up by two angels and has moulded finials; this is to show that it is a symbolic cross and not a picture of the Crucifixion. Saint John Fisher is clothed in the chasuble and wears the mitre and holds a crozier. Saint Thomas More is clothed in his long coat, and his favourite monkey is crouching at his feet with hands uplifted. Saint Thomas had a little zoo of his own at the house in Chelsea and among the inhabitants was a little monkey of whom (sic) he was very fond. The sculptor has introduced the little animal as indicating by its very incongruity the deeply human character of the Saint - so completely unlike the conventional stained glass window figure.

Moreover the animal does by its caricature of humanity remind us of our lowly state.'

Later Cardinal Griffin had the monkey removed, considering the note of whimsy out of place beside the cross of salvation. There was, it seems, a great furore at the time with the eventual result that the Art and Architecture Committee was re-established, which continues to watch over such matters.

Sir Giles Gilbert Scott was asked to prepare scheme for mosaics for the whole chapel. Gill objected to Scott's frame for the reredos and canopy. The Art and Architecture committee Committe agreed and the scheme for the mosaic was dropped.

New work in Saint George's Chapel was begun and completed in 1931, in time for the celebration of the Solemn Triduum (three days of liturgical celebration) in honour of the English Martyrs. It was greatly admired at the time. The richness of the floor is due to the choice of component marbles: red Griotte, Spanish pink, Belgian black and Italian white. The predominant reds and pinks were chosen to suggest the rose as emblem of England, and the stylised flower, inlaid with lapis lazuli and mother-of-pearl, is seen at the centre of the pavement. An ornate grille of polished bronze with enamels of champlevé cloisonné divides the chapel from the north aisle. In its lower part, space is allowed for those in the aisle wishing to kneel and pray before the shrine of Saint John Southworth, whose body lies in a glass casket just inside the chapel grille. The prie-Dieu, or kneeler, has an armrest of rosewood inlaid with ivory, padouk and ebony. The body of the martyr - of great importance to the Archdiocese of Westminster (as also to the Catholics of Lancashire) - was translated to this chapel on 1 May 1930.

The following year, work on the chapel was once more taken in hand under the direction of the Cathedral architect, Laurence H. Shattock. The chief feature

The reliquary of Saint John Southworth, 'Parish Priest of Westminster'

was to be a figure of Saint George, patron of England, to be set in the north wall. It was decided to execute this figure life-size in deep relief, Saint George taking his place as chief patron of the chapel, as well as providing a link between the chapel and the war dead, whose names appeared on the panels on each side. (Further memorials to the fallen were added later, including a tablet to Polish servicemen who gave their lives in the 1939-45 War.) The insertion of the relief meant rearranging the panels bearing the names symmetrically on either side. In place of the large column which stands beneath the windows in the other chapels, the architect provided for a carved corbel to be located near the springing of the ceiling.

The sculpted relief was the work of Captain Lindsey Clarke who had already provided the Cathedral with a group of figures for the Christmas crib in 1927 and the bas-relief of the Precious Blood at the back of the High Altar in 1929. The estimate for the new relief with its surrounding moulding was £400. The cost of the remainder of the marble-work brought the sum to be raised to £798. As part of the project, Shattock designed the bronze and enamel intention box, made by Blunt & Wray Ltd which is located in the east wall above the shrine of the martyr's body on the aisle side of the bronze screen.

Saint John Southworth, whose remains lie here, vested in an eighteenth-century red chasuble and an alb trimmed with lace, was born in Lancashire in 1592. He went to the English seminary of Douai, France.

He is next heard of in March 1630 in the Southwark prison known as the Clink where his name is listed in a banishment order for being a priest. Whether or not he left the country is not known, but during the devastating plague of 1636 he and the Jesuit Henry Morse organised the relief of the marginalised slum-dwellers in the district of Westminster, where the rest of his life was spent ministering to the Catholic poor. He came to be known as 'the Parish Priest of Westminster'. Southworth was arrested and imprisoned in October 1636 where he continued his ministry to the plague-stricken; he was released the following June but recommitted in November. His name is found again amongst the prisoners in the Clink in June 1640. It seems probable that he was in and out of prison until his final arrest in 1654. He was in bed when they came for him. At his trial on 26 June, John Southworth admitted he was a Catholic priest and the jury had no alternative under the law but to find him guilty of priesthood for which the penalty was death. The judge, Sergeant William Steele, is said to have been in tears, at length composing himself to pronounce the unavoidable sentence.

The Portuguese ambassador approached the Lord Protector for a reprieve but to no avail. On 28 June 1654 Father John was hanged and quartered at Tyburn, one of the last to suffer the death penalty under penal laws. His body was purchased from the hangman by the Spanish ambassador for forty shillings. The ambassador, Don Fluento de Cardenas, was apparently acting on behalf of the Howards of Norfolk who at the time had a home at Arundel House in the Strand. Evidence exists that the body was skilfully embalmed by a surgeon named James Clarke. Father Godfrey Anstruther, OP in his book *A Hundred Homeless Years* (1958) suggests that Father Philip Howard was in London at the time of the execution of John Southworth, and that he was responsible for having the embalming carried out and

The altarpiece by Eric Gill, 1947, shows Christ as Priest and King

the body transported to the continent. At all events, the remains were conveyed to the English College at Douai in northern France, where it was enshrined under the altar of Saint Augustine in the old chapel until around 1725. The body was then moved to a newly-built college chapel - probably placed in its lead coffin at that time - remaining there until the outbreak of the French Revolution in 1793. As a precaution, the body of the martyr was secretly re-interred elsewhere on the site, ahead of the confiscation of the buildings and the closure of the college for ever. The remains were only re-discovered by labourers building a new road through the area during 1926-27.

On 15 July 1927 they uncovered a leaden coffin containing the body of a man, believed to be that of Saint John Southworth. After protracted legal proceedings in France, it was brought to England where an official post-mortem was carried out on 14 December 1929. The following day Father John Southworth was solemnly beatified in Rome - declared one of the blessed of God. On 30 April 1930 the sacred relics were brought to London where they rested for a brief period at the convent

in Tyburn, a short walk from the place of John Southworth's execution - now Marble Arch. Finally they were brought to Westminster Cathedral, in the heart of his ancient 'parish', encased in a glass feretory and installed in Saint George's Chapel on 1 May 1930. On 25 October 1970, John Southworth was one of the Forty Martyrs of England and Wales solemnly canonised in Rome. His feast day is observed in the Cathedral and throughout the diocese on 27 June, the eve of the anniversary of his death as a martyr for the church.

Placed high on the west wall at the entrance to the Chapel of Saint George and the English Martyrs is a square mosaic by Michael Leigh completed in June 1952 and erected as a memorial to the officers and men of the Royal Army Medical Corps. The picture is inspired by two texts from the Book of Revelation, chapter 21, verse 5: '*See, I am making all things new ....*', and chapter 22, verse 2: '*On either side of the river is the tree of life, with its twelve kinds of fruit, producing a fruit each month, and the leaves of the tree are for the healing of the nations.*' The iconography is obscure, purporting as it does to represent Christ the Divine Healer.

Chapel of the Holy Souls

Completed in close accord with the wishes of John Bentley, the marble work of this chapel follows the architect's detailed plans

(Opposite)
Symons' altarpiece, 1904, in opus sectile, shows the Divine Redeemer enthroned in majesty

(Overleaf)
Symons' mosaic includes the figure of Adam ensnared by the coils of the serpent

West of the Chapel of Saint George we come to the Holy Souls Chapel and discover a completed scheme that includes shimmering mosaics and rich, dark marble. Here in the last of the Cathedral's chapels we encounter the most complete realisation of one of Bentley's designs. The chapel is virtually unique with all its elements fully integrated and in harmony with Bentley's conception of the whole edifice. Every detail of the marble-work and the enclosing grille emanates from the architect. In addition, the design and cartoons for the mosaics were produced under his continuous supervision, by an artist with an intimate knowledge of his mind and masterplan. It was in a letter dated 3 March 1900 that Bentley invited his friend Christian Symons to create the decoration for this Chapel of the Holy Souls. Given that the work could not have been undertaken without close attention to biblical theology and Catholic doctrine in particular, it might be worth reviewing these concepts before examining the artistry of the chapel. In a letter about Catholic beliefs, Pope Paul VI wrote as follows about mortality and eternal life:

We believe that in Adam, all have sinned .... We believe that Our Lord Jesus Christ redeemed us by the sacrifice of the Cross from original sin and from all those personal sins to which we confess .... We believe in eternal life (and that) the souls of all those who die in the grace of Christ - whether they must still make expiation in the fire of Purgatory, or whether, from the moment they leave their bodies they are received by Jesus into Paradise like the good thief - go to form that People of God which succeeds death; death which will be totally destroyed on the day of the Resurrection when these souls are reunited with their bodies.

We believe in the communion of all the faithful in Christ, whether they still make their pilgrim way on earth, whether, their life over, they undergo purification or they enjoy the happiness of heaven. One and all, they go to form the one Church. We likewise believe that in this communion we are surrounded by the love of a compassionate God and his saints, who always listen to our prayers, even as Jesus told us, 'Ask and you shall receive' (Luke 10:9-10, John 16:24). Confessing this faith and sustained by this hope, we await the resurrection of the dead and the life of the world to come ...
(*The Credo of the People of God*, Pope Paul VI, 1968.)

The chapel sets out to epitomise the Church's doctrine regarding Purgatory and the souls of those who have died in Christ. 'The Holy Souls' is the name given to those who, having passed through death, await the final purification which will enable them to enter heaven. They do not suffer uncomforted. United in the Communion of Saints they are assisted by the prayers of the living and those already sanctified who have gone before them into glory. In the lines of Cardinal Newman:

Angels to whom the willing task is given
Shall tend and nurse and lull thee as thou liest;
And Masses on the earth, and prayers in Heaven,
Shall aid thee at the throne of the Most Highest.
(*The Dream of Gerontius*)

Bentley told Symons he was convinced that they should 'avoid anything pictorial and the drawing must be severe and very Greek in character'. True to his wishes, the decoration symbolises theological concepts associated with life after death - rather than allowing scene-setting to take over. The primary theme of the chapel is expressed by the two figures which dominate the spandrels of the barrel vault. These figures are Adam, the progenitor of the human race and the author of its ruin - and Christ, the second Adam, restorer of the broken fortunes of mankind. Adam is shown standing in an open grave with his spade beside him beneath the fateful tree. The serpent is coiled around him with the forbidden fruit in its jaws in the form of a skull. Opposite Adam stands Christ, newly

risen from the tomb, holding the standard of his victory surmounted by a cross. The words SICUT IN ADAM OMNES MORIUNTUR and ITA IN CHRISTO OMNES VIVIFICABUNTUR (for as all die in Adam, so all will be made alive in Christ)(1 Cor 15:22) suitably interpret the two figures.

It was Symons who suggested the account of 'the three young men in the burning, fiery furnace' although it also conforms with an ancient iconographic tradition in mortuary chambers and chapels. The subject comes from chapter 3 of the book of Daniel, in which Shadrach, Meshach and Abednego elect to be cast into a furnace rather than worship an idol set up by King Nebuchadnezzar. Their attitude to the tyrant is 'Do your worst, we are not afraid. Our God can deliver us, but even if he does not, we still refuse to worship the image.' Thrown into the fire they remain unscathed. Bentley agreed that the scene should adorn the back elevation of the chapel. What might appear to be an angel is Christ bearing bread and wine. Above this scene is King Nebuchadnezzar of Babylon, conferring with his wise men, asking them, NONNE TRES VIROS MISIMUS IN MEDIUM IGNIS COMPEDIOS? ('Was it not three men that we threw bound into the fire?') and exclaiming, ECCE EGO VIDEO QUATTUOR VIROS SOLUTOS ET AMBULANTES IN MEDIO IGNIS, ET NHILI CORRUPTIONIS IN EIS EST, ET SPECIES QUATTUOR SIMILIS FILIO DEI ('But, I see four men unbound, walking in the middle of the fire, and they are not hurt; and the fourth has the appearance of a God') (Daniel 3:91,92).

Above the altar - directly opposite - the representation of Purgatory was Bentley's idea. The Archangel Raphael (the name in Hebrew means 'God has healed', 1 Chronicles 26:7) escorts penitent souls through the cleansing crucible, of which the fiery furnace on the facing wall is an Old Testament type and counterpart. On the right-hand side the Archangel Michael stands, crowned and holding the Devil (a

Cerberus-like creature) by a heavy chain, beckoning a man to come out of the fire. The latter is one of five figures moving across the picture in progressive stages of purification. A sixth emerges from behind Saint Michael's wings while the seventh, an individual soul but also an embodiment of the Church Triumphant, stands at the centre, receiving a crown from the hand of God.

Surrounding this figure and lower on the mosaic is a three-part Latin inscription based on the first letter of Saint Paul to the Corinthians, chapter 3 verses 13-15. *The work of each builder will become visible for the day will disclose it, because it will be revealed with fire and the fire will test what sort of work each has done. If what has been built on the foundation survives, the builder will receive a reward, if the work has been burned up, the builder will suffer loss. The builder will be saved but only as through fire.* (Rather a hefty text to choose to set in mosaic tesserae - even in the terser Latin!)

The front of the arch bears the inscription REQUIEM AETERNAM DONA EIS DOMINE ET LUX PERPETUA LUCEAT EIS (Eternal rest give unto them O Lord, and let perpetual light shine upon them). On the underside of the arch, above the altar we read the words BEATI MORTUI QUI IN DOMINO MORIUNTUR AMODO IAM DICIT SPIRITUS UT REQUISCANT A LABORIBUS SUIS: OPERA ENIM ILLORUM SEQUUNTUR ILLOS (Blessed are the dead who from now on die in the Lord: 'Yes,' says the Spirit, 'they will rest from their labours, for their deeds follow them!' Revelation 14:13. The entire tableau is a reminder that the late Victorian Church had a certain fascination with eschatology. *The Dream of Gerontius* by John Henry Newman, about the passing of a Christian soul from death to eternal life, was published in 1865. The choral work by Edward Elgar, based on Newman's poem, had its first performance in Westminster Cathedral on 6 June 1903, a year after this chapel was completed.

On either side of this central inscription are brief, non-scriptural Latin texts recording the corporal and spiritual works of mercy. The 'corporal works' (right) read from the top: to feed the hungry; to give drink to the thirsty; to clothe the naked; to house the homeless; to visit the sick; to visit the imprisoned; to bury the dead. The seven 'spiritual works' (left) appear in the following order from the top: to counsel the doubtful; to instruct the ignorant; to convert the sinner; to comfort the sorrowful; to bear wrongs patiently; to forgive injuries; to pray for the living and the dead. These, the first part of the mosaic to be erected, were, for Bentley, the key to the whole chapel.

Symons' altarpiece itself, with vibrant colours in *opus sectile* was finished by the artist in 1904. It represents Christ enthroned, his gaze at once tender and intense. He shows his five wounds, a repetition of the primary dedication of the entire Cathedral. The Redeemer is clad in a wine-dark robe, reminiscent of Isaiah 63:1, *'Who is this that comes from Edom, from Bozrah in garments stained crimson, who is this so splendidly clothed ....Why are your robes red, your garments like theirs who tread the winepress?'* Of this verse The Jerusalem Bible commentary states: 'Yahweh is represented as one who treads the grapes, his garments stained red. But what he has been treading are 'the nations, whose blood has spattered him and who are represented by Edom (a name that means 'red').' Some emend Edom and Bozrah in this verse and translate Who is this that comes all in red, in crimson garments like a wine-harvester?' Below him the Virgin Mary and Saint Joseph, who, together with Jesus in the centre, are the Holy Family of Nazareth. The mother and foster-father of Christ intercede for the Holy Souls with upraised hands. Behind the throne, the golden cross of the background displays the symbolic Alpha and Omega. These capitals of the first and last letters of the Greek alphabet which recur in Church iconography signify the beginning and the end of the cosmic creative process. ('I am the Alpha and the

Omega' says the Lord God, who is, and who was and who is to come, the Almighty)(Revelation 1:8; 21:6; 22:13).

The throne is surrounded by the six-winged seraphs of the apocalyptic vision - the seven spirits before the throne (Tobit 12:15; Revelation 8:2), the whole picture set against a background of deep blue with a pattern of interlaced gold circles. In the lower corners of the altarpiece are two small panels representing the donor of the chapel, Mary Etheldreda Walmesley and her husband Robert. The benefactress provided a down-to-earth £10,000 for the chapel to be completed. She was born in Rome on 8 November 1855, the eighth child of Thomas Weld-Blundell, of Ludworth Castle, Dorset, and his wife, Mary Teresa, daughter of William Vaughan of Courtfield. In the altarpiece Mrs Walmesley kneels on the left in the habit of the Order of Saint Benedict with Robert her husband on the right. Following the death of Robert Walmesley she entered the Benedictine Abbey at East Bergholt where she was clothed in the religious habit on 17 November 1898 by her brother, Dom Adrian Weld-Blundell. A year later she made her monastic profession, her cousin Cardinal Herbert Vaughan performing the ceremony. Mother Etheldreda, as she was latterly known, became prioress of the convent and died on 7 March 1934.

In the panel on the right, Robert Walmesley kneels before the *vernicle* - the towel of Veronica. A pious legend which gained popularity in the fourteenth century speaks of a woman taking pity on Jesus on the way to his Crucifixion and wiping his face, after which an image of his countenance remained on the towel she had offered him. The inscription reads VERA EFFIGIES SACRI VULTUS D N JESU CHRISTI (a true image of the sacred face of Our Lord Jesus Christ). The face of Christ in his suffering was an important preoccupation of Christian Symons at the time this chapel was being decorated. He would later work on a design for a mosaic of the face of Jesus in the Shrine of the Sacred Heart. His most

The experience of Purgatory is shown as a liberating process for every soul on its way to glory

The illustrious three young men (Daniel 3:91), unscathed in 'the fiery furnace' of King Nebuchnezzar's wrath, encounter a Christ-like figure amid the flames

prominent work in Westminster Cathedral is the great rood, or crucifix, which hangs in the nave. Interest in the work of W. Christian Symons has been growing in recent years, and a comprehensive exhibition of his paintings toured Britain in 1994.

In the pavement of the chapel the arms of the Walmesley family quartering those of Weld-Blundell are set into the marble at the foot of the altar steps. They include Siena, Canadian blue, and *grande brèche de Klaber* to provide the required hues of *or, azure,* and *gules.* On either side of the altar above the vaulted (apse-headed) niches are two panels, again in *opus sectile,* displaying the words IUSTORUM ANIMAE IN MANU DEI SUNT (The souls of the just are in the hand of God) and on the right ET NON TANGET ILLOS TORMENTUM MORTIS (And the torment of death shall not touch them).

The decoration of this chapel, completed in accordance with the precise and detailed instructions of John Bentley, is notable for the harmony of its design. The mosaics combine with the enclosing grille of gilt bronze, the marble-work, bronze candlesticks and crucifix forming a unity. The choice of marbles is appropriately sombre, giving a generally black and white scheme, complemented in the mosaics by the use of silvered tesserae rather than the usual gold. The column of black Norwegian labradorite at the entrance to the chapel sets the tone of mourning, combined with hope in the Resurrection expressed by a pure white capital. On the north wall, a column of figured white pavonazzo carries the arches of the window openings, its swag-decorated base resting on a dark pedestal of Tinos green. A wide variety of marbles are installed including broad slabs of *verde mare* on the west and north walls, grey Zola, red Levanto and imperial yellow. Notable effects derive from the figured grey of *Bardiglio fiorito*, seen in the floor and altar steps, the Greek cipollino of the dossal, the mensa of breccia and the distinguished altar front with its panels of

black and gold *portoro.* Running across the floor are lines of *rosso antico* while the green marble of Genoa covers the wall on either side of the altar below the level of the first cornice.

The marble facing of the window arches was ordered from Messrs Whitehead in December 1901 and completed in April 1902, the year in which the brick shell of the Cathedral could be said to be complete. In March they started a second contract for the main marble-work which they completed in nine months. By June the chapel was filled with scaffolding for the work of George Bridge and the women mosaicists on his team to start the application of tesserae. Portions of the design had been prepared in advance on canvas in the firm's Oxford Street studios which John Bentley visited frequently during the winter before his death in 1902. After eighteen months of continuous work the mosaicists completed the encrustation by November 1903. J. Whitehead & Sons finished the main marble-work in nine months. The firm laid the floor between March and June 1906 and in 1908 the chapel received its bronze gilt grille, the design of which had been fully detailed by the architect.

From the summer day in 1895 when the first stone had been laid, until the end of his life, John Bentley was totally absorbed by Westminster Cathedral, although he had other commissions including one project for a Gothic Cathedral in America. Every morning, on the journey between his home in Clapham and offices near the Strand he called in at the site. At the end of each day he was again to be seen - a solitary figure in frock coat and tall hat -strolling alone amidst the scaffolding and masonry, noting the day's progress in the fading light. The burden of responsibility he carried alone and the strain was undoubtedly immense.

John Bentley's health was delicate from 1898 onwards when he suffered a stroke at the age of 59. For weeks he had lain almost helpless, his speech impaired,

Arms of the donor set into the marble pavement

(Previous page)
(Left) Angels bearing exhortations from 'the corporal and spiritual works of mercy'
(Right) Christ, 'the new Adam', holds aloft the standard of his victory

although with the assistance of one of his daughters (almost certainly Winefride, his biographer) he carried on his correspondence and the process of decision-making. The sick-bed, she tells us, was littered with marble samples, and clay models of carving from the mason's yard were strewn about the room. By the autumn of that year, much recovered, he took up his normal punishing routine once more, admitting to himself that he would probably never see the opening of the Cathedral.

All his life John Bentley had been an insatiable worker, showing little interest in holidays. From the time of his recovery until the end of his life he worked ever more urgently under enormous pressure. He rapidly laid down the general scheme of the revetment for the nave, sanctuary and side chapels and produced the designs for the marble pavements. A decision from his client to substitute a woodblock floor pained him greatly. Similarly the Cardinal's decision to order from Rome a pulpit for the nave and a throne for the sanctuary was taken without consultation and the architect felt this keenly. Nevertheless he pressed on. On 1 March 1902 the whole shell of the Cathedral was completed, except for the last 50 feet of the campanile. This work on the tower would have been finished, if a hard frost had not prevented all building work for three weeks. On 28 February, the first slabs of marble had started to go up in the Chapel of Saint Gregory. It was all John Bentley would ever see of the revetments although he had envisaged everything we see in the Cathedral today and much more.

He was at his office as usual on Saturday, March and spent part of the morning showing the drawings of Symons' great crucifix and other work to Charles Hadfield who had come from Sheffield to see him. 'He was full of enthusiasm about the Cathedral's progress', says this friend, who noted how well he seemed that morning, speaking with less difficulty and talking of a probable visit to the United States in the summer. For the architect,

Saturday was a full working day, so his leaving the office in the early afternoon was unusual. It is thought that the last conscious hours of his life were spent in the Cathedral. Did he stand there alone in the Chapel of the Holy Souls, pondering its walls in the thin winter light, examining the window arches - the first marble-work of the Whitehead masons - and picturing what we now see? This would account for the lapse of time between his leaving 13 John Street off the Strand and arriving at the house of friends in Grosvenor Road. It was there that he collapsed. A priest from the Cathedral arrived to minister to him before he was taken home. At dawn on Sunday morning, without regaining consciousness, John Bentley passed away. The Cardinal's secretary Mr Austin Oates was with Vaughan at breakfast that morning when the news came. He reported that the Cardinal was overwhelmed by the tragic suddenness of his passing for which he was totally unprepared.

At the funeral Mass in Saint Mary's Church, Clapham, he spoke warmly of the man who had built him a noble Cathedral in seven years: 'Bentley was a poet. He saw and felt the beauty, the harmony and meaning of his artistic creations. He had a passion for truth and sincerity in his work. He was gentle and considerate in dealing with suggestions and objections. But he would have his own way whenever it was a question of fidelity to his standards. He was the best of architects for a cathedral or for any work that was to excel in artistic beauty. Whatever he produced was stamped with his own individuality. It was alive and original and he had a genius for taking infinite pains.'

Cardinal Vaughan pledged publicly and solemnly to carry on the work along the lines Bentley had indicated and for which he had left ample guidance. In view of this promise, it was decided to set up a new firm of John F. Bentley, Son & Marshall. John A. Marshall - who had become Bentley's chief assistant - became a partner, and provision was made for the architect's second son, Osmond, to join

Sicilian gold chalice by Giacinto Omodei, Palermo, 1691. A masterpiece of intricate chasing with myriad figures portraying the souls in Purgatory at the base, angels in the middle, and an entire 'Last Supper' scene on the cup

him as soon as he had gained sufficient experience.

The following year, the Jesuit Herbert Lucas wrote in *The Tablet*, that the designs in the Holy Souls Chapel could be taken as 'providing a norm for the completion of the vast undertaking of which they are the overture'. Throughout the twentieth century continuing work on the interior has taken account of Bentley's meticulous drawings and detailed instructions, particularly in marble-work, while the lofty interior, intended in due course to be ablaze with mosaic, awaits completion at the end of the century as it did at the beginning. But as with the great cathedrals of the Middle Ages, this is a task that spans the generations. One day it will be finished. Everyone who cares about the Cathedral, for whatever personal reason, need have no doubt about that. After all, Westminster Cathedral is a *building of faith*.

Mosaic archway above the altarpiece emblazoned with the works of mercy

Visions of the Future

A Victorian vision of how the Cathedral might look when completed

When we say Westminster Cathedral is incomplete we are not talking of the exterior which was a *fait accompli* as soon as the tower had risen to its full height in 1903. The challenge of today comes inside where the domes and upper walls remain unfinished.

Throughout this century the marble revetment of the lower half of the interior has gone ahead steadily so that it is now almost complete. In 1995 plans were set in motion for the completion of the Vaughan Chantry and Saint Edmund's crypt chapel. The main decorative work to be addressed however is the 22,000 square feet of the vaulting and domes of the nave. Some would be content to see this area remain unfinished in view of the solemn, dark and somewhat mysterious quality of these vast spaces.

It should be borne in mind that Bentley characterised Westminster Cathedral as a 'veneered' building - within and without. He was clearly acting in conformity with this principle when he used mosaics for surface covering as they are found in Santa Sophia. It was always the architect's intention that the mosaics would eventually be completed. He made provision for access to the domes by mosaic workers when he placed doors off the clerestories (called monk's dormitories in Cathedral lore) facing into the topmost spaces of the nave. These would lead on to a false ceiling erected for the duration of the work. It was estimated in 1903 that the mosaics would take a century to finish. Had it been started then, the domes would now be ablaze with gold.

Herbert Vaughan's successor, Cardinal Francis Bourne, was committed to the pursuit of Bentley's ideal and commissioned a great deal of decorative work during his long tenure as archbishop. In 1928 he attempted to set up a school of mosaic work on the lines of Saint Mark's, Venice, to create and maintain the Cathedral mosaics. In 1931 the Cardinal visited Monreale and Palermo in Sicily for first hand experience of the mosaics for which these places are renowned.

John Bentley had always intended drawing others in the work of decorating the Cathedral. At the close of 1898, with the imminent completion of the roof, he began considering decorative schemes. He decided to commence work with the Holy Souls Chapel treating it as a prototype for the whole. In any critique of Bentley's ideals it is essential to assess the mosaic technique and characteristics of this completed chapel.

Regarding religious themes, it was clear from the outset that a comprehensive plan would be needed for the entire mosaic surface, which could then be undertaken by degrees and systematically. Cardinal Vaughan, for example, had expressed the wish that the nave might tell the story of the Catholic Church in England. An article on the subject in *The Tablet* of 17 June 1899 was probably inspired, if not actually written by the Cardinal, stating that the 'biblical, allegorical, or mystical treatment of the domes, transepts, sanctuary, apse, and side chapels had better be deferred for the present.' The columns of *The Tablet* would be open to proposals for the mosaic themes of the nave and the writer proposed that one or two side chapels should be brought to completion by the proposed date of opening, 29 September 1900. It was an optimistic target. The name of Professor Seitz, a German mosaicist 'of the newer school' was put forward as a possible designer. He had recently restored the Borgia apartments in the Vatican, and decorated the choir of the basilica at Loreto but was widely considered unsuitable for the style of the Cathedral.

Seven schemes were submitted by interested parties: C. Boothman, Monsignor Moyes, Dom Aidan Gasquet, T. Longueville, Father Sydney Smith, SJ, Father Herbert Thurston, SJ, and F. Urquhart. These historical synopses included scenes to cover landmarks of British ecclesiastical history from the time of the earliest British missionaries down to the opening of the new Cathedral at Westminster. Exhaustive lists of saints were added from Saint

Alban to the sixteenth and seventeenth-century martyrs.

In an eighth scheme, Edmund Bishop proposed the principle that only genuine historical scenes should be included. Charles Weld-Blundell in a ninth scheme suggested that the Crucifixion be the central subject surrounded by martyrs from the early Church up to Tudor times.

In the tenth plan from Dudley Baxter (1900) the first dome (westwards) would illustrate the Creation of the World; the second, the Old Testament and the Old Law; the third, the Incarnation, leading to the Holy Rood of Redemption and the New Law. The fourth dome, overshadowing the sanctuary, would depict the Church and Christ's kingdom on earth. The space above the high altar would show Christ surrounded by the Blessed Virgin Mary and the apostles. Finally, in the apse heaven and the apocalypse would be depicted, focused on the Lamb of God.

Reverend Herbert Lucas, SJ, wrote in *The Tablet* of 28 December 1901 that a scheme could be devised based on themes from the writings of Saint Thomas Aquinas (*c.* 1225-74) The first dome would depict Baptism refering to the birth and infancy of Christ, *'Se nascens dedit socium'*, (being born, he gave himself as a companion). The second would be based on the Eucharist and associated miracles, *'Convescens in edulium'* (eating that which is to be eaten). The third dome would portray the sacrifice of the cross with scenes from the passion, *'Se moriens in pretium'* (dying he gives himself as a reward) and the fourth dome would show Christ the King in glory, *'Se regnans dat in præmium'* (ruling, he gives himself as the gift).

This entire discussion came to an end with the death of Bentley. The passing of the architect came as a paralysing blow to progress and no scheme has ever been adopted. As the decades rolled by the question of subject matter was supplanted by that of cost and the spectre of vast expenditure which would be required to create *any* scheme.

At the beginning of a new century, however, there is an ever-expanding range of new technologies which might be considered as aids to completion. For a glimpse of possible options it is necessary to turn to architects of the present day who are working with techniques which only a short time ago were unimagined.

The Art of the Possible: Technologies for 'Space-writing'
John Outram

It is a curious fact that while modern architecture has anathematised decoration, techniques for large-scale surface decoration are multiplying. One can, for example, either transfer a hand-drawn design into a computer or draw directly into the electronic medium. This design, which can be at least 15 feet by 10 feet in real size with the latest software, such as 'Live Image', can then be manipulated in the computer, changed into a 'mosaic' finish, complete with squared tesserae, and printed out as 'paper tiles' from a colour laser copier. The pigment from these sheets can then be transferred to a plaster surface by a process called 'Metamark Monoprinting'. This pigment can then be lacquered. The pigment has been tested and is extremely lightfast, with an indeterminate life-span in a shadowed environment like a ceiling. If a sheet requires replacing it is merely printed out from the computer archive and then re-transferred on to the plaster surface.

What ends up on the plaster surface is pigment only. The paper that is printed from the copier is thrown away.

Another technique can inkjet print off 10 inches by 8 inches photographic transparencies to relatively fine detail on to pieces of canvas or plastic that are 30 feet long by 9 feet wide. I do not have a test result on the longevity of these inks as yet. But the Printing Industry Research Association 'Blue Wall' test holds its samples at 45° to the horizon in open sunlight. The light on any ceiling is thousands of times less than this. There are three aspects to large-scale inscriptional technologies of a kind useful to architects. Firstly there is the creation of the image. Secondly there is the manipulation of the image. Thirdly there is the transfer of the image into a lasting form. The first two technologies are in rapid development in the printing industry. Images can be scanned into a computer, changed, organised and broken down ready to be printed as individual sheets of paper that will 'tile' into the original large-scale design. The researches of my own firm have, therefore, been mainly concentrated into the third aspect: fixing images in a permanent form.

We began our researches with stencil. This old technique is really a form of large scale printing, where each colour is put on separately. If the pigment is thick and pure and bound with casein it will last for centuries. Then there is fresco, again a very long-lasting technique and not as expensive or as slow as one might imagine. Fresco costs between five to ten times as much as the most complex stencil or the most expensive wall-paper. Then we explored inlaid plaster and concrete; masonry marquetry, we could call it. We are using inlaid concrete on the exterior of a building in Cambridge, England, and one in Houston, Texas; both for universities.

The most cost-effective technique that we have found is monoprinting, in which a printed page transfers its image to another surface. It is solid and lightfast. Its limitation is the size of the pages and the difficulty of registering the edges of neighbouring pages so that they form a seamless join into a continuous sheet. If the 'joins' can be disguised as joints in an apparently 'tiled' surface this problem can be 'designed out'.

Large-scale printing is the latest technology to become commonly available with sheets up to 200 feet long and 4 feet wide being possible in heavy paper or plastic. These can then be fixed side by side to create graphics of truly vast size.

In short there are very many ways to decorate a wall or a ceiling with designs which can be as complex or as simple as the artist can imagine. Invariably, today, it is not the technology, or the money that is lacking, but the literacy, willpower and experience of the commissioning body.

In the case of Westminster Cathedral the original plan for mosaic decoration, had it been carried out to the original timetable, would be coming to its completion date at the millenium, roughly 100 years later. It seems appropriate to use twentieth-century technology, created by the culture that failed to support the original ambition, to shortcut and meet the proposed completion deadline for the Cathedral ceilings. There is probably no other practical way to decorate the vaults.

As to whether these vaults *should* be decorated, one can only say that 'figura', the surface of a building, is its intelligence: 'forma', the three-dimensionality of a building, is its body. Form renders architecture credible (the 'doubting Thomas' factor). Figure renders it intelligible. This is why figuration has been absent from twentieth-century architecture. We have been asked to *believe* in 'the Future'. But the Future has never been vouchsafed *intelligibly*. Belief is not enough. It has crumbled under the strain of supporting actions, and ways of living, that make no sense. A culture that can explain itself can describe itself and picture itself. Such a culture can employ the pictorial, iconographical, intellectual, aspect of architecture.

Mosaic, it is true, has no modern technical substitute. However, if what matters are the images and their meanings and cross-references, if there is a desire to use an interior to bring ideas into a relation to each other and to our bodies both singular and ecclesiastical, then there are techniques available today to effect this at an expenditure in human labour which makes it altogether practical.

The Liturgical Treasury

For a church that is no more than a hundred years old, it is perhaps surprising to find that Westminster Cathedral's treasury includes a number of important artefacts stretching back over 600 years: a piece of Byzantine silk from the shroud of Saint Edward the Confessor, a mitre associated with Saint Thomas à Becket, a prayer book of Mary Tudor, the last Catholic Queen of England, a gold chalice dating to the time of the Reformation Parliament and King Henry VIII, a gold pyx from the time of Charles I. The treasury contains these items because the continuity of faith ensured such survivals, with certain of the old Catholic families handing down their few liturgical treasures from a dimly-remembered past. Only when the Cathedral and other new churches were being built, did they consider the option of returning such possessions to the care of the Church. Although many items had been in use in private chapels, with the return to legality of worship according to the Roman Rite, Westminster Cathedral must have seemed a worthy repository for certain historic and sacred objects. Some date back to the English College at Douai, France, founded in 1569, yet reached the Cathedral via Saint Edmund's College, Ware, Hertfordshire, established in 1793. Some items have been in the possession of former Archbishops of Westminster, some were gifts of popes or kings, others were specially commissioned.

Catalogue

Manuscripts

1. **Westminster Cathedral,**
    Treasury MS 1
    by Michelle Brown

Book of Hours
France (Tours?); late 15th-early 16th century. *Latin.* Stylistically and textually this volume resembles Bodleian, MS Liturg 80, and was probably made for use in or near Tours.

Books of Hours were the most popular volumes used in private devotions from the 13th-16th centuries and enjoyed particular popularity in France and Flanders. Also known as horae or primers, they essentially represented a shorter version of the devotions performed by religious at the eight canonical hours, thereby assisting the laity to participate in the prayer-life of the Church by following a similar round of devotions.

A 17th-century *ex libris* inscription ('*Bibliothecae communitatis Archicaenobii praemonstratensis*', f. 1) indicates ownership by the canons of Prémontré at that time. However, the binding carries the arms of the French diplomat, Philippe de Bethune, Comte de Selles et de Charost (died 1649), and Ker has noted that inscriptions in Bethune books, such as the Prémontré inscription noted above, are often suspect. See N.R. Ker, *Medieval Manuscripts in British Libraries. I. London* (1969), pp 415-16; L. Delisle, *Cabinet des manuscrits*, i (1868), pp 267-9; E. Olivier, *Reliures Armoriees Françaises* (1924), pl. 422.

ff. i+132+ii. 175 × 122mm. Written space 112 × 70mm. Secundo folio: 'est et'. Ruled in ink for single columns of 18 lines. Gatherings (18) of 8, except 3⁴, 5⁸ (wants 1 before f. 29), 6⁸ (wants 1 before f. 36), 8⁸ (wants 3 and 6, ff. 51, 56), 9⁸ (wants 6 before f. 62), 10⁶, 11⁸ (wants 8, blank, after f. 76), 17¹⁰, 18⁴ + two leaves after 4 (ff. 127-132). Script is a French 'bastard secretary'. 17th-century binding of red morocco with arms of Bethune, and interlaced 'PP' beneath a coronet repeated at corners and on spine. Marbled endpapers. Probable 19th-century Westminster Cathedral shelf-mark, 'G.3.10'.

Contents:
1. ff. 1-5v. Gospel sequences.
2. ff. 6-8v. Prayer to the Blessed Virgin Mary, '*Obsecro te ...*'
3. ff. 9-11v. '*O intemerata ... orbis terrarum. De te enim ...*'
4. ff. 12-13v. Prayer to the Blessed Virgin Mary, '*Stabat mater dolorosa ...*'
5. ff. 13v-15. *Aves.*
6. ff. 15v-19v. Prayers to the Blessed Virgin Mary, '*Missus est Gabriel angelus ...*', '*Te deprecor ergo mitissimam ...*'
7. ff. 19v-20v. Prayer to St Francis, '*Benoist et glorieux ...*'
8. ff. 21-28v. John xviii.1-19, '*Egressus est ihesus trans torrentum cedron ...*'

9. a) ff. 29-64v. Hours of the Blessed Virgin Mary (Use of Rome), 5 leaves missing. A memoria '*de sanctis*' and hours of the Cross and of the Holy Spirit are worked in after lauds and each subsequent hour.
    b) ff. 64v-65v. '*Salve regina*'.
    c) ff. 65v-71. Psalms 44, 45, 86 for use on Tuesdays and Fridays, and Psalms 95-97 for use on Wednesdays and Saturdays.
    d) ff. 71-76. Special offices in Hours of the Blessed Virgin Mary during Advent and special forms at other seasons.
10. ff. 77-91v. Penitential Psalms and Litany of the Saints (including Sts Blasius, Lutropius, Gatianus, Lidorius, Genovefa and Radegond).
11. ff. 91-116v. Office of the Dead.
12. ff. 117-118. Prayers to the Persons of the Holy Trinity.
13. ff. 118-132v. Memorials of the Holy Trinity, Sts Michael, John the Baptist, John the Evangelist, Peter and Paul, Andrew, James, Bartholomew, Stephen, Laurence, Christopher, Sebastian, Denis, Gatianus, Martin, Nicholas, Claud, Anthony, Fiacre, Francis, Anne, Katherine, Barbara, Mary Magdalene, Margaret, Apollonia, Genovefa.

Decoration consists of the following:
1. 8-line miniatures of the Evangelists as scribes, with their symbols. f. 1 John; f. 2v. Luke; f. 3v. Matthew; f. 5 Mark.
2. 8-line miniatures of the Virgin and Child, ff. 6 and 9.
3. 8-line miniature of the Annunciation, f. 15v.
4. Half-page miniatures with full foliate borders: f.34 the Betrayal (detached miniature, apparently slightly misplaced?); f. 44 the Crucifixion; f. 45 Pentecost; f. 46 the Nativity; f.49 the Annunciation to the Shepherds (detached miniature, apparently slightly misplaced?); f. 57 the Flight into Egypt.
5. Half-page miniature with full foliate border of King David at prayer, f. 77.
6. Half-page miniature with full foliate border of the Resurrection of Christ (a man in loincloth rises from the grave, watched by three men in contemporary dress), f. 92.
7. 6-line miniatures of: f. 117 Christ holding orb; f. 118 the Holy Spirit in the form of a dove; f. 118v the Trinity, with Christ crucified.
8. 6-line miniatures with partial foliate borders depicting the saints, with their identifying attributes; f. 119 Michael; f. 119v John the Baptist, and another of John the Evangelist; f. 120 Peter; f. 120v Andrew; f. 121 Jacob; f. 121Bartholomew; f. 122 Stephen; f. 122v Laurence; f. 123 Christopher; f. 124 Sebastian; f. 125 Denis; f.125v Gatianus; f. 126 Martin (depicted with his soul ascending, accompanied by mourners); f. 126v Nicholas, and another of Claudius; f. 127v Anthony; f. 128 Fiacre; f. 128v Francis; f. 129 Anne, teaching the Blessed Virgin Mary to read; f. 129v Katherine; f. 130 Barbara; f. 130v Mary Magdalene; f. 131 Margaret; f. 131v Apollonia; f. 132v Genovefa.

The style of illumination is typical of Touronian work of this period, with rather plump, sweetly round-faced figures. Initials are set on red or blue grounds with gilded decoration.

2. **Westminster Cathedral,**
    Treasury MS3
    by Michelle Brown

Premonstratensian Ordinal and Customary
Germany; 1510. *Latin.* Copied in the Premonstratensian abbey of Arnstein, Nassau, by Brother Iohannis Anre (see colophon, ff. 1 & 69v).

An Ordinal is a manual or guide to the celebration of all or part of the liturgy. Its contents may vary and this version contains directions used by the Premonstratensian Order. A Customary contains certain rites and ceremonies for services and/or rules and disciplinary customs of an ecclesiastical establishment. The Premonstratensian Canons ('Norbertines' or 'White Friars') were founded by St Norbert at Prémontré, near Laon, in 1120. Their 'rule' of life was an austere version of that of St Augustine. For a previous description, see Ker, *Medieval Manuscripts*, pp 417-18.

Contents:
1. ff. 1-69v. Premonstratensian Ordinal. Incipit: '*Incipit Ordinarius premonstransis. De reuerentia circa altare. Pia fides habet presentiam Christi ...*'; explicit: '*... requiesant in pace. Amen ... Sit laus Deo qui est benedictus in secula seculorum. Amen*'. The Kyries and other chants are accompanied by Gothic musical notation on four-line staves (ff.62-64, 67). See M. van Waefelghem (ed.), *Liber Ordinarius* (1913), pp 23-394.
2. ff. 69v-82. Premonstratensian Customary. Incipit: '*Incipiunt consuetudines ordini Premonstratensis de tempore et de sanctis per circulum anni. Dominica prima in aduentu domini ...*'; explicit: '*... Si in dominica post ascensionem*' (ends abruptly at '*Inuentio sanctae crucis*'). Usus II, see P. Lefevre (ed.), *Coutumiers liturgiques de Prémontré du xiiie et du xive siècles*, Bibliotheque de la Revue d'histoire ecclesiastique (1953), sects I-XXIX/6.
3. ff. i+82+i. 151 × 108mm. Written space c. 115 × '*Omnibus diebus*'. Ruled in ink for single columns of 32-36 lines. Gatherings (9) of 8, except 2-5¹⁰, 6⁸ + single leaves after 1 and 8 (ff. 49, 58), 7⁶ + 5 single leaves (ff. 59-69; ff. 59, 60, 62, 67, 69 singletons), 9² + 3 single leaves (ff. 78-82; ff. 78-80 singletons). Script is a German *hybrida* with calligraphic elaboration and attenuation to top and bottom lines of script. Initials and rubrics in red (with signs of oxidisation). The scribe provided guideletters to instruct the artist. Systematic leaf-signatures (al-a4 etc.) were added contemporaneously to assist the binder in assembly. 19th-century binding of marbled boards. Front and back leaves worn, possibly acted as outer cover at some point. Probable 19th-century Westminster Cathedral shelf-mark 'H.5.39'.

1

2

3

3

3. Westminster Cathedral, Treasury MS 4
by Patricia Basing

Florilegium

A collection from mystical works ascribed to Walter Hilton, who died c. 1396, and Julian of Norwich, the female anchorite who flourished 1373-c. 1413; c. 1500. *English*. The four texts in this compilation are translated into modern English from the present manuscript, with an introduction, in *Of the Knowledge of Ourselves and of God*, edited by J. Walsh and E. Colledge (1961). See also: *Index of Printed Middle English Prose*, edited by R.E. Lewis, N.F. Blake and A.S.G. Edwards (1985); *Middle English Prose*, edited by A.S.G. Edwards (1984), pp 61-81, 97-108; Ker, *Medieval Manuscripts*, p 418. The names 'Thomas Lowe' and 'Fraunces Lowe' are repeated in different scripts, late 16th-early 17th century, f. 112v. Heraldic bookplate of James Yorke Bramston (1763-1836), Vicar Apostolic and Bishop of Usulae. Westminster Cathedral shelf-mark 'G.3.11'.

Vellum, with paper flyleaves; ff. iii + 112 + iii. Early series of foliation, probably 17th-18th century, cropped (see f. 33). 157 x 100mm. Gatherings of 8. Catchwords regular from f. 8v. Written space 113 x 73 mm. Single columns. English bastard secretary hand. Two-line blue initials with red decoration. Marginals 16th-17th century, chiefly *English*, some *Latin*. '1368' written in a 16th-17th century hand, foot of f. 1: see also front flyleaf, where 1368 is subtracted in pencil from 1821 in an early 19th-cenury hand. Brown leather binding, probably late 18th century. Marbled endpapers.

Contents:

1   ff. 1-25. *Commentary on Psalm 90*, by? Walter Hilton. Beg: 'He that wonyth in the helpe of the hyeste in helyng of god of heuen he shall dwel. He wonyth in the helpe of the hyeste'. Ends: ' ... for who so loueth me I shall loue hym. and I shall shewe me vnto hym'. *Lewis et al., Index of Printed Middle English Prose*, no. 554. Cf. H.E. Allen, *Writings ascribed to Richard Rolle* (1927), pp 196-7. Printed from other manuscripts by B. Wallner, *An exposition of* Qui Habitat *and* Bonum Est *in English*, Lund Studies in English, xxiii (1954), pp 2-50.

2   ff. 25-35v. Commentary on Psalm 91, *i-v* by? Walter Hilton. Beg: 'It is good to shryue to or lord god and synge to his name. By shryfte is the soule clensed.' Ends: ' ... ryghtfully. wysely. and godly in all thyngis'. *Lewis et al.,Index of Printed Middle English Prose*, no. 115.5. Wallner, *An exposition*, pp 52-65; the text in the present MS ends with several lines not in Wallner's edition.

3   ff. 35v-72. Extracts in 14 paragraphs from the *Scale of Perfection* of Walter Hilton. From bk 2, ch 30; bk 1, chs 40-43; bk 2, chs 30, 32-38, 27, 39, 30, 42, 41, 28; bk 1, chs 48, 70; bk 2, chs 42-46. Beg: 'Hit nedyth to a soule tht wold haue knowyng of goostly thingis'. Ends: ' ... perteynyng to this mater the whiche is open'. *Lewis, et al., Index of Printed Middle English Prose*, no. 255.

4   ff. 72v-112v. Extracts from Julian of Norwich, *Revelations of Divine Love*: Sheweings 1-2, 9, 10, 14, 15, written without a break. Beg: 'Oure gracious and goode lorde god shewed me in party 'e wisdom and 'e trewthe'. Ends: 'It is godis wyll that we sett the poynt of our thought in this blessed beholdyng as often as we may and as long'. *Lewis et al., Index of Printed Middle English Prose*, no. 321.

4. Westminster Cathedral, Treasury MS 5
by John Goldfinch

Summa angelica de casibus conscientiae (An angelic treatise about mistakes of the conscience), Angelus de Clavasio. With additions by Hieronymus Tomieli. Venice: Georgius Arrivabenus, 2 May 1495. 8°.

This comprehensive handbook for   confessors was composed by the Observant Franciscan Angelo Carletti (died 1495), and first published in his native town of Chivasso in 1486. A great success, it was reprinted numerous times, and was singled out by Luther as 'mehr als teuflisch' (more than devilish) and a copy was publicly burnt.

5. Westminster Cathedral, Treasury MS 6

Postilla super epistolas et evangelia (Treatise on the epistles and gospels), Guillermus Parisiensis. [Basel: Michael Furter, about 1502?]. 4⁰.

This guide to the liturgical epistles and gospels enjoyed enormous popularity in print, and at least a hundred editions are known from the fifteenth and early sixteenth centuries. Attributed in printed editions to Guillermus, supposedly a Paris Dominican of the early fifteenth century, the manuscript tradition suggests that the true author is probably Johann Herolt (d. 1468), prior of the Nuremberg Dominicans, and author of widely-read collections of sermons.

In an unlocalised but probably German blind-stamped binding of the early sixteenth century, apparently repaired in England with pieces taken from vellum documents of the fourteenth and fifteenth centuries.

Binding continental, with clasp fastening onto upper board. The vellum pastedowns appear to have come from the same source and carry an early 14th century *cursiva anglicana* relating to manorial accounts (records of income from individual parishes etc) for the Leet of Brinklow, County Warwickshire. Brinklow was the site of the meeting place for the Hundred of Brinklow, and the use of the title Leet implies that it was the centre of some special local jurisdiction/court. The paper pastedown overlying the vellum on the upper board carries later English court hands of 15th century date. Presumably the binding was 'doctored' soon after importation.

6. Westminster Cathedral, Treasury MS 7

Diaeta salutis (A course of life for salvation), Pseudo-Bonaventura. Venice: Caesar Arrivabenus, 24 Dec. 1518. 8°.

[Bound with:]
Ibid. *Meditationes vitae Christi* (Meditations on the life of Christ). Add: Bonaventura, *Lignum vitae* (The tree of life); Johannes de Peckham, *Canticum de sanctissimo nomine Jesu Christi*. Venice: Manfredus de Bonellis, de Monteferrato, 14 Dec. 1497. 8°.

[and]
Ibid. *Meditationes vitae Christi [Italian] Le deuote meditatione sopra la passione del nostro signore* (Devotional meditations on the passion of Our Lord) (with text ending: 'scripto di me nele prophetie e psalmi'). Venice: Lazarus de Suardis, de Saviliano, 16 Mar. 1497. 8°.

Three popular devotional works generally attributed in printed editions to Saint Bonaventure. The manuscript tradition assigns the *Diaeta* to a Guilelmus de Lanicia, supposed to be an early fourteenth century Franciscan, while the authorship of the *Meditationes* remains obscure, but is clearly a century or more later than its supposed author. The *Meditationes* are regarded as a key text for the *devotio moderna* of the fifteenth century, and the popularity

of the text is here attested by its appearance in Italian.

7. Queen Mary's Manual for blessing cramp rings and touching for the evil: the rituals of the royal healing ceremonies, written and illuminated for Mary I (1553-58)
by Janet Backhouse

Latin with rubrics in *English*. The two ceremonies, traditionally performed on Good Friday, were peculiar to the appointed monarch and were enthusiastically adopted by Mary, the first female ruler to whom they were appropriate. For general discussion of both ceremonies, with additional references, see Marc Bloch, *Les Rois Thaumaturges: étude sur le caractère surnaturel attribué a la puissance royale particulièrement en France et en Angleterre* (1924), esp. pp 178-83 and 317-20; an English edition of this book, *The Royal Touch, Sacred Monarchy and Scrofula in England and France*, translated by J.E. Anderson, was published in 1973. Mary I's performance of both rites at the Greyfriars Church in Greenwich at Easter 1556 is the subject of an eyewitness account by Marco Antonio Faitta, secretary to Cardinal Pole, see *Calendar of State Papers: Venetian*, vi pt. i (1877), pp 435-7. References to the distribution of cramp rings blessed by her occur soon after Easter in 1554 (*Calendar of State Papers: Spanish*, xii (1949), pp 173, 177 and 195), 1555 (*Calendar of State Papers: Foreign, 1553-1558* (1861), pp 164-5 and 167) and 1557 (*Calendar of State Papers: Venetian*, vi pt. ii (1881), p 1118). The manuscript was apparently intended for her personal use on these occasions. Armorial evidence (see below) places it after her marriage to Philip of Spain in July 1554.

Vellum; ff. 19 (arranged 1+4+5+1+4+4) +4 contemporary ruled blank leaves + 15 blank leaves associated with the 19th-century binding. 205 × 155mm. Secundo folio: *levamenta*. Bound in 1850 (according to a note on the flyleaf), in gold-tooled black morocco powdered with the monogram MR, the Tudor rose and the fleur-de-lys, by J. Wright (probably John Wright of Wardour Street. see Charles Ramsden, *London Bookbinders 1780-1840* (1956), p 154).

Contents:
1 'Certayn prayers to be used by the quenes heighnes in the consecration of the Cramperyngs', ff. 2-10b; printed by Gilbert Burnet, *The History of the Reformation of the Church of England*, ii (1681), pp 295-7.
2 'The Ceremonye for ye heling of them that be diseased with the Kyng Evill', ff. 12-19; printed by W. Sparrow Simpson, 'On the forms of prayer recited "at the healing" or touching for the King's Evil', *Journal of the British Archaeological Association* (1871), pp 295-8. This is apparently the earliest record of a text for the ceremony. Its rubrics, unlike those of the previous ritual, remain in the masculine form, indicating that it was copied from an earlier version used by one of Mary's predecessors, possibly Henry VII.

Decoration:
1 The arms of Philip of Spain and Mary I impaled, surrounded by the garter and surmounted by a crown, f.1. They are accompanied by the traditional pomegranate and red rose symbols of the two kingdoms. A shield of the cross of St George and a fleur-de-lys, each surrounded by a garland, are incorporated in the marginal decoration. Philip was elected to the Garter on 24 April 1554, invested on his arrival at Southampton for his marriage on 21 July, and installed as joint sovereign of the Order on 3 August.
2 Three full-page miniatures. Two represent Mary performing the two ceremonies, each facing the opening passage of the appropriate text, the blessing of cramp rings at f. 1b and the touching for King's Evil at f. 11b. Each scene corresponds

very closely to Faitta's eyewitness description mentioned above. The third, marking the division between the two elements of text at f.11, represents the Crucifixion in acknowledgement of the fact that the ceremonies were performed during the services of Good Friday.
3 Elaborate decorated borders on all four sides of both recto and verso of all of the 19 leaves of the core of the manuscript. These contain fashionable renaissance motifs of fruit and flowers, grotesque masks and other symbols. A figure of St George and the dragon appears below the miniature on f. 1b, the arms of the City of London are at f. 2b, Mary's personal motto 'Veritas temporis filia' is at f. 3, the royal arms of England appear on ff. 4 and 16b, the portcullis badge at f. 5, the Tudor rose at f. 5b and the pomegranate at f. 11b. Figures of the virtues are included in a sequence between f. 6 and f. 9b. The border decoration has been compared with panels connected with Nonsuch Palace (see E. Croft-Murry, *Decorative Painting in England 1537-1837* (1962), pls 17-20) and with ornament in Thomas Geminus, *Morysse and Damashin renewed and encreased very profitable for Goldsmythes and Embroiderars* (1548).

The miniatures of Mary, and by implication the rest of the decoration of the volume, have been attributed to Levina Teerlinc, see R. Strong et al., *Artists of the Tudor Court: the Portrait Miniature Rediscovered, 1520-1620* (1983), pp 52-7, this manuscript no. 39. Mistress Teerlinc, a daughter of the famed Flemish illuminator Simon Bening, entered the service of Henry VIII in 1546 and remained in England until her death in 1576. She is documented as a miniaturist and is known to have painted various subjects for both Mary I and Elizabeth I, including some in which the latter is seen participating in various ceremonies of the royal year. However, no miniature can as yet be associated with her beyond doubt. Furthermore the manuscript work of the mid 16th century has still to be exhaustively investigated. The attribution must therefore remain open.

Later ownership

According to a note by Gilbert Burnet (*History of the Reformation*), the manuscript was 'in Biblioth. R. Smith. Lond' when he used it in or about 1681. This was wrongly identified by Edmund Waterton ('On a remarkable incident in the Life of St Edward the Confessor, with notices of certain rings hallowed on Good Friday by the Sovereign of England', *Archaeological Journal* (1864), p 112 n 3, followed by Sparrow Simpson, 'On the forms of prayer', p 285) as the collection of Richard Smith (1566-1655), titular Bishop of Chalcedon and Vicar-Apostolic in England from April 1625. It is in fact a reference to another Richard Smith (1590-1675), a book collector widely known among contemporary scholars and bibliophiles, see C.E. Wright, *Fontes Harleiani* (1972), p 307. Smith's impressive library was not dispersed until 15 May 1682, more than seven years after his death, when it was offered for sale by Richard Chiswell at Great St Bartholomew's Close. Queen Mary's manuscript does not appear in the catalogue of the sale (a copy in the British Library, 821. i.3 (1)), but is listed on f. 5 in one of his own autograph catalogues of his collection, now Additional MS 21096 in the British Library.

The autograph catalogue and not the manuscript itself was also the source of Thomas Hearne's knowledge of Queen Mary's Ritual, mentioned in *Notes and Queries*, first series, vii (January-June 1853), p 89, from his autograph diary, Oxford, Bodleian Library, MS Rawlinson K. 55, f. 190, which has been taken as evidence of the manuscript's whereabouts early in the 18th century. The subsequent published edition of the diary, *Remarks and Collections of Thomas Hearne*, editor D.W. Rannie, v (1901), pp 143-4, entry for 27 November 1715, reveals that the catalogue was loaned to Hearne on that day by William Fleetwood (1656-1723), Bishop of Ely, whose mother had been one of Richard Smith's daughters. The Queen Mary entry is transcribed.

Against the relevant entry in Smith's autograph catalogue (Additional MS 21096, f. 5) is a note in Fleetwood's hand which reads: 'ys book, ye Executor of M. Smith (?himself) presented to K. James ye 2d. W.F..' James II came to the throne on 6 February 1685. 'The Ceremonies for Healing', claimed to be in the form used in the time of Henry VII (i.e. by the last pre-Reformation King) was published for his use in Latin and in English, see Sparrow Simpson, *op.cit.*, pp 289-90 and 301-3, where the English text is printed. The Latin varies very little from Queen Mary's text, which may well have been its immediate source.

No further reference to the manuscript has been found before it came into the hands of Cardinal Wiseman in or about 1851.

8. Westminster Cathedral, Treasury MS 9
by John Goldfinch

Breviarium Romanum: pars hiemalis (Roman Breviary: the winter section). Paris: Jacob Kerver, 28 Jan. 1571. 16°.

A rare early Tridentine breviary (the new text first appeared in 1568). Apparently the first to be printed in Paris, it is also the first to be printed in such a small easy-to-carry format. Bound in contemporary limp vellum. This breviary belonged to St John Southworth (1592-1654) and was presented by Jane McGiveney and Gerald McGiveney.

4

5

5

6

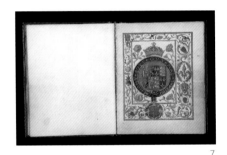

7

7

7

7

8

The Bulley Bibles

The complete Old and New Testaments of the Bible written by Edward Bulley (died 8 October 1986) between 1969 and 1983. The calligraphy is Johnson's 'Fountain' hand, slightly compressed which was based on the Winchester School of Caligraphy of the 10th century.

9. Old Testament: the Pentateuch
10. Old Testament: the Historical Books
    Vol 1
11. Old Testament: the Historical Books
    Vol 2
12. Old Testament: the Wisdom books excluding the
    Psalms
13. Psalms in the Douai and RSV
14. Old Testament: the Prophetic Books
15. Four Gospels
16. New Testament without the Gospels
17. Hymns of St Ambrose and St Augustine

Bibliography

Avril, F., and Reynaud, N., *Les Manuscrits a Peintures en France* (Bibliotheque Nationale, Paris, exhibition catalogue, 1993-4)

Backhouse, J.M., *Books of Hours* (1985)

Brown, M.P., *A Guide to Western Historical Scripts from Antiquity to 1600* (1900; 2nd edn 1993)

Brown, M.P., *Understanding Illuminated Manuscripts* (1994)

de Hamel, C., *A History of Illuminated Manuscripts* (1986)

Hughes, A., *Medieval Manuscripts for Mass and Office* (1982)

Ker, N.R., *Medieval Manuscripts in British Libraries. I. London* (Oxford, 1969)

Lewis, R.E., Blake, N.F., and Edwards, A.S.G. (editors), *Index of Printed Middle English Prose* (1984)

9

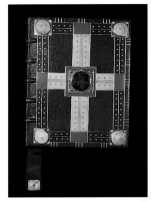

10

11

12

13

14

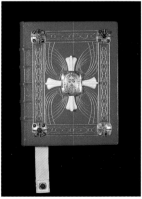

15

16

17

Ecclesiastical Plate
by Charles Truman

The Cardinal Howard Plate
An Italian silver-gilt service of ecclesiastical plate, formerly the property of Cardinal Edward Henry Howard (1829-92), and presented for the future Cathedral of Westminster on 10 November 1893, each piece decorated in the 17th-century style with scrolls, foliage, putti and clouds over a matted ground and set with bloodstones, the majority with an applied shield of arms of the Cardinal, comprising:

18. A chalice on shaped circular foot. 14^{1}/$_{8}$ inches high (48 ounces).

19. A ciborium on circular foot with domed cover. 12^{1}/$_{2}$ inches high (28^{1}/$_{2}$ ounces).

20. A ciborium, similar, smaller. 7 inches high (10 ounces).

21. A pyx. 3^{7}/$_{8}$ inches diameter (10 ounces).

22. A pyx, similar, smaller. 1^{7}/$_{8}$ inches diameter.

23. A pair of cruets on an oval stand. The stand 9^{3}/$_{4}$ inches long, the cruets 7^{3}/$_{4}$ inches high (27 ounces).

24. A pair of silver-gilt mounted cut glass decanters with silver stoppers and oval stand. The decanters 8^{3}/$_{4}$ inches high, the stand 12^{7}/$_{8}$ inches wide.

25. A crozier similarly decorated and engraved - three knops to the stem. 74 inches high.

26. Chrismatory, and circular stand. 5 inches high (12 ounces), the stand 7^{1}/$_{2}$ inches diameter (4 ounces).

27. Another smaller. 3 inches high (2^{1}/$_{2}$ ounces).

28. A thurible. 10 inches high excluding chains (32 ounces).

29. An incense boat and spoon. 6^{1}/$_{2}$ inches high (11^{1}/$_{2}$ ounces).

30. A holy water stoop and sprinkler. 11^{1}/$_{2}$ inches high with handle (24^{1}/$_{2}$ ounces).

31. A pax, with scroll handle and stand. 8^{5}/$_{8}$ inches high (18 ounces).

32. A bugia. 12^{3}/$_{4}$ inches long (9^{1}/$_{2}$ ounces).

33,34. A ewer and basin. The ewer 12^{1}/$_{4}$ inches high (17^{1}/$_{2}$ ounces). The basin 12^{1}/$_{2}$ inches diameter (14^{1}/$_{2}$ ounces).

35. A silver-gilt mounted hammer. 8^{3}/$_{4}$ inches long.

36. Four circular dishes. 9 inches diameter.

37. A knife with a Victorian blade by F. Townsend. 10^{3}/$_{4}$ inches.

38. A double-ended spatula. 9^{1}/$_{2}$ inches.

39. A shell. 5^{1}/$_{2}$ inches maximum (4 ounces).

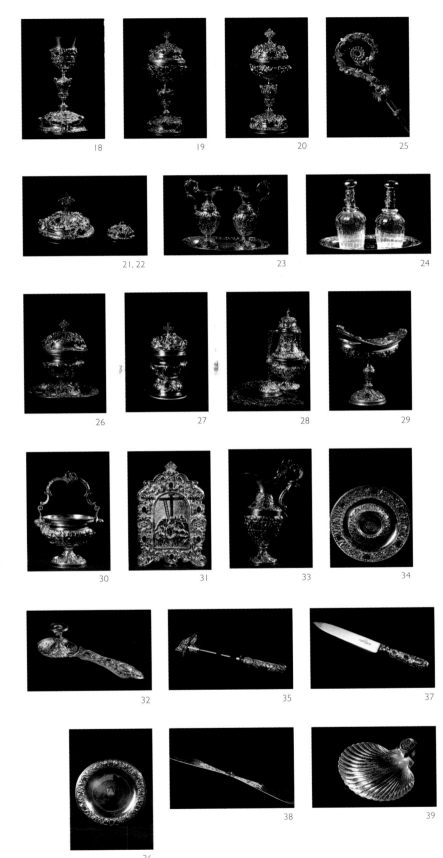

18 19 20 25

21, 22 23 24

26 27 28 29

30 31 33 34

32 35 37

36 38 39

40. An Italian silver-gilt chalice and paten, the chalice on shaped circular foot chased with putti holding symbols of the Passion between foliage and scrolls, the baluster stem with further symbols, and a similarly chased calyx to the bowl, engraved under the foot with the arms of Cardinal Howard, c. 1880, the paten unmarked. Chalice 11 inches high (22 ounces).

The Cardinal Wiseman Plate

41. A silver-gilt chalice and paten, the flared bowl with engraved bands inscribed + *Calicem Salutaris Accipiam + et Nomen Domini Invocabo* (I will take the chalice of salvation and I will call upon the name of the Lord), applied calyx of vesicas with foliated decoration on matted ground, circular stem with rope mouldings and engraved lozenge pattern enclosing floriated crosses, hexagonal knot engraved with fleurs-de-lys on a matted ground, set with carbuncles, with six bosses with engraved vine pattern on blue enamel ground. At the junction of stem and foot a frieze of engraved foliated ornament, set with turquoise, on a hexagonal lobed foot with panelled design on matted ground, enclosing six applied panels depicting the Crucifixion on red enamel, with five saints on green enamel, the intervening spaces with foliated decoration and set with carbuncles, the edge of the base with quatrefoil tracery, the paten engraved with the Holy Lamb in a roundel within a quatrefoil, within a larger roundel inscribed +*Agnus Dei qui tollis peccata mundi* (Lamb of God who takes away the sins of the world), Birmingham, 1848, with the maker's mark of John Hardman & Co, designed by A.W.N. Pugin. Chalice 10¹/2 inches high, paten 6⁵/8 inches diameter.

42. A Victorian silver-gilt ewer, in the 16th-century taste, on a circular foot cast and chased with three bands of ovolo and a wreath of foliage, the gourd-shaped body chased with foliage and strap-work, engraved twice with arms of Cardinal Wiseman, the scroll handle with winged demi-figure terminal, by C.T. and G. Fox 1846. 15³/4 inches high (35¹/2 ounces).

43. A Mexican silver-gilt shaped circular basin with fluted border, chased with scrolling foliage, flowers and shells engraved with the same arms, and with central well, on shaped circular trumpet foot, Mexico City, c. 1800, maker's mark BAIIEJO. 16 inches diameter (40 ounces).

The Cardinal Manning Plate

44. A French silver and enamel chalice and paten, the chalice on hexafoil foot, the lobed stem enamelled in opaque blues, green and red, with granulated borders, the knop set with garnets and enamelled in green with the inscription *Sanguis et acqua exivit* (Blood and water flowed forth), the bowl with further enamel and granulated borders inscribed under the base: *Ad Dei gloriam et pro S.S. Vaticani Concilii mnemosyno novi testamenti calicem in ecclesia Westmonast Cathedrali reponendum in festo S. Thomae Cantuar totius in Anglia Cleri Saecularis Patr MDCCCLXXI Obtulit Henricus Eduardus Archiep Westmonast II* (To the glory of God, and as a souvenir of the Sacred Vatican Council. Henry Edward Second Archbishop of Westminster presented [this] chalice of the New Covenant to be preserved in the Church of Westminster Cathedral on the Feast of St Thomas of Canterbury, Patron of the secular clergy in England, 1871), Paris, c. 1871, maker's mark ACS. Chalice 10⁵/8 inches high, paten 6⁷/8 inches diameter.

45. A matching ciborium, similarly decorated with

domed cover and cross finial, by the same, inscription under the base: *Ad Dei gloriam et pro S.S. Vaticani Concilii mnemosyno verbi incarnati tabernaculum in ecclesia Westmonast Cathedrali reponendum in festo S. Thomae Cantuar totius in Anglia Cleri Saecularis Patr MDCCCLXXI Obtulit Henricus Eduardus Archiep Westmonast II* (To the glory of God, and as a souvenir of the Sacred Vatican Council. Henry Edward Second Archbishop of Westminster presented [this] vessel of the incarnate word to be preserved in the Church of Westminster Cathedral on the Feast of Saint Thomas of Canterbury, Patron of the secular clergy in England, 1871, Paris, c. 1871. 14 inches high. Both presented by Cardinal Manning.

46. A chalice on moulded domed foot, with baluster stem and plain slightly everted bowl, inscribed beneath the vase *Eminentissimo ac Reverendissimo Domino Henrico Eduardo Cardinal Manning Archiepiscipo Westmonasterienis Joannes Marchio Bothae ad memoriam baptismatis Columbae Edmundi Crichton Stuart Die 5 Aprilis 1886* (To His Most Eminent and Reverend Lord Henry Edward Cardinal Manning Archbishop of Westminster from John Mark Botha in memory of the Baptism of Columba Edmund Crichton Stuart on 5 April 1886), unmarked, partly old. 10 inches high (10¹/2 ounces).

47. A large silver-gilt ciborium on circular moulded base, with broad baluster stem and short cylindrical bowl, with double-domed cover and cross finial, the foot inscribed IN MEM H.E. CARD MANNING DD LG CAN VERE AD MCMIV, unmarked. 15¹/2 inches high (56 ounces).

48. A Victorian silver-gilt and gilt metal and enamel crozier, the stem of three knopped tubes of gilt metal, the octagonal architectural knop with chamfered enamelled silver plaques depicting the Virgin and angels within gothic tracery, the scrolling terminal with applied foliage and fruiting vine, apparently unmarked. The head 12³/4 inches high. Presented by Cardinal Manning.

The Cardinal Vaughan Plate

49. A French silver-gilt chalice and paten, the chalice on circular foot chased with scrolls and masks and with applied plaques depicting the Passion, Crucifixion and Resurrection with baluster stem, the calyx chased with Faith, Hope and Charity, with grapes, corn and bullrushes between, the foot engraved 'Presented to Herbert Cardinal Vaughan. Abp. Westmon by his Cousin Chas. Weld-Blundell of Ince Blundell on the Silver Jubilee of his Episcopate AD 1897', by H. Puche, Paris, c. 1880, the paten unmarked. Chalice 12³/4 inches high, paten 6³/4 inches diameter (24 ounces).

The Bishop Fenton Plate

50. A Victorian Cellini pattern ewer cast with scrolls and strap-work after a model by François Briot, engraved with initials and with the inscription 'Hunt and Roskill, late Storr and Mortimer 4382' by Hunt and Roskill, 1867. 12¹/2 inches high (27¹/2 ounces).

51. A Victorian shaped circular basin with a border cast with lion's masks, shells and strap-work, engraved with initials and the inscription 'The Rt. Rev Patrick Fenton Bp of Amycla, V.G. of Westminster. Presented to Westminster Cathedral for the use of the Archbishops of Westminster when Pontificating in the Cathedral or any Bishop deputed by the Archbishop to Pontificate therein. This silver-gilt bowl and ewer, six silver-gilt plates after the same pattern, and a set of crystal wine and water cruets mounted in

silver-gilt with a silver-gilt tray for the same. This plate was used for the first time in Westminster Cathedral by His Eminence Cardinal Bourne, Archbishop of Westminster on the Feast of Epiphany MCMXIV', stamped 'Hunt and Roskill late Storr and Mortimer 1651' by John S. Hunt, 1850. 14 inches diameter (38 ounces).

52. Five dishes (one missing), to match, by Ball Brothers, Birmingham, 1903. 10 inches diameter.

53,54. A ewer and basin, the ewer on moulded foot, the pear-shaped body with applied collars and border, with scroll handle and everted spout, the plain basin with scalloped border, each engraved with an inscription from the Sisters of Nazareth (worn), London, 1907. Ewer 8 inches high, basin 9¹/4 inches diameter (39¹/2 ounces).

55. A silver-gilt flagon set with twenty-two carbuncles and lobed foot inscribed 'PF'. Makers' mark Mark Thomas and Edward Cox, Southampton Street, London, 1870-1871. 13 inches high (22 ounces).

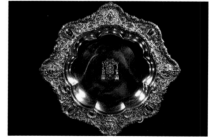

51

40

41

42, 43

44

45

46

47

48

49

50

53, 54

55

Chalices

56. A Spanish silver-gilt chalice, the hexagonal foot on pierced border and chased with symbols of the Passion on a matted ground and the name PEDRO DEAINON, and applied with a crucifix, the baluster stem with gadrooned knop with foliate girdle, the gadrooned calyx with foliage border, Saragossa, mid 15th century. 8³/₄ inches high (14¹/₂ ounces).

57. An English silver-gilt chalice on trumpet foot set with a crucifix over an engraved cross, the stem engraved with a trellis, the pierced hexafoil knop with letters MARIA in lozenges, and a Tudor rose, with shallow bowl with modern lining, English late 15th century, the outer bowl rehammered and possibly later. 6 inches high (13¹/₂ ounces). Presented by the Swaythling family.

58. A Henry VIII silver-gilt chalice, the hexafoil foot with rouletted border and engraved with a crucifixion and the inscription *Crux XPI Salva nos* (Cross of Christ, save us) and *Crux XPI Protege nos* (Cross of Christ, protect us), the hexagonal stem with rope-twist borders, the lobed knops with six marks, the bowl engraved *Vere Pcepio Corporis et sanguinis Dni Jesu Xpe* (Truly the receiving of the body and blood of Christ - prayer used at communion according to the Sarum Missal), London, 1529, maker's mark a sceptre. 6⁷/₈ inches high. See C. Oman, *English Church Plate 597-1837* (1957), plate 21. Note two other chalices by the same maker in Wylye Church, Wiltshire (1525) and Royal Scottish Museum (1527). 6³/₄ inches high (12 ounces). Presented by Baron Antonio French and his sisters Georgine and Blanche French.

59. A silver-gilt chalice and paten, the octafoil trumpet foot on pierced border, one lobe set with a medallion of the Holy Family and a donor and engraved IENNI VÃ I BINS HEFT MICH DOEN MAKREN BIT GOT VOI HEM (Jan Van Bins had me made, pray to God for him); the octagonal stem bordered above and below with foliage cast with pilasters and windows, the compressed knop chased with gadroon engraved with straps, and set with enamelled bosses containing letters 'IHESUSMA', with plain flaring bowl, engraved under the foot PAA; maker's mark a lower-case gothic D in a shaped shield struck three times. The paten is engraved in the centre with the Man of Sorrows and a cross, marked once with the same maker's mark probably Flemish, c. 1500. Chalice 8¹/₂ inches high, paten 6³/₄ inches diameter (24 ounces).

60. An Italian copper-gilt chalice, on octafoil foot each panel chased with scrolling foliage or set with an enamel plaque depicting the Virgin and Child, and saints, and a coat of arms, the stem engraved *GRACIA* beneath a cushion shaped knop with six enamelled portrait plaques, engraved above with *AVE MARIA*, the calyx with enamels of the Virgin and Child and three saints, and with two vacant reserves, the silver-gilt bowl with inverted rim, inscribed beneath the base BMJ 1534 and a later inscription *Orate pro animabus Claudii Watney et Adae M Hildae Conjugis quae hunc calicem Domino redemit MCMXX* (Pray for the souls of Claude Watney and Ada Hilda his wife who procured this chalice for the Lord in 1920). Probably Sienna, 1534, the bowl later. 7⁷/₈ inches high. Presented by Claude Watney and Ada Hilda his wife.

61. A continental silver-gilt chalice and paten, the chalice on hexafoil foot, the domed centre engraved with accole coats of arms with hexagonal stem, the knop chased with winged masks, the calyx of pierced straps and with plain bowl dated 1619, with plain paten with Dutch import mark. Chalice 8⁷/₈ inches high (18 ounces), paten 6 inches diameter.

62. A Spanish silver-gilt chalice, the circular foot engraved with foliage and set with plaques enamelled in transparent red and opaque white, the baluster stem rising from a cylindrical base similarly decorated, and with an engraved calyx, set with enamelled panels and imitation enamelled 'stones', apparently unmarked, c. 1620. 10³/₈ inches high (40 ounces). Presented by the Earl of Craven.

63. An English silver-gilt recusant chalice on hexafoil foot engraved with a border of stylised foliage and an ovolo, with applied Crucifixion, the stem with two mereses and baluster knop with three winged masks and slightly everted plain bowl, c. 1650. 8 inches high (11 ounces).

64. An English recusant silver-gilt chalice and paten, the chalice on hexafoil foot engraved with a border of stylised leaves and a Crucifixion, the stem rising from a merese, the baluster knop with three applied cherubs' masks, and with slightly flaring bowl, the paten engraved with IHS, a cross above, and a wounded heart below, unmarked, c. 1680, the gilding modern. The chalice 8¹/₂ inches high, the paten 5¹/₄ inches diameter (15¹/₂ ounces).

65. A Sicilian silver-gilt chalice, the cast base with figures in purgatory, beneath a representation of Christ feeding the five thousand, the knop formed as angels, and the calyx cast with the Last Supper, mark of Palermo 1691, Giacinto Omodei, as Consul and maker. 12 inches high (52 ounces). C. Truman (ed.), *The Sotheby's Concise Encyclopedia of Silver* (1993), p 82, ill.

66. A German chalice on hexafoil foot chased with three cherubs' heads in high relief between vacant cartouches with trumpet stem and small knop, the calyx with three demi-angels between scrolls, Augsburg, early 18th century, maker's mark IH or HI; the interior of the bowl a modern replacement. 9 inches high (20 ounces).

67. An Irish chalice on moulded octagonal foot engraved with the Crucifixion and two Marys and inscribed 'Blessed be the most holy sacrament of the altar', the octagonal stem with cushion knop chased with quatrefoils in lozenges and with plain bowl with slightly everted lip, engraved under the foot 'Pray for the souls of Mr Patrick fiz Gerald and Mrs Cecily Darsy his wife who caused this chalice to be made for theirs and their posterity Anno Domini 1719', the foot by Mark Fallon and the bowl by Richard Joyes, Galway, c. 1719. 8⁵/₈ inches high (10 ounces). Presented by Dudley Fitzgerald.

56

57

58

59

60

61

62

63

64

65

66

67

68. A recusant chalice, the domed foot bordered by lobes and engraved with a Crucifixion and *Ex dono Georgii Lovelock pbn 1721* (From the gift of George Lovelock, Prebendary 1721), the circular stem rising from a merese and with a cushion shaped knop chased with three stylised flowers with plain slightly flaring bowl, by George Gallant, Dublin, c. 1720. 7¹/₂ inches high (10 ounces).

69. A George IV parcel-gilt chalice and paten, the hexagonal foot applied with a Crucifixion and the two Marys above engraved foliage, the hexagonal stem with pierced knop, with six bosses engraved with stylised flowers and with plain bowl, the paten engraved IHS, a cross above, three nails below, with a glory, by Robert Gainsford, Sheffield, 1827. The chalice 6³/₄ inches high, the paten 4 inches diameter (10¹/₂ ounces).

70. A William IV chalice on circular moulded foot, chased with passion flowers, with baluster stem and similarly chased bowl, engraved with Sacred Monogram, the foot engraved *Sacerdote Revd. Dno A. Magee Donum Capellae Westminster Datum an Dni 1831* (Given by the priest the Reverend Father A Magee as a gift to the Church of Westminster in AD 1831). By Robert Hennell, 1830. 10¹/₄ inches high (17 ounces).

71. A French silver-gilt chalice and paten, the chalice on circular foot chased with a border of water leaves, flowers and cartouches, the dome chased with the Marriage of the Virgin, the Adoration of the Shepherds and the Magi, with baluster stem and calyx with the Presentation in the Temple, Christ before the Doctors, and Christ with the Apostles, the paten with the Coronation of the Virgin, Metz, 1819-38, maker's mark FG. Chalice 13¹/₂ inches high, the paten 7³/₄ inches diameter. Gift of the Very Reverend Monsignor T. Croft-Frazer.

72. A Victorian silver-gilt chalice on hexafoil foot chased with foliage and berries and set with enamelled bosses depicting the instruments of the Passion, the knopped stem with enamelled letters 'IHESUS', with a calyx of fruit and foliage, and the bowl with an engraved band of foliage, the base with a plate inscribed *R. adm. Cui: Ant: Can: Johnson grato animo d.d. Clerus Westmon. Mense Decemb MDCCCLXXVIII* (The clergy of Westminster gave this to the Reverend Administrator Anthony Canon Johnson with grateful thanks. December 1878), by John Hardman & Co, Birmingham, 1875, and a paten engraved with a foliate cross, 1878. Chalice 9 inches high (21 ounces), paten 6¹/₄ inches diameter.

73. A French parcel-gilt chalice and paten, the chalice with hexafoil foot set with enamelled plaques of the Crucifixion, the Spanish Royal arms, the monogram of King Alfonso XIII between engraved foliage and fruit, the stem with a shallow knop inscribed *Hoc facite, in commemorationem meam* (Do this in memory of me), the bowl with a calyx of scrolling foliage, the paten with an enamelled boss of the Sacred Monogram within etched scrolling foliage, Paris, 19th century, maker's mark of D. Freres and the Madrid retailers of G. de Ansorena Hijos. Chalice 9 inches high, paten 6 inches diameter. Presented by King Alfonso XIII of Spain, 1905.

74. An Italian gold and silver-gilt chalice on shaped circular foot chased with scrolls and putti, the stem formed as Christ, the Virgin and St Joseph, with calyx of scrolls and putti, and with a gold bowl, maker's mark G.G., the base engraved *MDCCCLXXXVII Leoni Papaenn XIII ob cuius sacerdotale jubilaeum universa*

exultat Ecclesia Genuensis Ephemeris L'Amico delle Famiglie Eiusque Lectores venerabundi offerunt - Bme Pater ad quem ibimus verba vitae aeternae habes (Ephemeris L'Amico delle Famiglie of Genoa and his Lectors offered this to the Venerable Pope Leo XIII for whose priestly jubilee the universal Church rejoices. Most Blessed Father, to whom shall we go, you have the words of eternal life) and *'coppe d'oro' 'Piede Argento'* and *'Baldi F',* the paten unmarked. 11¹/₂ inches high (32 ounces).
Presented by Pope Leo XIII, 1896.

75. A French silver-gilt, jewelled and enamelled chalice and paten, the chalice on a circular foot enamelled with a band of zig-zag and set with diamonds and an amethyst, the stem with enamelled lines and shallow beaded knop, the calyx with stylised enamelled flowers and inscription *Calicem salutaris accipiam et nomen domini invocabo* (I will take the chalice of salvation and I will call on the name of the Lord), the chalice with an etched scene of the Crucifixion, French, imported by Vanpoule, 1931. Chalice 8¹/₈ inches high, paten 5⁷/₈ inches diameter.

76. A silver-gilt chalice on shaped hexagonal foot, the trumpet stem set with a cross and an opal, the knop with ivory disc and with funnel shaped bowl, inscribed beneath the foot 'Leonard and Aimee Longstaff to their son John, June 11 1938', by Charles Boyton, 1937, and with plain paten by the same, 1937. Chalice 8¹/₄ inches high, paten 3 inches diameter.

77. A silver chalice and paten, the chalice on circular trumpet foot, the stem with an applied gold cross and ivory disc knop with celtic border and plain hemispherical bowl, inscribed under the base *Vincentio McEvoy, Sacerdoti, Patris memoriale Mater Vidua ad III ID JUN MCMXXXVIII* (To Vincent McEvoy, Priest, from his widowed mother in memory of his father, 11 June 1938), by The Faith Metal Company, 1937. Chalice 8¹/₄ inches high.

78. A silver-gilt chalice and paten, the chalice on domed foot with rope-twist borders and set with diamonds and emeralds, the stem decorated with a diamond and the knop with rubies and diamonds, the calyx of the bowl chased with flutes and scrolls and set with pearls and diamonds, inscribed under the foot *Quae olim dilectam conjugam condecorabant gemmae nunc ex dono Joannes Prosser calicem divini sponsi exornant* (The gems which once graced with beauty his beloved wife now adorn the chalice of the divine spouse, given by John Prosser), designed by John A Marshall, the paten plain, by E.E. Davis, 1949. Chalice 8¹/₂ inches high. Presented by John Prosser.

79. An Italian silver-gilt chalice, plain paten, and spoon, the chalice with a funnel-shaped base with celebrating angels, the knop chased with vines and the bowl with the Last Supper, a detachable plate to the base inscribed 28-5-1982 beneath the Papal arms. Chalice 8 inches high, paten 6³/₈ inches diameter. Presented by Pope John Paul II on the occasion of the Papal Mass in Westminster Cathedral, 28 May 1982.

68

69

70

71

72

73

74

75

76

77

78

79

Ciboria

80. A composite silver-gilt ciborium, the hexafoil foot cast with an ovolo, and chased with the symbols of the Passion, the trumpet foot chased with the Crucifixion and saints, with gothic knop, the calyx chased with cherubs' heads and scrolls, with plain bowl and the cover with an ovolo border and chased with auricular cartouches containing the Resurrection, Christ appearing to the Apostles, Pentecost and the Last Judgement, with an open crown surmounted by a crucifix, the foot with Amsterdam mark (c. 1650), the rim to the foot a modern addition. 20 inches high. Presented by Viscount Anthony Furness.

81. A German silver parcel-gilt ciborium on hexafoil foot chased with fruit, foliage and shells, with plain baluster stem and pierced calyx of straps, foliage and flowers, the gilt bowl with a dedicatory inscription dated 1714, the domed cover with further pierced straps, foliage and flowers, with replaced cross finial, Hildesheim, c. 1714, maker's mark IPW. 19 inches high (45 ounces).

82. A continental silver-gilt ciborium on shaped circular domed foot chased with flowers and altars between strap-work, with knopped stem and bowl chased with shells, flowers and lambrequins, the domed cover with further flowers and altars, probably Maltese, mid 18th century, with Victorian additions marked London 1840. 16¹/₂ inches high (45 ounces).

83. A French silver parcel-gilt and enamel ciborium, the octafoil foot set with garnets, and with enamelled plaques, with applied figures of the Evangelists, the knopped stem with plaques enamelled with cherubs' heads, the bowl with an open-work calyx with applied enamel plaques of saints and garnets, the cover similarly decorated and with garnet set cross finial, the base inscribed 'Les dames du diocese de Cambrai en souverain Pontife Pie IX Pape et Roi: 21 Mai 1877' (The ladies of the Diocese of Cambrai to the Sovereign Pontiff and King Pope Pius IX, 21 May 1877), by H. Thierry, Paris, c. 1875. 15 inches high. Presented by Pope Pius IX, 1898.

84. A French silver-gilt ciborium in the gothic taste on hexafoil foot chased with reserves stamped with mullets and engraved with foliage, with hexagonal trumpet stem, the knop embossed with 'jewels' and with a calyx of open-work tracery, the cover engraved with tracery and with cross finial, late 19th century. 10¹/₂ inches high (18 ounces).

85. A pair of silver ciboria, each formed as a shallow bowl on trumpet foot, one inscribed *Hic est Panis de coelo descendens; ut si quis, ex ipso manducaverit non moriatur* (This is the Bread which comes down from heaven; so that whoever eats of it shall not die); the other *Portas coeli apervit Dominus, panem coeli dedit eis, panem angelorum manducat homo* (The Lord has opened the gates of heaven and has given them the bread of heaven, and man eats of the bread of the angels): by Dunstan Pruden, 1971. 8⁵/₈ inches diameter (33¹/₂ ounces).

80

81

82

83

84

85

Crosses

86. A French gilt copper processional cross, engraved overall with scrolling foliage, the arms terminating in trefoils, and set with quatrefoils mounted with crystals and blue glass, the front with an applied corpus, the back engraved with Christ in Majesty, the lower quatrefoil to the stem a replacement. Limoges, 13th century. 23¼ inches high. Presented by Viscount Anthony Furness, 1960.

87. An Italian copper-gilt altar cross, the shaped octofoil base on an open-work border and chased with scrolls and foliage, and set with coloured stones and four enamelled bosses of the crown of thorns around a cross, the stem rising through two tiers of architectural tracery enclosing enamelled silver plaques, the knop with six enamelled plaques of the four Evangelists, the risen Christ and an episcopal coat of arms, the fluted stem with a further knop beneath a rectangular socket, the cross of shaped outline, the trefoil terminals set with crystals and with applied busts of the Virgin and St John, St Mary Magdalene and a male saint, the corpus with enamelled silver nimbus, the reverse with the symbols of the Evangelists around a seated figure of God the Father, the stem with an enamelled inscription *MAISTER ANTONIUS DE MACERATA SERVUS CRISTI INUTILIS 1481* (Master Anthony de Macerata, useless servant of Christ, 1481) dated 1481. 43½ inches high. Presented by Consuela Vanderbilt, sometime Duchess of Marlborough.

88. A Spanish silver processional cross of shaped outline, the arms decorated with grotesque masks, beasts and foliage, the borders of stylised shells, the terminals with foliate finials (some wanting), each side with four silver-gilt plaques depicting the Evangelists and saints, at the centre of one side a plaque depicting Christ(?) overcoming evil, the other with the eternal city, c. 1560. 22½ inches high. The staff-head in silver with foliate collar, the knop chased with grotesque masks, a large spool-shaped central element similarly chased and engraved supporting a rectangular socket with pilasters at the corners, unmarked, c. 1560. 13 inches high.

89. A Louis XIV altar cross on oval domed foot bordered by foliage, and supported on a knop chased with winged cherubs' heads, the cross with foliate terminals, titulus and corpus, probably Paris, 1661. 12¾ inches high (14 ounces).

The Metropolitan Cross

90. A jewelled silver and enamelled processional cross, the head with applied crucifix over a *cloisonné* enamelled ground, flanked by roundels of the two Marys, a pelican in her piety above and a skull below, the arms of the cross chased with scrolls and set with amethysts, moonstones and garnets and further enamels, the reverse with the arms of the diocese, Archbishop Bourne and St Edmund of Abingdon and the centre inscribed 'To the Glory of God and in homage to Francis Bourne, Cardinal Archbishop this cross is dedicated and offered by the Catholic Women's League of the Province of Westminster 1912' and with two open-work pendent quatrefoils pierced A & O, the stem joined of three parts, the two shorter with moonstone set knops, chased with trellises and a spiralling engrailed ribbon, by Blunt and Wray, London, 1912. 85 inches high.

Cruets

91. A Regency silver-gilt cruet, the shaped oval stand on four fruiting vine feet, and chased vine border, the two cruets with borders of vine, and with bird's-head spouts and scroll handles, one with a pierced A, the other with V, by Joseph Angell, London, 1822 (22 ounces). Made for the Roman Catholic Chapel at Westminster.

92. A French silver-gilt pair of altar cruets and stand, the shaped oval stand chased with bullrushes and grapes, and with four applied plaques of the Evangelists, the vase-shaped cruets with grapes and the head of Christ, and bullrushes and the head of the Blessed Virgin Mary, and with scroll handles, by H. Puche, Paris, c. 1880, engraved 'Pray for Nanolo & Jose and Louis Lapiz, Burning Hill'. The stand 13½ inches wide, the cruets 6½ inches high.

Maces

93. Cathedral Mace. An ebony staff with three knopped bands, the head rising from a shaped cylindrical collar chased with foliage, the inscription *Ecclesia Metropolitana Westmonasteriensis* (The Metropolitan Church of Westminster) and the *pallium*, beneath two scrolling brackets set with moonstones, supporting a fluted orb set with further stones and four plaques of the Evangelists, and two of the Sacred Monogram, the whole surmounted by a figure of St Peter, by Blunt and Wray, 1915. 61 inches high.

94. Mace of the Guild of the Blessed Sacrament. A silver, enamel and rock crystal mace, the stem with two bands enamelled in red, white and blue, the collar inscribed in red enamel: *ECCLES MET WESTM. SODALITAS S S SACR MCMXI* (The Guild of the Blessed Sacrament of the Metropolitan Church of Westminster 1911) beneath a knop chased with the emblems of the four Evangelists, between enamelled open-work straps, from which rises an octagonal enamelled section, the head formed as a domed building with four rock crystal pillars at the corners, between figures of Christ, the Blessed Virgin Mary, St Peter and St John, the pierced dome rising between four crosses and surmounted by a cupola supported by a pelican in her piety mounted on a coin, signed *HAROLDUS STABLER ME FECIT LONDIN MCMXI* (Harold Stabler made me in London in 1911), by Harold Stabler, 1911. 50½ inches high.

86

87

88

89

90

91

92

93

94

Monstrances

95. A Spanish jewelled, enamelled gold monstrance, on shaped square silver-gilt foot, set alternately with strap-work in enamel, with rubies, and emeralds, the domed foot enamelled with strap-work and set with rubies and diamonds and with panels of translucent blue, the baluster stem similarly decorated and set with stones, the rays around the oculus enamelled with blue and white and set with further rubies and emeralds, the finial formed as St Dominic holding a riband above with inscription *MET E DEVM ET.DATE*, the base with an applied diamond button, apparently unmarked, c. 1620. 18¹/2 inches high (84 ounces).

96. A continental monstrance on circular foot with four-winged cherub and scroll feet, the domed base cast with straps, foliage and two further cherubs' heads, the baluster stem similarly decorated, and the frame with further heads amidst wheat husks, flowers and grapes and with plain sunburst engraved with stylised flowers, probably Flemish, c. 1650, unmarked. 18⁷/8 inches high.

97. A Flemish jewelled silver-gilt monstrance on shaped oval base with pierced foliate border, the domed foot chased with two putti, and the Israelites gathering manna, and the Last Supper, the knopped stem with symbols of the Evangelists supporting an upper knop with applied swags and angels beneath a chased cloud on which kneel two angels supporting a further cloud and putti either side of the Holy Spirit supporting a crown with a pelican in piety finial and set with an amethyst around the glory and oculus set with garnets and white stones, by Jan Moermans, Antwerp, 1669. 31 inches high (225 ounces).

98. A Victorian silver-gilt monstrance on shaped oval foot with ovolo border, the domed base chased with foliage and symbols of the Evangelists, the stem rising from praying angels, the knop chased with putti and foliage and set with a carbuncle heart embellished with a diamond, the cross chased with foliage and set with diamonds and carbuncles, and the glory set with diamonds and issuing from almondine garnets, the back of the oculus inscribed 'Pray for the children of Charles Weld-Blundell of Ince Blundell and Mary Richard Lewis Alice'. By S.B. Harman, 1899. 29¹/2 inches high (145 ounces). Presented by the Weld-Blundell family.

99. An Edward VII silver-gilt monstrance, supported on a shaped oblong base engraved with the inscription *OSTENSORIUM HOC E SUO CONFLATUM IN NATIVITATE B.V.M. ANNO MCMVII. CATHEDRALI WESTMONASTERIENSI GRATA OBTULIT IN FIDEM AC RELIGIONEM VOCATA JAMQUE VOTA NUNCUPATURA CLARISSA AMBIANENSIS* (A Poor Clare of Amiens, called to the religious life, and about to make her vows gave in thanks this monstrance to Westminster Cathedral made from her property on the Feast of the Nativity of the Blessed Virgin Mary, 1907) below a fluted trumpet foot chased with the arms of Cardinal Bourne supporting a stem with four figures of saints (St Peter, St Francis, St Clare and St Colette) in niches each surmounted by a jewelled cross. The cruciform head of the monstrance set with eight enamel panels, the four on the front with the symbols of the Evangelists and the four on the back representing the risen Christ, the Virgin and Child, Christ blessing the Host and Christ crucified. The diamond set oculus surrounded by a square panel chased and pierced with grapes and vine leaves and wheat, all enclosed in a nimbus chased with stylised clouds and set with amethysts. The nimbus supported by wire rays terminated with amethysts and four glass spheres set in a wire work cage. Engraved on the

stem *FECERUNT NOS ARTE ET OPERA SUA OMAR RAMSDEN ET ALWYN CARR MCMVIII* (Omar Ramsden and Alwyn Carr made us with skill and as their own works in 1907) by Omar Ramsden and Alwyn Carr, 1906. The monstrance is supported on a gilt metal base set on four scrolling buttresses on a rectangular foot. Height 30 inches. Presented by Margaret Stella Nickols.

100. A copper gilt and hardstone monstrance, the oval base set with red stones, and engraved with the inscription: 'This monstrance is the gift of Elena - D: 17 Jan 1907 - And Anita O'Callaghan - D 29 May 1908, it is enriched with jewels bequeathed by them to the glory of God RIP' with fluted stem, the knop set with a cameo of the Virgin Mary and chased with the Sacred Monogram, beneath two scrolling arms supporting a shaped oval frame of sodalite set with red stones and foiled crystals around a glory and stylised clouds, designed by John Marshall, c. 1910. 37³/4 inches high.
Presented by Elena and Anita O'Callaghan.

95

96

97

98

99

100

Morses

101. A cruciform morse (a clasp for a cope), each branch and the central boss set with sixty-one amethysts set in scrolls and flowers with gilt metal supports, 1890. 7³/₄ inches diameter. Presented by Mrs Crawford, 1895.

102. A George V silver-gilt morse in the form of a cross moline set with a cut crystal on each arm and in the centre with an earlier jewel of nine stones set in a gold square with traces of enamel on the edge, the back with an abstract pattern in *champlevé* enamel in red, green, white and blue, issuing from the arms of the cross are floral sprays set with carbuncles, cairngorms, cut crystals, pearls and turquoise, the corners decorated with four small crosses set with pearls and turquoise, engraved on the back *OMAR RAMSDEN ME FECIT* (Omar Ramsden made me), by Omar Ramsden, 1935, in original presentation case. Overall size 6³/₄ × 5 inches. Presented to Cardinal Hinsley.

Pyxes

103. An English silver-gilt circular pyx, the cover with the Crucifixion, surrounded by a glory and ovolo border, the back with the Agnus Dei within a similar border, the interior of the lid with the Sacred Monogram, maker's mark a unicorn's head, c. 1620. 2³/₄ inches diameter. C. Oman, *English Church Plate* (1957), pl. 181. With the original gold embroidered burse with the Sacred Heart and a crown of thorns around a cross and a heart, both being bordered by wreaths.

104. An Edward VII silver pyx, the square box with a hinged lid chased with four panels surrounding a circular boss pierced out, on a red enamel ground with the Sacred Monogram IHS in a wreath of wheat sheaves, the plain box with one side hinged and engraved on the base *OMAR RAMSDEN ET ALWYN CARR ME FECERUNT MCMX* (Omar Ramsden and Alwyn Carr made me in 1910), by Omar Ramsden and Alwyn Carr, 1910. Overall size 3³/₄ × 3³/₄ × 1¹/₂ inches. Presented by Anthony Bartlett.

Reliquaries

105. A silver and parcel-gilt reliquary, with enamels and semi-precious stones, designed to hold a relic of the True Cross, the four arms edged with roll mouldings and pierced with quatrefoils, set with crystals and decorated with foliage reserved on green enamel. The arms terminate in trefoils similarly decorated with enamel and set with cabouchons, at the intersection a quatrefoil, each spandrel set with a pearl, enclosed by a roundel set with trefoil cresting and the inscription: *Ecce Lignum Crucis in quo Salus Mundi pependit Venite Adoremus* (Behold the wood of the cross on which hung the salvation of the world; come let us worship). The circular stem descends from a compressed spherical knot engraved alternately with crosses and trefoils, the bosses enamelled to form the words: *Ave O Crux* (Hail O Cross). The base is eight-lobed with moulded edges and spandrels of foliated ornament set with eight crystals, the back of the cross engraved, Birmingham, 1845, maker's mark of Hardman and Iliffe. 11¹/₂ inches high. The Hardman day-book, 1845-49.

106. A German jewelled silver-gilt cruciform reliquary, on circular base engraved with scrolling foliage and applied with four plaques of the Annunciation, Birth of Christ, Resurrection and Transfiguration, with knopped stem set with amethysts, the cross chased with rosettes and anthemions, with foliate truncations set with amethysts, the centre containing a relic of the

True Cross, by August Witte, Aachen, c. 1875. Presented by Monsignor (later Cardinal) Weld to St Thomas's Seminary, Hammersmith, 1888.

107. Reliquary of St Oliver Plunket. A jewelled silver *châsse* decorated with celtic scrolls, coloured stones and two hinged handles, the base sliding to reveal a wooden casket with a silver plaque engraved 'Blessed Oliver Plunket, Archbishop of Armagh martyred at Tyburn July 1st 1681', containing a glass ossiary and relic of the saint. Dublin, 1921, maker's mark worn (probably Edmond Johnson). 6³/₄ inches long.

107

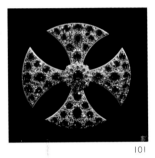

101

102

104

103

105

106

Miscellaneous

108. A Scandinavian circular brass basin, with vertical sides and everted rim, the centre embossed with the Annunciation bordered by two black-letter inscriptions, the rim with a further inscription dated 1642, c. 1640. 18¹/₂ inches diameter.

109. A German silver-gilt beaker on moulded foot beneath a rouletted border, the flaring cylindrical body engraved with a band of scrolls, foliage, flowers and birds beneath a band of ovals containing images of Sts Andrew, Thomas, Matthew, Philip, Bartholomew and Matthias, with swags between, and an upper frieze of further ovals containing views and arms of the towns of Cologne, Mainz, Speyer, Hamburg, Regensburg, and Augsburg, the underside of the base later engraved with the initials IFW and date 1706, Cologne, about 1620, maker's mark of a key, the gilding modern. 7³/₄ inches high (4 ounces 15 pennyweight).

110. A silver-gilt cup and cover, the spool-shaped foot chased with jewels and bosses, the stem formed of a baluster cast with shells and bracelets, the bowl with cartouches of animals and fruit between strap-work, with a border etched with scrolls, the domed cover chased with scrolls and fruit and with a classical warrior finial, bearing Augsburg marks and maker's mark ⧢K, 19th century. 13³/₄ inches high.

111. A pair of George III goblets, each hexagonal foot with baluster stem, the bell-shaped bowls engraved with two vacant cartouches and a band of flowers and foliage, by Napthali Hart, 1811. 6¹/₂ inches high (18 ounces). Presented to Cardinal Hume by Josephine Belfrage from her family chapel in Langley Castle, Northumberland.

Bibliography

Birmingham City Museum, *Omar Ramsden 1873-1939, Centenary Exhibition of Silver*, Exhibition Catalogue, Birmingham (1973), *Birmingham Gold and Silver 1873-1973*, Exhibition Catalogue (1973)

Blair, C. (ed.), *The History of Silver* (McDonald Orbis, 1987)

Bury, S., 'Pugin and the Tractarians', *Connoisseur* (January 1972)

Clayton, M., *A Collector's Antique Dictionary of Gold and Silver of the British Isles and North America* (Antique Collectors Club, 1971)

Clayton,M., *The Collector's Dictionary of the Gold and Silver of Great Britain and North America* (1971; revised edition 1984)

Glanville, P., *Silver in England* (Unwin Hyman, 1987)

Hayward, J.F., *Virtuoso Goldsmiths and the Triumph of Mannerism 1540-1620* (Sotheby Parke Bernet, 1976)

Hennell, P., 'The Hennel Family of silversmiths', *Proceedings of the Society of Silver Collectors* (I, 11, 1968)

Hemmarck, C., *The Art of the European Silversmith 1430-1830* (Sotheby Parke Bernet, 1977)

Jackson, C.F., *English Goldsmiths and their Marks* (1921)

Jackson, C.F., *English Goldsmiths and their Marks*,

Pickford, I. (ed.), (revised edition, Antique Collectors Club, 1986)

Jackson, C.F., *An Illustrated History of English Plate*, 2 volumes (1911)

Jervis, S., *The Penguin Dictionary of Design and Designers* (1984)

Oman, C., *English Church Plate 597-1837* (London, 1957)

Oman, C., *The Golden Age of Hispanic Silver* (London, 1968)

Pugin, A.W.N., *Designs for Gold and Silversmiths* (1836)

Pugin, A.W.N., *The True Principles of Pointed and Christian Architecture* (1841)

Tardy (ed.) *Les Poinçons de garanties internationaux pour l'argent* (Tardy, 1985)

Taylor, G., *Silver* (Harmondsworth, 1956)

Truman, C. (ed.), *The Sotheby's Concise Encyclopedia of Silver* (1994)

Victoria and Albert Museum, *Victorian Church Art* (exhibition catalogue, London, 1971)

Wardle, P., *Victorian Silver and Silver Plate* (1965; New York 1970)

Watts, W., *Catalogue of Chalices and Other Communion Vessels in the Victoria and Albert Museum* (1922)

109

110

108

111

Vestments
by Linda Woolley

112. Silk from the tomb of Edward the Confessor. Eastern Mediterranean or Western Asia, about the middle of the 11th century. A small fragment of undyed silk, originally cream, in weft-patterned weave. Weft-patterned tabby with pattern in weft-faced 1:2 twill. The silk shows part of the body and neck of a bird with a scarf flying behind the bird, the former a symbol seen frequently on early medieval Persian and Byzantine textiles *et al.* To the left part of the border of a roundel.

This was found in the tomb of Edward the Confessor (King of England 1042-65) in Westminster Abbey when it was accidentally broken into during preparations for the coronation of James II in April 1685 (not 1886 as stated on labels which were found with three fragments, probably from the same silk, which are now in the Victoria and Albert Museum, Numbers T2, 3, 4-1944).

The original pattern was of paired birds and animals in roundels. For a more detailed analysis of the Victoria and Albert fragments see British Museum catalogue, Byzantine Treasures from British Collections (British Museum, 1995).

The accompanying label states that 'this came out of ... Edwards S(h)rine a great ...', last word undeciphered. It is uncertain at the moment if this is in the same hand as the script of the labels mentioned above which were found with the Victoria and Albert pieces. There are certain differences which may suggest that another person wrote this description.

113. Mitre. English, 1160-1220. Pattern of foliate scrolls and circles; between the horns of the mitre are small lozenges. One lappet is original; the other which has a human figure, possibly an apostle, was formerly attached to another mitre, of about 1180-1210, at Sens Cathedral.

The embroidery is worked in silver-gilt thread in underside couching, on white silk woven with a pattern of lozenges. Applied ornaments, possibly enamels or gems, have been removed from the bands of red silk and from the circular compartments in the embroidery.

Underside couching was an extremely labour-intensive and therefore costly method of embroidery, and was particularly favoured in the finest quality *Opus Anglicanum.* It was created by laying the gold (or silver-gilt) thread on the face of the ground material and fixing it at intervals by a linen thread which was on the back of the material. At these points a tiny loop of the gold thread was pulled through to the back so that the linen couching thread was not seen on the front.

Although the tradition of the 19th century associates the mitre with St Thomas of Canterbury (21 December 1118?-29 December 1170), this is too recent to be taken as clear evidence, although it is not completely incompatible with the style of the foliate ornament.
Mitre 27cm × 23.5cm; original lappet 3cm (extending to 6.5cm at base) × 44cm.

112

113

114. Chasuble with matching stole, maniple and burse Chasuble of deep red velvet, 19th century, in the Gothic style, made up in the 19th century with applied late 15th/16th-century English embroidered orphreys. Edged with braid of two different kinds, one woven in silver-gilt and yellow silk with scalloped edges round the hem and bordering the orphreys, and the other at the neck in silver-gilt and yellow silk. They are presumably of the same date as the velvet, ie 19th century. Lined with modern red silk. The history of this vestment has been traced back to the private chapel of Mapledurham House, which was built in the 16th century by the recusant Blount family by the Thames near Pangbourne.

Orphreys: linen embroidered with silks and silver-gilt thread mainly in split stitch and laid and couched work. Front or straight orphrey: panels of saints beneath architectural canopies. Reading from the top downwards: St Paul with sword and book. St Helen? (Empress, mother of Constantine the Great) with cross and wearing a crown. St Jude, bearded saint with club. Back or cross orphrey: reading from the top downwards: God the Father with the Dove representing the Holy Spirit. Christ crucified with ministering angels catching his blood in chalices. This was a particularly popular iconographic composition on English cross orphreys of the 15th and first part of the 16th century. The Virgin Mary. Saint with book (he may be a Doctor of the Church and the fact that he is wearing a cap may also suggest a learned figure). The bottom part of this panel is missing. At the end of each crosspiece is a border of silk thread couched in a herringbone pattern.

Stole and maniple in the same 19th-century velvet as above, edged with braid and with a fringe at each end. The braid and fringes are also of 19th-century date. The crosses on these are embroidered in floss (unspun) silk.

Burse with a red velvet back which is a similar velvet to that of the chasuble, stole and maniple. The front of the burse is a panel which was originally part of an orphrey, English, late 15th century. Embroidered in silk, floss silk and silver-gilt thread. The area behind the saint is worked in laid and couched silver-gilt thread, much worn. The figure and most of the architectural canopy are embroidered in split stitch, with some laid and couched work and stem stitches. The burse is edged with striped braid, probably 19th century, and lined with modern linen. The figure is that of St Bartholomew with butcher's knife.
Chasuble 105.5cm x 126cm
Stole 223.5cm x 15cm
Maniple 94cm x 15cm
Burse 23cm x 19.5cm

115. Burse of red velvet, much worn. English, date uncertain, 16th century? Applied motifs in linen embroidered with silk in split stitch with some laid and couched work in silver-gilt thread. Edged at the top and sides with silk braid. At the top left and right are decorative devices covered in silk and floss silk thread and at the middle of the top there is a bobble of wood with thread wound round it. It has been mounted on to modern pink silk. Symbols of the Passion and the Sacred Monogram IHS within a shield shape edged in metal thread.

Chalice veil of red velvet, edged with braid, English, 20th century. The embroidery was probably worked between 1912 and 1926, perhaps by Mrs Elizabeth Riddell-Blount. Embroidered with silk principally in split stitch. Angels holding chalices and a cross at each

corner and in the middle.
Chalice veil 56cm x 58.5cm

116. Chasuble, stole and maniple. Chasuble, in the Gothic style, ground of woven silk and gold thread, possibly French, 1860s-1880s? Such designs were produced from about the 1860s but the patterns may have been used for some time. Edged with gold braid of similar date. Embroidered orphreys, English, late 15th/early 16th century.

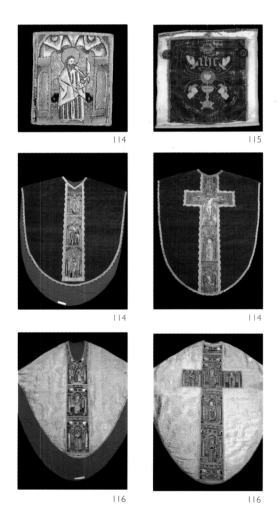

114   115

114   114

116   116

Orphreys: linen embroidered with silk, floss silk and silver-gilt thread in split stitch and laid and couched work. Some later re-working of the embroidery has been done, presumably at the time when the chasuble was made. Edged with braid woven in silver-gilt, 19th century. Front or straight orphrey: three panels with saints beneath architectural canopies. Around the neck area, pieces from several other orphrey panels have been joined together to make up the length of the orphrey. Reading from the top downwards: a figure in contemporary dress of the second half of the 15th century. Unidentified martyred saint (female?) with palm leaf. A figure in contemporary dress of second half 15th/early 16th century. Back or cross orphrey: at the top, three pieces from orphrey panels have been joined (the uppermost piece being upside down) to produce the length of the orphrey. The main part of the orphrey has been made up from a straight orphrey with a panel added at each side to compose the cross pieces. At the bottom, two pieces from orphrey panels have been joined to make up the length of the orphrey. Reading from the top downwards: Saint with chalice or Mary Magdalene with ointment jar in the centre of the crosspiece. On left crosspiece an unidentified figure in contemporary 15th-century dress carrying a purse or bag. On the right crosspiece it might be St Peter with key although the symbol looks more like a flag with cross and St Peter is usually depicted as an old man. Moses with tablets of the law? St Thomas the Apostle? with spear or lance.

Stole and maniple made of the same silk as the chasuble above. Areas at each end made up from different woven material, which has been embroidered over in silk, with a cross in the centre in silver-gilt thread. The cross in the middle of the stole and maniple is in gold braid. The fringe at each end is of torsade, a thick twisted gold thread.
Chasuble 128cm x 123cm
Stole 239cm x 21.5cm
Maniple 104cm x 21.5cm

117. Cope of woven silk, English, about 1912-26. Orphreys and morse (ie clasp) embroidered, English, about 1912-26. Cope hood embroidered, English, late 15th/first half 16th century. Edged with gold braid and lined with silk of same date as the main part of the cope.

Orphreys and morse are embroidered with silk in split stitch and some laid and couched work. These were embroidered by Mrs Elizabeth Riddell-Blount between 1912 and 1926 according to her daughters. The morse has the Sacred Monogram IHS embroidered in split stitch. The cope hood is embroidered with silk, floss silk and silver-gilt thread in split stitch and laid and couched work. The Assumption of the Virgin with four angels.
Cope 152.5cm x 305cm
Cope hood 37cm x 41cm

118. Edmund Riddell-Blount chasuble. English, first half 16th century. Red velvet with applied front or straight orphrey and back or cross orphrey, both of blue velvet with applied motifs. Lined with the original blue linen. This has been severely cut down from its original shape. Perhaps there was only sufficient material left in good enough condition for this shape. Front or straight orphrey: applied motifs, M, a heraldic shield, W, M. Back or cross orphrey: applied motifs, linen embroidered with silk and silver-gilt thread in split stitch and a little laid and couched work. Stylised

flowers between the letters MWM and in the middle a coat of arms with the letter M to the left and W to the right. The heraldry may well be connected with the Riddell-Blount family who donated this and other vestments to the Cathedral in 1930.

Purse, possibly French, 17th century. Canvaswork embroidered in *or nue* technique (a technique whereby silver-gilt thread is couched down with silk thread at different intervals to give a shading effect). On one side a heart with the Sacred Monogram IHS and cornflowers, on the other side a heart and cross with vine leaves and grapes. The braid strings are of green silk with metal bobbles at the ends.

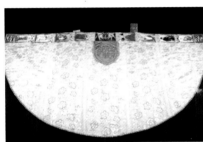

117 117

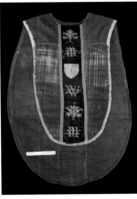

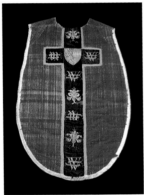

118 118

119. Vestments on St John Southworth
by Clare Browne and Wendy Hefford

The lace at cuffs and hem of the alb are second half
of the 19th-century bobbin-made tape lace, which
could have been made in one of a number of
European centres in France, Belgium or even England.
The cuffs are trimmed with Maltese style bobbin lace.

The red silk velvet of the chasuble may date from the
beginning of the 18th century to about 1735 and is
probably French. It is also possible that it is a 19th-
century copy of an 18th-century style. The red silk
damask with the sprigs of flowers and areas of zig-zag
geometric patterns dates from the late 1740s-1750s
and is probably French.

The silk braid at the edges and down the seams is
extremely difficult to date accurately and could be
18th, 19th, or even 20th century, but is most
probably 19th century when the vestment was
presumably assembled. Vestments presented by
Anthony Bartlett.

119

120, 121. Challoner-Talbot Vestments
by Paul Harrison

Fabric is yellow silk with silver thread with ornaments
of woven braid. The hood has a fringe with spangled
hangers. The vestments probably date from the
second half of the 19th century and are continental,
possibly Italian. These vestments are thought to have
been made to commemorate the work of two great
bishops, Richard Challoner (1691-1781) and James
Talbot (1726-90) and the main vestments bear the
arms combining the quarterings of both men with the
motto *Prest d'accomplir* (Prompt to achieve).
1 Cope 154cm x 304cm
2 Dalmatics 102cm x 132cm
1 Chasuble 101cm x 75cm
2 Stoles 206cm x 11cm expanding to 23cm
3 Maniples 104cm x 11cm expanding to 23cm
1 Burse 28cm x 28cm

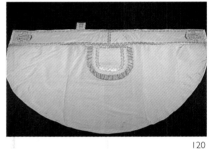

120

121

122-126. Howard Vestments. Fabric of white [?] silk with silver thread and embroidered with silver-gilt plain thread, purl thread and plate, in a style based on rococo ornament of the mid 18th century. These vestments date from the second half of the 19th century and are continental, possibly Italian, and belonged to Cardinal Edward Henry Howard (1829-92). Coat of arms embroidered on chasuble with motto *Sola virtutus invicta* (Only virtue is unconquered).
1 Chasuble 119cm × 76cm
1 Stole 184cm × 13cm expanding to 27cm
1 Chalice veil 71cm × 74cm

127. Manning Cope. Fabric of red silk with silver thread and embroidered on the hood and orphrey in raised and padded work, with silver-gilt purl thread, plate, and spangles. This cope probably dates from the second half of the 19th century and is continental, possibly Italian. Coats of arms at the base of the orphreys with motto *Malo mori quam foedari* (I prefer to die than compromise). This cope belonged to Cardinal Henry Edward Manning (1808-92) and was reputedly worn at the First Vatican Council which he attended between 8 December 1869 and 1 December 1870.
Cope 150cm × 304cm

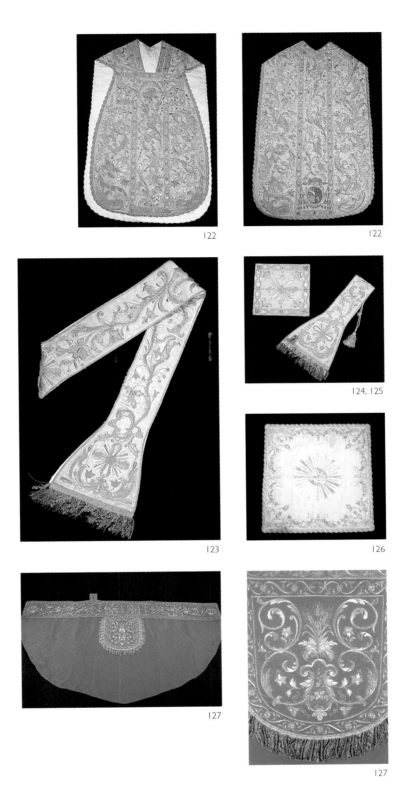

122

122

124, 125

123

126

127

127

128-136. Wiseman Vestments. [The state of our knowledge concerning Pugin and vestments has improved considerably recently, and we can confidently correct some of the guesswork published in *Raiment for the Lord's Service* and *Victorian Church Art:* this set of vestments was not designed in 1848, was not designed for the opening of St George's Cathedral, Southwark (witness the crossed keys and Westminster martlets), was not embroidered by Lonsdale and Tyler ... and was possibly not designed by Pugin!]

The fabric consists of a yellow silk with silver thread with applied red and green velvet ground embroidered with a variety of silver-gilt plain threads, purl threads, plate, spangles, and cord, and silver purl threads and spangles; the cope hood has, in addition, blue velvet. The cope hood and humeral veil have a block trellis fringe of red silk and silver-gilt thread; the stoles and maniples have a block knotted fringe in the same threads.

The style and technique of the embroidery on these vestments matches work on vestments made to Pugin's designs in Mrs Powell's workshop in Birmingham. This attribution is confirmed by the survival of designs for details of the embroidery of these vestments among drawings from this workshop of Mrs Powell.

The vestments for St Mary's College, Oscott (1838), and for St Chad's Cathedral, Birmingham (1840/1), were made to Pugin's designs by Lonsdale and Tyler of Covent Garden, suppliers of silver and gold 'lace' (woven braids) and military embroiderers. In 1842 a workshop dedicated to the production of vestments was established under the direction of Louise Powell, sister of John Hardman who executed Pugin's metalwork designs and wife of Hardman's partner, William Powell. From this time Pugin seems to have passed all his vestment work to Mrs Powell, simply supplying her with designs. Although trading as a separate company, Mrs Powell's workshop collaborated closely with Hardman and was undoubtedly responsible for the embroidery on Doctor Wiseman's mitre.

Since the embroidery designs may not be in Pugin's hand, and since Cardinal Wiseman (1802-65) does not seem to have worn these vestments at his enthronement at Saint George's Cathedral, Southwark (*Illustrated London News,* 7 December 1850 - 'robed in scarlet and white'), it is difficult to be certain to what degree Pugin contributed to their creation. At this period Pugin was working frantically on the Palace of Westminster and the Great Exhibition, and was increasingly afflicted by illness and madness until his death in September 1852. However, Mrs Powell's later advertisements proclaimed that they produced vestments '... from the Designs by the late AWN Pugin, Esq.' (*Catholic Directory,* 1853) suggesting that, although Pugin's death deprived them of new designs, vestments continued to be produced from existing drawings. John Hardman Powell, Mrs Powell's son who became Pugin's pupil, said of Pugin's fecundity as a designer: '... he poured out fifteenth century detail like a conjurer' ('"Pugin in his home" A memoir by J.H. Powell', edited by Alexandra Wedgwood (1994), reprinted from *Architectural History,* volume 31, 1988). In addition to their own stock of designs, Mrs Powell and her colleagues could turn for inspiration to Pugin's lavish and famous book, *Glossary of Ecclesiastical Ornament and Costume* (1844).

1 Cope 140cm x 288cm

Orphrey band 288cm x 15cm
Hood 58cm x 53cm
4 Dalmatics 114cm x 180cm
Chasuble 122cm x 117cm
Humeral veil 298cm x 49cm
2 Stoles 292cm x 10cm
3 Maniples 113cm x 10cm
Chalice veil 58cm x 60cm
Burse 20.5cm x 20cm
Gloves

128

128

130

129

137. Mitre. 'Mitre: cloth of silver and velvet decorated with panels of silver enamelled copper plaques and semiprecious stones. 1848. Presumably embroidered by Lonsdale and Tyler, the metalwork by John Hardman and Co. This mitre designed by Augustus Welby Northmore Pugin (1812-1852) was by far the most splendid thing of its kind that had been made by English craftsmen since the Reformation. It was made for Cardinal Wiseman. The entry in Hardman's day book dated June 30th 1848 reads: Revd H.D. Haigh for Dr Wiseman A precious mitre of rich raised embroidery work on velvet, set with stones and jewels, enamels and beaten plates of silver with gilt crockets running up sides and gilt cross set with pearls etc £65. A week after delivering on July 4th on the occasion of the consecration of St George's Southwark Wiseman wore this mitre for the first time' (from Victorian Church Art, Victoria and Albert Museum, 1971).
Mitre 36.5cm × 24cm
lappets 19cm × 4.5cm

138, 139. Byzantine red vestments. Fabric of red and yellow lampas, the chasuble decorated with gold flames on velvet bands, the dalmatics with applied pendants set with moonstones. This set was made in 1928 for Cardinal Francis Bourne (1861-1935) by A.E. Grossé of place Simon, Stevin 15, Bruges, Belgium.
6 Copes 156cm × 308cm
4 Dalmatics 100cm × 142cm
1 Chasuble 113cm × 142cm
1 Tunicle 100cm × 142cm
Humeral veil 164cm × 53cm
2 Stoles 132cm × 9cm
3 Maniples 69cm × 10cm
Chalice veil (large) 61.5cm × 64cm
Chalice veil (small) 50.5cm × 53cm
Burse 20cm × 20cm
Book cover 61cm × 64cm
Lectern cover 52cm × 131cm

Bibliography

Atterbury, P., and Wainwright, C., (editors), *Pugin: a Gothic Passion* (Yale, 1994)

Byzance: L'art byzantin dans les collections publiques françaises (exhibition catalogue) (Paris, 1992)

Christie, A.H., *English Medieval Embroidery* (Oxford, 1938)

King, D., *Catalogue of the Opus Anglicanum Exhibition* (London, V&A Museum, 1963)

Martinari-Reber, M., *Soieries sassanides, coptes et byzantines Ve-XIe siècles Musée historique des tissus* (Lyon) (Paris, 1986)

Mayer-Thurman, C., *Raiment for the Lord's Service: A Thousand Years of Western Vestments* (Chicago, 1975)

Pugin, A.W.N., *Glossary of Ecclesiastical Ornament and Costume* (1844, second edition 1846, third edition 1868)

Staniland, K., *Embroiderers* (in the British Museum's 'Medieval Craftsmen' series) (1991)

Victoria and Albert Museum, *Catalogue of English Ecclesiastical Embroidery of the 13th-16th centuries* (London, 1930)

Victoria and Albert Museum, *Victorian Church Art* (exhibition catalogue, 1971)

131

132

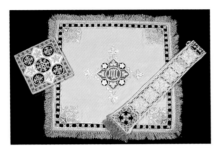
133, 134, 135

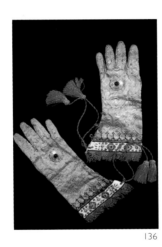
136

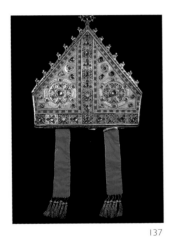
137

138

139

Select Bibliography

Our primary sources of information have been the two-volume biography of John Bentley by his daughter, Winefride de l'Hôpital, the *Westminster Cathedral Record*, 1896-1902, the *Westminster Cathedral Chronicle*, 1907-79, and the *Westminster Cathedral Bulletin*, which continues to the present day. In the earliest days the latter publications kept the public abreast of developments in the building and decoration of the Cathedral. The artists involved often wrote about their work themselves. We also refer to occasional writings and reminiscences of Monsignor Francis Bartlett, (1912-1992), Administrator of Westminster Cathedral from 1967 to 1977.

Psalms are taken from *The Psalms: A New Translation* published by Harper Collins and from *The Divine Office* by permission of A. P. Watt Ltd on behalf of The Grail, England.

Scripture quotaions are from the *New Revised Standard Version* of the Bible copyright 1989 by the Division of Christian Education of the National Council of the Churches of Christ in the USA. Used by permission. All rights reserved.

An Architectural Student, *The New Westminster Cathedral: A Free Criticism* (T. Fisher Unwin, London, 1905)

Bamm, P., *The Kingdoms of Christ: the story of the early Church* (Thames & Hudson, 1959)

Beck, G.A.(ed.), *The English Catholics 1850-1950* (Burns & Oates, 1950)

Beckwith, J., *Early Christian and Byzantine Art* (Yale University Press, 1993)

Bence-Jones, M., *The Catholic Families* (Constable, London, 1992)

Blair, S., *Art and Architecture of Islam* (Penguin, 1994)

Bossy, J., *The English Catholic Community 1570-1850* (Darton, Longman & Todd, London, 1975)

Butler, A.S.G., *John Francis Bentley: the Architect of Westminster Cathedral* (Burns & Oates, 1961)

Catechism of the Catholic Church (Geoffrey Chapman, 1994)

Cathedrals of England (B.T.Batsford Ltd, 1960)

Congar, Y.M.J., *The Mystery of the Temple* (Burns & Oates, London, 1962)

Cumming, E. and Kaplan, W., *The Arts and Crafts Movement* (Thames and Hudson, 1993)

De l'Hôpital, W., *Westminster Cathedral and its Architect* (Hutchinson and Co, London, 1919)

Doyle, P., *Westminster Cathedral 1895-1995* (Geoffrey Chapman, London, 1995)

Duffy, E.(ed.), *Challoner and His Church* (Darton, Longman & Todd London, 1981)

Duffy, E., *The Stripping of the Altars* (Yale, 1992)

Ferguson, G., *Signs and Symbols in Christian Art* (Oxford University Press, 1954)

Flannery, A., *Vatican Council II: the Conciliar Documents (2 volumes)* (Dominican Publications, Dublin, 1988)

Foster, M., *The Principles of Architecture: Style, Structure and Design* (Phaidon, 1982)

Fothergill, B., *Nicholas Wiseman* (Faber & Faber, 1963)

Garner, P., *Twentieth-Century Furniture* (Phaidon, 1980)

Gray, N., *A History of Lettering: creative experiment and letter identity* (Phaidon, Oxford, 1986)

Gwynn, D., *The Struggle for Catholic Emancipation* (Longmans, Green & Co, 1928)

Gwynn, D., *A Hundred Years of Catholic Emancipation* (Longmans, Green & Co, 1929)

Hales, E.E.Y., *Pio Nono: A study in European politics and religion in the nineteenth century* (Eyre and Spottiswoode, London, 1954)

Hastings, A., *A History of English Catholicism 1920-1985* (Collins, 1986)

Heim, B.B., *Heraldry in the Catholic Church: its origins, customs and laws* (Van Duren, Gerrards Cross, 1981)

Hill, A.G., *The Architectural History of the Christian Church* (A.R. Mowbray, Oxford, 1908)

Howell, P. and Sutton, I., *The Faber Guide to Victorian Churches* (Faber and Faber, London, 1989)

Hughes, P., *Rome and the Counter Reformation in England* (Burns & Oates, 1944)

Kelly, J.N.D., *Oxford Dictionary of Popes* (Oxford University Press, 1988)

Ker, I., *John Henry Newman* (Oxford University Press, 1988)

Kollar, R., *Westminster Cathedral from Dream to Reality* (Faith & Life Publications Ltd, Edinburgh, 1987)

Krautheimer, R., *Early Christian and Byzantine Architecture* (Yale University Press, 1986)

Lethaby, W.R. and others, *Ernest Gimson: His life and work* (Basil Blackwell, Oxford, 1924)

Lindstrom, R.S., *Creation and Construction: European Churches since 1970* (The American Institute of Architects Press, Washington, 1988)

MacCarthy, F., *Eric Gill* (Faber and Faber, London, 1989)

Mango, C., *Byzantine Architecture* (Faber & Faber, London/Electa, 1978)

Masson, G., *The Companion Guide to Rome* (Collins, 1965)

Moloney, T., *Westminster, Whitehall and the Vatican* (Burns & Oates, 1985)

Nairn, I., *Nairn's London* (Penguin, 1966)

Neuner, J. and Dupuis, J., *The Christian Faith in the Doctrinal Documents of the Catholic Church* (Collins, 1983)

Nineteenth Eucharistic Congress, Westminster, 1908 (Sands & Co, 1909)

Norman, E.R., *Roman Catholicism in England* (Oxford University Press, 1964)

Norman, E.R., *Anti-Catholicism in Victorian England* (George Allen & Unwin, 1968)

Norman, E.R., *The English Catholic Church in the Nineteenth Century* (Clarendon Press, Oxford, 1984)

Norman, E.R., *The House of God: church architecture, style and history* (Thames & Hudson, London, 1990)

Nuttgens, P., *The Story of Architecture* (Phaidon, 1983)

Pepper, C.B., *An Artist and the Pope based on the personal recollections of Giacomo Manzù* (Catholic Book Club, 1969)

Pevsner, N. and Metcalf, P., *The Cathedrals of England* (Viking, 1985)

Port, M. H., *Imperial London: civil government buildings in London, 1851-1915* (Yale University Press, New Haven and London, 1995)

Pothom, H., *A Guide to Architectural Styles* (Phaidon, 1982)

E. S. Purcell, *Life of Cardinal Manning, Archbishop of Westminster* (2 volumes) (Macmillan, 1895)

Rice, D.T., *Art of the Byzantine Era* (Thames and Hudson, 1993)

Rosser, G., *Medieval Westminster 1200-1540* (Clarendon Press, Oxford, 1989)

Rossi, F., *Mosaics: A Survey of their History and Technique* (Pall Mall Press, London, 1970)

Rossiter, S., *Rome and Central Italy* (Ernest Benn, London, 1964)

Scarisbrick, J.J., *Henry VIII* (Eyre & Spottiswoode, London, 1968)

Scott-Moncrieff, W.W., *John Francis Bentley* (Ernest Benn, London, 1924)

Smart Jr., C.M., *Muscular Churches: ecclesiastical architecture of the high Victorian period* (University of Arkansas Press, Fayetteville & London, 1989)

Smith, R.J., *A Directory of Specialist Crafts for Architects and Builders* (Robert Hale, London, 1990)

Snead-Cox, J.G., *Life of Cardinal Vaughan* (2 volumes) (Herbert & Daniel, 1910)

Stamp, G., *Robert Weir Schultz: Architect and his work for the Marquesses of Bute* (Mount Stuart, 1981)

Thomson, D., *England in the Ninteenth Century* (Penguin, 1983)

Ward, B., *Catholic London a Century Ago* (Catholic Truth Society, 1905)

Ward, W., *William George Ward and the Oxford Movement* (Macmillan, 1893)

Ward, W., *William George Ward and the Catholic Revival* (Macmillan, 1893)

Ward, W., *The Life and Times of Cardinal Wiseman* (Longmans, Green and Co, London, 1897)

Weinreb, B and Hibbert, C.(eds.), *The London Encyclopaedia* (Macmillan, 1983)

Westminster Cathedral Guide (1923)

Westminster Cathedral Handbook (1950)

Wheeler, W.G., *In Truth and Love* (Gowland and Co, 1990)

Wheeler, W.G., *More Truth and Love* (Gowland and Co, 1994)

Whone, H., *Church, Monastery, Cathedral: a guide to the symbolism of the Christian tradition* (Ridley Enslow, New Jersey, 1977)